Mirrors Strike Back

a memoir

By Rebekah Mallory

An Unkind Press, LLC Publication

This is a work of creative nonfiction, memoir. All events described in this book happened to the best of the author's memory including dialogue and location. Only a few small liberties were taken regarding certain occasions and their timelines; some events depicted herein are composites of different experiences. Names and identifying details of the people described in this book have been altered (and at times embellished) to protect their privacy. Any offenses are unintentional.

Cover Design by Ryan Ashcroft at BookBrand
Formatting by Jo Harrison
Copy Editing/Proofreading by Kayli Baker
First printing edition 2022
Rebekah Mallory
www.rebekahmallory.com

UNKIND PRESS

ISBN Paperback: 978-1-7358221-2-9
ISBN ebook: 978-1-7358221-4-3

"Brutally honest and heartbreakingly self-aware, Mallory's second memoir is an unpredictable (and yet oh-so-addictive) ride on the rollercoaster of self-discovery. It should be required reading for anyone engaged in the deep work of personal growth and evolution."

Lauren Sapala, author of *The INFJ Writer* and *West is San Francisco*

"Mallory's raw emotion and potent honesty demand to be heard. Hers is not a memoir for the faint heart, but rather a fiercely authentic journey for the open mind and the searching soul."

J. A. Plosker, author of *An Audible Silence* and *The Nobody Bible: Uncovering the Simple Wisdom in Ordinary Life*

"Rebekah Mallory's remarkable storytelling ability again brings the reader into the mind, the heart, and the soul of a woman struggling to find herself and her place in the world. You'll laugh, you'll cry, you'll see the world through different eyes as you devour her words, and each page will leave you breathlessly thirsting for more."

Katherine Turner, author of *resilient: a memoir*

"In *Mirrors Strike Back,* Rebekah Mallory continues her beautifully crafted and all-consuming memoir. Her story will resonate with cult survivors, CODAs, but also with anyone who's dealt with a challenging family or who's made regrettable choices but have grown stronger and smarter because of them. Mallory's writing is honest, edgy, and addictive, and her story will stay with you long after you finish it."

Patricia Kirsch, author of *Bring Me to Life* and *Gia*

Also by Rebekah Mallory

Train Gone: A CODA Ex-Jw Memoir

"Whoever fights monsters should see to it that in the process he does not become a monster. And if you gaze long enough into an abyss, the abyss will gaze back into you."

~Friedrich Nietzsche

"For it was an unjust mirror, this mirror of his soul that he was looking at."

~Oscar Wilde

"How many people did you know who refracted your own light to you?... How rarely did other people's faces take of you and throw back to you your own expression, your own innermost trembling thought?"

~Ray Bradbury

For RKP Jr.

You asked me
to meet you for coffee.
I said, *Shit, that was today?*
I really just wanted to go home.

We met.
Coffees turned into beers,
we relayed our misery,
casualties of infidelity.

You made me forget my pain.
You invited me in,
made me part of your family.

Though I came kicking and screaming,
here we are,
twelve years later,
still holding each other's pain.

Sometimes with beer.
But only if it's really good beer
because we both don't care for beer.

Here's a bit more pain.
Will you hold it for me?
I luve you.

Table of Contents

Introduction

I HADN'T PLANNED on writing a sequel, or anything much after getting my memoir, *Train Gone*, out of my system.

But something happened.

When I set up my website and began writing blogs, I didn't think I'd publish a book. I was just getting shit out, you know? While I was in the rewriting and editing phase of the memoir I hadn't initially planned to publish, I received a message from a Jehovah's Witness (J-Dub) I used to know.

It totally threw me.

I thought she was getting in touch to maybe say hi or tell me she'd just left the Truth. But that wasn't at all why she sent the message.

She said she'd stumbled upon my website and was appalled. She asked how I could possibly say the things I was saying, how could I write what I was writing? And why was I so angry? She further stated that, since we were from the same area and grew up going to the same Kingdom Hall, she didn't understand how my experiences could have been so different from hers.

I was speechless. "How could our experiences be different?" Um, we're two different people. I was raised by Deaf parents that I interpreted for all the time. I have four older brothers. I couldn't believe that her blinders were on so tight. I couldn't believe she wasn't able to understand that people, regardless of how much they might have in common, have different experiences happening inside them. Clearly, it didn't occur to her that two people could look at the same painting, watch the same movie, play with the same My Little Pony, or read the same book and feel something completely different.

And why was I still so angry? Well, in certain blogs and in many parts of *Train Gone*, I'm sure I *did* seem angry; *Train Gone* is sort of my "before" photo. I was quite the rebellious and unhappy teen, and later—a confused young woman. But still angry? Nah. It may look like anger to someone who's told to think that leaving the fold, living life in a different kind of truth, is a terrible thing, but no, not angry.

Do I still go through parts of a grief cycle whenever I'm confronted with J-Dub bullshit? Yes, but a deep explanation of the grief cycle isn't anything you'd see in a *Watchtower* magazine. Quoting *Psychology Today* would be blasphemous to the ol' GB (Governing Body) and their feigned infallibility. And maybe she didn't know about the grief cycle?

Then it hit me.

Kyrie eleison! It would probably make her feel better to know that the Society *is right; I'm living under a bridge somewhere,* mentally diseased, *and my life is just utter chaos because I'm not in the Truth.* Knowing that would make some J-Dubs feel so much better, and they'd get to be right about who they think I am. They'd get to be right about how they're living their lives.

Well, sorry to break it to you darlin' but I'm doing okay these days; writing all this is an attempt to mend my own wounds independently. Memoirs are a snapshot in time; outdated upon publishing. This book? Already old and, if I'm being completely honest, written for me and RKP Jr. If by chance others benefit, even better.

As with the first book's introduction, there are some heroes, some villains, some poor choices, and some sexually explicit content. A note about the raw sexuality: when one finally understands the source of their own overactive libido, and is comfortable talking about it so openly, it can often be linked to earlier, unfortunate experiences. At least that was the case for me. There were some events I wish I'd remembered to forget.

Rest assured, things do get better for our narrator (me). She confronts some dark memories. She falls in with a couple of organizations that remind her of her cult upbringing, which lead to her further understanding herself and her own world theories.

There are many bumps and stark realizations along the way, including self-medicating with lots of alcohol. I sort of knew I had a problem with alcohol then, but at the same time, I didn't know, if that makes sense. Regardless, the excessive drinking and harsh realizations might cause a knee-jerk reaction for some. Take care of yourselves while reading.

This book picks up where *Train Gone* leaves off because I read and watched *Misery*. I know how pissed Annie Wilkes was over her "Rocket Man" chapter plays; that whole skirting-past-the-cliff-hanger shit ticks me off, too.

Flattened Wishes

I BREATHED IN the last trail of steam and coal from the line of Pullman train cars that had just rumbled by and committed the moment to memory.

I looked down and this adorable little version of me, humming with her arms wrapped around my waist, looked up into my face with sincere happiness. The sparkles in her eyes were surrounded by twinkling lights, sleeping teddy bears, and erratic fairies darting to obscure parts of the universe in whimsical haste. She was simply magical. Perfect.

"C'mon!" She ran to the fence, pushed it down, and hopped over it. I followed.

Squatting at the tracks, she collected her pennies, counting them again. I crouched beside her, picked up the pennies Joel had given me, and put one in her grubby, little playing-outside hand. She then put one of her pennies in my hand and smiled.

"Penny sisters," she said.

"Penny sisters," I said, smiling.

A high-pitched bellow came from the back door. "Make-ay!"

We both jerked our heads toward the back of the house.

I know that sound.

"Oh, I gotta go, that's my mom!" she said, standing up.

She hopped the fence, and her Trax sneakers stomped the path that she, I, and the boys knew oh-so-well. I couldn't let her just leave, though. My heart called out to her before my mouth knew what was happening.

"Bek!"

She turned around just as Mom shouted again. "Yeah?"

"Um, I love you."

She tilted her head and smiled; flattered with no idea why. Then, she ran to the back door.

I turned and reluctantly started walking back from whence I came. Along the tracks, I felt heavy sadness, overwhelming despair all around me. The ferns still cried, drooping with shame. I could hear an uprooted tree squealing in pain, lying next to the rails, begging for another chance at life.

Stepping on each railroad tie, I couldn't help but notice the broken glass and beer bottles from parties gone by, leaving behind this indescribable melancholy—almost as if I'd never trekked the magical path or dared leaving pennies on the rails, turning them into flattened wishes.

Why—after this amazing chance encounter—was there still so much sadness here? I stopped, dead on the tracks, once I realized that the devastating sadness I felt stemmed from the manipulation that was about to happen to her. Something had definitely happened, something I didn't remember to forget.

Reunited with my purple freedom ride, I sat quietly in the driver's seat, wondering how I even got there. I looked to the passenger's seat and saw a small, faded version of her...*me*. Her tiny body sat patiently—legs dangling, long dark hair bound in two ponytails by Goody bobble hair-ties, bangs, huge brown eyes, Frederick the Bear, and a handful of squashed dreams.

I started the engine and pulled up to a gas pump. With each gallon that flowed into my tank, I could see her vanishing into thin air. Although details were fuzzy, I knew that something had happened, and it affected everything.

On the open highway, en route to Massachusetts, my spirits lifted a bit. I don't know what it was about crossing that state line from NH into Massachusetts, but I always felt lighter. You would think Massachusetts drivers would have me going in the opposite direction, but nah. They could honk at me, cut me off, whatever. I'd been through worse than road-rage.

On Interstate 84 in Connecticut, and through the hills of Pennsylvania on I-81, I heard my father's voice echo, "Always take back road, no toll, no line, no traffic; maybe little longer but pretty."

He was right. It was beautiful. Every time.

Once home in Silver Spring, I wasted no time dialing Joel's number.

"Hello?"

"Hey, Joel. I need to see you sooner than our next scheduled session."

"Okay. Everything all right?"

"Yes and no. I don't know. Are Thursdays still kind of my night?"

"Yes. Same time?"

"Yeah. Thank you."

"See you then."

That helped but didn't necessarily stop childhood demons from making a nest in my psyche. I lay on the couch, spooning Bartok while Moron quietly played with his stuffed dragon at my feet.

Think, think. What was it you saw at the tracks after she ran inside?

Something told me I didn't want to remember, so I got up and made myself one strong Cosmopolitan with an extra drop of lime juice for that extra bitter taste. Like me.

While the deafening sound of Kelly's ghost sobbed from the other end of the couch—and *Sex and the City* played episode after episode from a Netflix DVD—I drank until several strong Cosmos, many uninvited memories, a few detailed vignettes of Dean's excitable libido, and everything that had happened since came shooting from my mouth into the toilet.

Memories swirled in the form of pink bile, mocking me from the commode I clung to. I heard Joel's voice after puking, "You were abused—plain and simple."

He was right. I knew that, but I didn't know it while it was happening, and that made me feel stupid. *How could I not know? Was any of it my fault?*

My hands slid down the side of the toilet. I rested my cheek on the seat and passed out to the sounds of two little snouts sniffing the bathroom floor.

●●●

"What couldn't wait, Rebekah?" Joel turned in his chair just as I walked into his office.

I sat on the couch, kicked off my shoes, and immediately teared up. "I got back from New Hampshire this past Sunday."

"How was it?"

I avoided eye contact, dug into my pocket, and handed him a flattened penny.

He smiled while looking it over. "This is special. Thank you."

I covered my face with my hands.

"What is it?"

I grabbed the tissue box Joel shook at me, and said, "I saw something happening to me."

"I gather you were at the tracks. What happened there?"

I looked at him, with tears in my eyes, and said, "I saw her. *Me*."

Joel leaned back in his chair.

"She was confident. Carefree. Intelligent. Adorable. Filthy. Unafraid...and it's all about to change."

"Why?"

"When I left her, after Mom called her inside, these movies started playing in my mind. I saw things that were about to happen to her that I couldn't stop. It's like I saw the crimes before they were committed."

"What did you see?"

I blinked, wishing I could *un*see it. I stared at the wall past Joel. Another version of me took over, then said, "I see a dark closet and a boy."

That was all I could say. I didn't feel right relaying her story, though it was part of mine.

We sat in silence until Joel said, "Let's resume a weekly schedule."

I looked at the clock. Top of the hour came slow but fast just the same. I nodded my head while dressing my feet.

"And I'd like you to continue journaling."

"Okay."

• • •

FOR AS LONG as I've known me, I've been hard. A challenging person to love. My presence adds a disquieting tension to most rooms, and I can feel uneasiness stirring in the people around me. Eggshells are strewn all over the floor and no one knows quite where to step, including me.

I've lived in this callous shell, powerless to find comfort inside my own hardened casing, and unable to cope with the haunted, jellied mush buried deep within.

I've always been envious of softness. Some people float—like the velvety filter of an Olan Mills photo—effortless, easy, gentle, and delicate. I grind with the graininess of an old-timey Western photo—harsh, serious, rough, and troubled. I think I know why.

When something is taken from you at such a young and impressionable age, you risk losing so much more than your innocence. Pieces of you fall off, trailing behind you, trying to keep up and find places to fit before fading away altogether. Lost smiles long to widen, sparkling eyes wish to wonder, and the heart wants desperately to beat with joy instead of fear.

Seeing my younger self at the tracks, before anything had happened, reminded me how carefree I was and just how much one seemingly insignificant event would change it all. It opened me up to experiences I wasn't ready for, things I didn't understand, dares I should never have accepted, people I shouldn't have trusted.

To forget it all, I drank. While drinking and watching bad television, I fell in love with an old piece of me found in random episodes of *Sex and the City*, a piece of me I thought I'd lost, a piece that tied in nicely with journaling.

What I loved most about the show was the narration. It didn't matter that the show was mostly about sex, who was fucking who, who got off, who didn't—the *writing* captivated me. Carrie Bradshaw poked at my middle school fantasies of being a writer until they awakened.

On nights I couldn't see past my own misery—suffocating the memories that were trying to breathe at the surface—I listened to my favorites on vinyl, drafting album reviews in my head. I became a walking cluster of song lyrics; the Siskel and Ebert of music.

I played "Fast Car" by Tracy Chapman, looking for an escape route between the grooves. The player's tone arm found "Human Nature" by Michael Jackson, constantly reaching for happier childhood memories. I rested the needle on Boston's "Amanda," wishing to ride away on Brad Delp's passionate vocal cords. And I spun "Alison" by Elvis Costello regularly because my aim was true.

I'd stumbled upon a book called *Love is a Mix Tape* by Rob Sheffield—a contributing editor for Rolling Stone—and fell madly in love with his heart, story of lost love, album reviews, and of course, his writing.

I vowed to research the art of writing album reviews during my next book run.

My Sunday mornings were one hundred percent reserved for hours upon hours of book browsing at Borders. I'd start in one section of the bookstore and wind up on the other side, shuffling more than I could carry while deciding which books were coming home with me.

Italian Vegan Cooking, Star Wars Darth Bane: Path of Destruction, The Tao of Pooh, and *Endometriosis and You* had made the final cut.

At the SLA office one day, I used a company computer to check my Myspace profile. In bold, there was a new message. I clicked on the profile picture. Travis was a gorgeous, bald, blue-eyed man. *Shit, this won't work;* his profile stated he was a Yankees fan.

We exchanged a few messages.

When I said I made weekly book runs to Borders, he asked which books I'd recently bought, then mentioned he'd just finished rereading *Candide* by Voltaire. A hot, well-read man curious about my book haul?

Welcome, Travis.

We went out on one date. I didn't want to admit that I really liked him and could see myself falling hard, fast. I fought it. Not only because I was still reeling in Kelly-covered grief but because I was coming to some dark realizations about things I remembered while at the tracks. And could there be a future between a Yankees fan and a Red Sox fan?

I told Joel.

•••

"Rebekah, slow down. It's only been a week since you recalled something very significant from your past. We haven't even worked through it yet. Your actions are becoming cyclical."

I looked at him, my eyes blinking rapidly. "Meaning?"

"Well, because of this incident from your youth, your sexual misconduct tribunals at the Kingdom Hall, your licentious

Dean years, your extramarital affair, and your recent dates with Ben... Do you think jumping into anything right now is wise?"

He was right. I hated him for it. I felt my presence changing. The softness I'd felt a moment ago, transformed into harsh grittiness. I wanted to be velvet, but I was sandpaper through and through.

"Maybe Travis could soothe me somehow."

"Just give yourself a little time. Some space. Have you been journaling?"

"And drinking. Journaling and drinking."

He sighed, then pursed his lips. "Let me see what you've scribbled."

I handed him my journal. It was a bit worn but still kind of elegant looking, regal—what I wished for myself. He flipped through it and stopped suddenly. His eyes widened, begging for elaboration.

"This poem," he said, showing me the journal, tapping the page with his pointer finger. "What's it about?"

I leaned closer and saw:

> *"Yellow water and moldy popcorn*
> *surface from something evil.*
> *Trapped but not resisting,*
> *frozen and warm, skin on skin.*
> *She screams.*
> *Rusted red pressure underneath,*
> *pushes the door open.*
> *She's confused.*
> *She's wet.*
> *It smells.*
> *It's over."*

"Oh, yeah. That's the movie reel playing in clips." I leaned back and Joel shook the journal with subtlety, indicating he was finished with it.

I leaned forward again, took it, and set it beside me.

"Do you want to talk about this?"

I shrugged. "It's what I told you about last week with more detail; something I felt from mentally putting myself back there."

"How do you feel about it?"

"I mean, I wish I didn't remember it. I wish the things that happened afterward didn't happen. But they did. I guess I can sort of get why I've always felt so..." I paused, searching for the right word.

"Eager?"

"I was thinking 'promiscuous,' but eager does sound nicer." A bit offended that he already knew what I thought of myself, and slighted that he agreed, I was amenable just the same.

"Well, children who've experienced varying types of sexual trauma and abuse can develop precarious sexual behaviors. Research shows that, in most cases, cycles start repeating," he said.

I nodded, filing that tidbit for future contemplation, then said, "Speaking of things repeating, something you told me recently is on a loop in my head. You said, 'You were abused—plain and simple.' I didn't know it then. I thought what I went through with family, old boyfriends, and my first husband was normal; like, everyone experiences abuse. But that's not true; abuse *doesn't* happen to everyone. It makes me feel stupid, weak."

"You're anything but. You're like fire; powerful."

"Then why can't I just blaze through this? If I'm fire, then why did I allow paralyzing fear and submission to control me for so long? Where did it all stem from?"

"For you, it started with the Governing Body."

I scoffed. "Isn't that *too* easy?"

"Yes and no. It unintentionally began with your parents, and perhaps even before them. Abuse cycles are difficult to catch, let alone stop completely. Remember when we discovered—" Joel opened one of his desk drawers, fishing out a steno pad. He flipped through it. "Ah, here it is, right here: 'because of the institutionalized techniques and twisted programming at your parents' school, they easily fell prey to another type of mind control.' Remember that session?" He closed the steno pad, tossed it on his desk, and smiled at me like he'd just cracked the cipher of the Zodiac Killer.

Amused, I looked at him. "And?"

"Time and time again, they were abused in a variety of ways: hushed, pushed aside, unable to use their own voices; they find another programmed community that stifles them and their children, but they don't see it that way. They feel rescued even though, unbeknownst to them, another cycle of abuse is about to start. Fast forward to you here now, knowing all you know about them and yourself, and it's easy to see where the cycle began for them and where it began for you. The most amazing part of that is you have the power here and now to see it all for what it is and choose accordingly. You can forgive past hurts, stop the cycle, or let it continue, whatever... The choice is yours."

"Don't be late?" I asked, quoting a Nirvana song.

"Huh?"

"Nothing." I smiled, shaking my head.

Nirvana aside, he was right and deep down I knew it. My parents unintentionally started the cycle. In different ways, my brothers took part in keeping the wheel of abuse spinning via stonewalling, physical abuse, abandonment. And Dean had mixed pain and fear with warped affection during our four-year relationship.

"Everyone in my cycle of abuse probably suffered in ways I could never understand. Someone else is responsible for their cycle."

"That right there is what makes you the caring person you are. Now that you're coming to terms with what you know was abuse, don't lose that quality—your concern for others, your compassion. True compassion is having the ability to put yourself in someone else's shoes and literally empathize. I've watched too many folks harden. Don't harden, Rebekah. Don't let the hushed voices of your parents become your hushed voice. Find your voice and use it," he said, leaning forward and patting my knee.

Studying the lines and wise crevices scattered about Joel's Larry David-like face put me at ease. While dark, uninvited nightmares and stark realizations whorled around me, he and his calming presence felt like home.

"Next week?" he asked.

"I'll be here."

• • •

FIND YOUR VOICE and use it. Just give yourself a little time, Joel's words echoed as I got ready for date number three with Travis.

I know, I know. Don't jump into anything, I said to the mini-Joel perched on a tiny nerve in my brain—legs dangling, finger wagging.

On our date, Travis creeped around the topic of sport sex, I could tell he hoped I was athletic. Well, I've never been good at sports. And sport sex? Too dangerous for someone who just uncovered a traumatic memory on her therapist's couch. Not to mention, as soon as the dick hit the lips, I was liable to start getting attached. For me, the two were not mutually exclusive.

Exhibit A: Ben, right after I called it quits with Kelly.

Despite knowing the danger, I let it happen. Though Travis was sexy as hell, there was nothing athletic about it; my mind lingered near the tracks, floating between the sleepers.

After sex on his living room floor, we lay on his carpet, and he told me a story while stroking my hair.

"Once upon a time—" he began.

"Oh, my god." I rolled my eyes.

"Shh, listen. There was a couple with less than two dollars between them come Christmastime. The wife, very much in love with her husband, stared into the mirror at her long hair and cried while cutting it all off."

Gazing into his blue eyes, I asked, "Why?"

"To sell it, so she could buy her husband a platinum chain for his watch. Her hair sold for twenty dollars—just enough to buy the chain. When her husband got home, he was shocked by her short hair, since, until recently, it fell past her knees. When they exchanged gifts, she opened hers and cried."

"Why?"

"Her husband had given her combs she'd been wanting for her hair, only—"

"Now it's short."

"And when he saw the watch chain, he laughed—"

"Laughed?"

Travis nodded. "He'd sold his watch to buy the combs for his wife."

I laid there awestruck. I could feel myself falling for him. To push him away, I asked, "Why the Yankees?"

He sighed and stared at the ceiling, falling into a distant memory, before answering. "I used to listen to the games on the radio with my grandfather. I don't know, there was just something special about it."

Shit.

Later that week I lay in my bed, snuggling my furry sausages. While listening to the radio, I fell asleep. I woke, about 3 a.m., to a song that sounded familiar, though I knew I'd never heard it before.

The singer sang about knights in armor, saying something about a queen, and his voice transported me to another dimension. I saw myself in a filthy medieval peasant's dress, awaiting my fate. Why? I'm not sure, but the song...I couldn't get it out of my head.

At Travis' a few nights later, I mentioned the mysterious song.

"I have no idea who it is, what the song means, or why I can't get it out of my head. It's an annoying earworm."

"Knights in armor? A queen?" Travis got up from the couch and went into a back room. He came out holding a vinyl record album belonging to Neil Young.

"You...you have vinyl?" I was falling even harder than I had during his Gift of the Magi story.

He put the record on, moved the tone arm, and I heard the haunting melody of a lonely piano begin for the second time that week. I sat, completely stunned.

"Was this it?" he asked. "It's called 'After the Gold Rush.'"

I felt my mouth open, but I was speechless; suspended somewhere between falling in love and the crackle of a needle scraping wax was the perfect place.

We talked almost every day. The Red Sox and Yankee banter became a flirtatious dig between us; a cute story I could see telling our grandkids someday. We were becoming a thing.

Until I learned I wasn't the only woman Travis was dating.

To be fair, we never agreed to be exclusive. I just assumed we were, and I had no problem being a one-man woman once I saw his vinyl collection. I wasn't angry with him; he was a genuinely good man with a kind heart. But the damage had already been done.

I remembered why I rarely ever wanted to make it past date number two. I fell too hard, too fast. Having recently peeled back layers of my bitter, trauma-flavored onion, I understood why having sex early on in any relationship wasn't a huge deal for me.

She's confused. She's wet. It smells. It's over.

I decided to end it before things got ugly, promising myself I'd take the space Joel said I needed. I sent Travis a message on AOL Instant Messenger via my Sidekick (it was wildly popular in the early aughts, shut up).

> Leialuvs: I really like you. I have to stop seeing you or I'll fall in love. I don't think that's where you are and it's okay.

I half-lied. I was already in love with him, but I wasn't telling him that. I figured he had dates lining up at his door and he wouldn't miss my company much at all. I was wrong.

> Trav-nine: I get it. I'm not happy about it, but I understand. I also don't want to lose you. You're important to me.

I'd considered responding, salvaging something; just one more date, one more fuck, but when I saw his away message:

> Trav-nine: ...*but my dreams, they aren't as empty as my conscience seems to be...*

I left it alone because like The Who sang, I knew my love was vengeance, that's never free.

The few guys I'd dated since Kelly had at least one thing in common: no matter how long or short our time together, I fell hard and could see a future—sometimes within minutes of date, or fuck, number one. I hoped that didn't mean I was a lonely, pathetic, desperate woman, needing to find validation of her existence living in—or underneath—someone else's shadow.

Struggling with my damaged self-worth, I didn't want to think about reasons why I instantly attached myself to people. I'd always suspected that my upbringing and subsequent banishment from my own family was the culprit. But that's too easy, right? Too easy. It went much deeper than that, and I was beginning to see it, living among the insanity I wished I could forget.

Unrecognizable Shapes

NEW YEAR'S EVE.

I peeled myself off the couch to meet Kara and a few others in DuPont Circle. And while in one of the gayest pockets of D.C., at one of the gayest clubs, I planned to drown unlikeable pieces of myself in enough alcohol to forget recent memories.

Four bitter Cosmos in, I left the New Year's crowd behind, jumping onto an elevated platform, gyrating uncontrollably.

The club's deep, rhythmic bass vibrated my earlobes. The beat moved my body, almost involuntarily. Gorgeous gay men hopped up onto the pedestal, bathing themselves in the desperate aura I emitted.

While grabbing me around the waist and grinding, my dance partner shouted, "You're fabulous! Are you straight?"

"I'm all about the cock!" I shouted into his ear.

He laughed. "Me too!"

I smiled, keeping in sync with the beat. Slinking down to his waistline, I grabbed the edge of his shirt with my teeth. While dancing my way up, I brought the shirt up to his neck, grinding against him.

"Oh, my god! You have to do something for me!" He grabbed my hand, we hopped off the pedestal, and he led me through the dancefloor, stopping at the bar. He pointed to someone sitting on a barstool.

"He has coke," he said.

"I don't do coke."

"You don't have to, honey. Just score some for me."

"Why don't you?"

"Girl, please," he said, looking me up and down as if I were a hard cock on-a-stick. "You can get anything you want, and you could get it a lot faster than I could. He's stingy, but he won't be with you. Go!"

He gave me money and pointed again to who he believed I'd have no problem manipulating. I slithered up to the man at the bar, tilted my head playfully, and before I knew it, I held a tiny plastic baggie in my hand. The minute-long exchange was shockingly pedestrian. I hand delivered the goods to my dance partner near the porn-room door.

"You are a fucking queen, I love you!" he said.

He waltzed into the bathroom, snorting himself into ecstasy.

Standing against the wall of the porn-room, I lit a Parliament and looked around. Ass-fucking and dick-sucking took place on the screen before me, the bass bounced, my chest vibrated.

Bending my own warped-and-barely-intact principles felt oddly familiar. I had gotten used to being whatever anyone needed at any given moment. I was certain, more than ever, that I possessed some sort of chameleon muscle—that was a given.

I was beginning to understand where it stemmed from. Actively concealing who I was all those years as a J-Dub, while hiding inside the armor I'd created for my own protection, my chameleon-like abilities were less mysterious. And darker; much darker than I'd realized. Left unchecked, they had the power to contort into unrecognizable shapes.

Seconds after midnight, my flip-phone buzzed with several "Happy New Year!" messages.

Receiving a text message from Travis opened the door of communication again. I peeked inside our recently shared space and tiptoed carefully, so as not to fall again.

Recovering from my New Year hangover the next day, I laid on my sofa, Sidekick in hand, instant messaging Travis.

Trav-nine: I miss hanging out.

Leialuvs: Hanging out or having your dick sucked?

Trav-nine: Rebekah. C'mon. I miss you. Can we hang out soon?

Leialuvs: Sure. Just don't tell me any more love stories.

Trav-nine: Deal. Come over for *Family Guy* and beers on Sunday?

Leialuvs: Okay.

The truth was, I did miss hanging out with him. He was easy to be around. Though the two of us together didn't equal a love connection, he was honest, sincere, and trustworthy. I needed to get used to things not working out with people the way I envisioned, then resume some type of relationship with them after the fact. It was far too easy to slam the door on people who didn't deserve it, while keeping it wide open for folks I never should have let inside.

Bravo, Watchtower.

Beers and *Family Guy* on Sunday nights quickly became one of my favorite pastimes, taking place week after week.

"Hey, c'mere. I want to show you something," I said, sitting at Travis' computer, logging into Myspace. Travis leaned in behind me, peering at the monitor. I showed him the profile of a guy I'd started talking to a few weeks after the New Year. "Cute, right?"

"Um, well, sure. But he's in New Mexico?" Travis sipped his beer. "What can come of that?"

"Nothing now, but at least it'd be less pressure physically." I was certain I'd benefit from a large personal bubble while sifting through the memories that had recently surfaced. "His messages are sweet. Look."

"No, Rebekah. No. Walk away now." Travis shook his head.

"Why? Jealous?" I was half-teasing and one hundred percent still hopeful.

"You can do better than this guy. His message says: 'Feel free to *baroose* my profile.' I think he meant to say, peruse."

"Maybe a typo?"

"That's not a typo, sweetie. No. Just, no." He wagged his finger at me. "C'mon. *Family Guy* is back on."

We spooned on the couch—because that's what friends do—and zoned out to the sound of Peter Griffin's annoying laugh. I lay there, snuggled against Travis, wondering if I was desperate enough to *baroose* someone's Myspace page.

●●●

Joel, the only man in my life that made any sense, spun in his leather chair, greeting me with a smile. "How are you this week?"

I sat on the couch and kicked off my shoes. "Okay? I don't know."

"Well post-traumatic stress disorder, PTSD, is a beast to work with."

I tucked my socked feet under my ass and said, "I thought PTSD was reserved for war veterans."

"At one time it mainly applied to them, when it was referred to as 'shell shock,' but more and more people are relating to the experience for a host of reasons—abuse, sexual or not, is one of them. One of the big ones, actually."

"I won't be doing anything to exacerbate it," I muttered.

"Why do I feel like there's something you're not telling me?"

I hate that he knows me so well.

I shifted on the couch before answering his question with a question. "What do you mean?"

He tilted his head to the side and squinted while raising his eyebrows just a hair. "Rebekah, how long have you and I been meeting?"

I shrugged. "A year or so?"

"Mm-hmm," he said.

"Why?"

"Long enough for me to guess that you've accepted a platonic relationship with Travis, a man you were recently dating and quite fond of, because you're already distracting yourself with someone new." He exhaled, setting his elbow on the arm of his chair, thumb under his chin, two fingers pressed into his cheek, waiting like a perturbed parent.

I stared at my hands, embarrassed. "He's no one. I mean, his messages are chock-full of grammatical errors, misspellings," I said, knowing full well I was lonely enough to overlook that.

Joel laughed. "That doesn't mean you won't. Where'd you meet him?"

"Online. He lives in New Mexico."

He turned his lips down and bobbed his head. "New Mexico, huh?"

"Yeah. I thought I'd take my imminent heartbreak across state lines, heh." I was only half-joking. "Meeting someone as you both reach for the same free *Express* newspaper before hopping the Metro are fading fast. People meet online now."

He bobbed his head again. "I don't envy your generation. How long have you been talking with him?"

"A few weeks? We started out texting, now he's calling. Maybe being time zones away might slow things down?" I heard myself try to convince Joel.

"Maybe," Joel said, sounding doubtful.

I was too.

• • •

DOUBTFUL AND STUBBORN. I had already resolved to see it through—*baroosing* and all. The distance was perfect; I could fall, the way I typically did, without his dick meeting any of my orifices. No lines could be blurred. No misunderstandings. No awkwardness. Nothing.

Caleb and I talked about life, love, religion, and sex. As I got to know him, his brokenness clicked on like a flashing, neon billboard in a crowded city. So, I unplugged it. Despite its persistent jabs, I forced my gut-poking flagpole to hush and soldiered right into an actual, long-distance relationship with a man I had yet to meet in person. Since my gut had never been in an online, long-distance relationship before, it continued to poke, and I continued to silence it.

Caleb and I sent care packages full of personal effects—t-shirts, pictures, keepsakes from both the D.C. Metro area and New Mexico. We were exclusive for about a month until I got a phone call.

"Hello?"

"Hi. How do you know Caleb?" a young woman asked.

"We met on Myspace. Who's this?"

"His girlfriend." *Girlfriend? She's got to be joking.*

She wasn't.

I apologized, saying I had no idea. She said they shared a cell phone account, and when she received the bill, she was dying to know who he'd been calling in the middle of the night. I didn't blame her.

Rather than accept that he'd been caught, rather than come clean, Caleb insisted this woman was in the wrong.

"She's my *ex*-girlfriend. We share an account because after we broke up, she offered to keep me on until I went into the Navy—"

"The Navy? You have a girlfriend and are joining the Navy? What...how..." Words failed me; my head spun. I hung up. On whom, I had no idea.

He sent text after text. "Please, let me explain. You're my reason to change. Reason to be better."

"You barely know me, let alone well enough for me to be your 'reason.' Stop texting and calling me." *I should just listen to Joel from now on.*

I'd had it with people I couldn't trust. Was I attracting these bozos, or was I just so damn tired of the dating cycle Mark had predicted for me that I simply allowed these fools into my life? I felt as though I was wearing a sign: LIARS, POOR SPELLERS, THOSE EASILY ATTACHED, FUCK-BUDDIES, PLAYERS—I'M OPEN FOR BUSINESS.

I needed to get away.

With the raise I received after my security clearance was granted, I saved a bit of money and booked myself a trip to Oahu. Alone.

Having never been anywhere alone before—aside from the long, familiar drive from Silver Spring, Maryland to NH—I was nervous but by no means backing down. I wasn't going to let fear, resurfacing memories from my childhood, or anything that had happened afterward stunt my growth. I'd just turned thirty. I had a shit ton of living to do.

●●●

"I booked myself a trip to Oahu," I said, walking into Joel's office.

"That's great! Going with friends, or…?"

"No," I said. "I'm going alone."

I told Joel about the phone call I got from Caleb's 'girlfriend', but I didn't tell him I was plagued by Caleb's fierce insistence that it was his *ex*-girlfriend. *What if she's the one lying? A woman scorned?*

"Red flag, steer clear of that one. Rebekah, you've got to stop selling yourself short. This is one way the cycle of abuse just keeps on spinning."

"What is?" I asked, defensive.

25

"You, not recognizing and accepting your own worth. The abuse wheel will just keep circling around and around. If you don't take some control, you'll spin out."

"Well, tell me how to start accepting myself, then. I mean, we've been meeting for over a year now. Share some friggin' secrets, tell me what to do!"

I'd never scolded Joel before. He was my voice of reason, my Thursday evening champion, but I needed more. I wanted some goddamn direction. Now that I knew all these things about myself, and why I was how I was, what's next?

He smiled and said, "Good. You're using your voice."

I sat with my arms folded, looking out the window.

"How's work?" he asked.

I shrugged. "Fine. You know I can't talk about work." I had RID's confidentiality tenant from the Code of Ethics almost memorized. "I think I can share one thing with you, though."

I leaned forward and fished around in my bag for a stapled packet I received while on a recent assignment. I handed it to him.

Joel adjusted his glasses and flipped through the packet. When he was through, he handed it back to me.

"Well?" I asked, stuffing the papers back into my bag.

Joel crossed his leg and leaned back in his chair. "That's the Myers-Briggs Type Indicator. Some say it's valid, others don't think it's worth its salt. It might help you understand different facets of your personality, your behaviors. What you or others see as a 'weakness' or 'personality flaw,' could very well be a strength. For you, answering the questions in the packet may further your own self-awareness, perhaps even your own self-acceptance."

Did I need some test to tell me how fucked I was? To tell me I was uncomfortable around most people? Untrusting though I cling easily? Or that I attract even-more-fucked-than-I-am (if that's possible) types of people that never say it outright but secretly want me to fix them in some undefined way? Or how I don't feel right around anyone, and no one gets me? There's a test for that?

"How's...everything else?" he asked.

I knew what he was asking, and I didn't want to talk about that. How is anyone after remembering scattered bits of their past that flood to the surface—unable do anything to protect the little version of themselves, unable to stop the horrors about to befall them—then sandwiching those memories somewhere between too much alcohol and dates that didn't go anywhere? How is anyone after that?

"Everything is... I'm, you know, doing okay, I guess."

Chameleon Girl

I ENLISTED KARA to assume all apartment and dachshund-sitting duties. The boys were crazy about their auntie Kara, and she loved them just as much in return.

After booking a Circle Island Tour, a seat at the Paradise Cove Luau, and a romantic sunset dinner cruise as part of my all-inclusive package, I was on a plane to the magical island of Oahu to find and woo myself.

With hours to kill, I grabbed the Myers-Briggs packet and a pen from my bag, pulled down the tray table in front of me, and started grazing the test.

Highly agree or highly disagree:

1. People rarely upset you. DISAGREE.
2. You spend time thinking about unrealistic/intriguing ideas. AGREE.
3. You are still bothered by mistakes from the past. *Um, hello. I'm in therapy.* AGREE.

*Oh, my god I'm already exhausted and there are...*I flipped to the last page...*ninety-seven more questions.* I returned the test to my bag, put my tray table up, leaned my seat back as far as it would go, and tried to sleep before laying over in O'Hare.

In Honolulu, time stopped. My body's tension subsided as sweet Oahu air whorled around me, holding me in the center of its super-coiled spiral of warm protection.

While driving past Don Ho Lane, his song "Tiny Bubbles" echoed between my ears and I just...let...go; fully let go for the first time since Kelly had softened my edges two years before. My body relaxed; my breathing stabilized; Oahu had me in a trance.

After checking into my hotel, I walked down Liliuokalani Avenue toward the ocean. Steps away from Waikiki Beach, I stood before these massive Banyan trees.

The tree branches fell to the ground, re-rooted, and grew back into themselves—tall, proud, strong. I wanted to do that: catch my own falls, use my mistakes to re-root myself, and become whoever I was meant to be. White pigeons found their home within the crevices of the Banyan trees, nuzzling with content. If they could find a place they belonged, why couldn't I?

Leaving the beach, I turned a corner and came to King's Village. I treated myself to '50s diner grub and a small gift from Rock Island Café. Saying aloha to the ghosts of Elvis, James Dean, and Marilyn Monroe, I hopped the city bus and rode around the island in search of the perfect shave ice. I was told repeatedly that it's not shave*d* ice. In Hawaii, it's just shave ice. Either way, I found it: lilikoi. Hawaiians take the art of ice and fruit syrup in a cup to a whole new level—worth a city bus trip.

The next morning, I woke early. The shift in time zones had me up at 4 a.m. I went to the lobby and saw other restless souls roaming the hotel like aimless zombies. I made my way outside and drifted down Liliuokalani Avenue again, toward the beach; it was calling me.

Sitting, listening to sounds of the Pacific Ocean, I thought about my childhood incident. It was as grainy as the sand beneath my feet and played like an old silent movie. I stared at the many miles of ocean ahead of me, wanting to ride those waves into sweet oblivion. Instead, my mind's eye replaced a wondrous beach experience with scattered images of the Dagobah System, my childhood bedroom's brick-red colored carpet, the darkness of a closet, the smell of urine.

What is my subconscious trying to convey?

I watched the sunrise, waiting for the morning waves to tell me. But they didn't.

Back in the hotel lobby, fidgety zombies held coffee and made grumbling noises. I slid past folks, avoiding ritualistic good mornings, empty pleasantries, and slithered into the elevator alone.

Soap suds still glistening from my rushed shower, I dressed, grabbed my bag, and saw the Myers-Briggs test peeking out from one of its pockets. I pulled out the packet and tossed it on the other double bed to force a prompt, reminding myself to look at it later.

Sitting on the tour bus, for the Grand Circle Island tour, in a row all to myself, I realized I was surrounded by newlyweds and anniversary celebrators. It was unnerving.

A newlywed couple noticed my discomfort and befriended me. I felt pity oozing from the bride's mouth as she asked in slow motion, "Are you here alone?" It sounded like she was underwater.

"Yes." I smiled, looking out the window while the tour guide rambled on about Hawaii's state fish, state flower, and other island trivia.

I was the newlywed couple's third wheel for most of the morning until the husband bounded to my side each time I asked someone to take a picture of me at the landmarks we visited.

The husband grabbed the new digital camera I'd bought especially for the trip, (thus far it only had photos of Travis, playfully, but literally, climbing the walls in a parking garage just before my vacation) and I heard it click several times.

Instead of taking one, maybe two pictures, he snapped several. He was a professional photographer, and I, his model. While snapping picture after picture, his wife came up beside him.

"I think you got it," she said, glaring at me as if I'd slinked up to him at a bar, giving him the key to my hotel room.

Dipping his head, he handed me the camera and walked away with his bride.

I scrolled through the pictures while walking around a koi fishpond and counted eight. Eight pictures of gentle Hawaiian breezes flitting my hair in different directions. Eight pictures of me moving hair away from my face. Eight pictures of my head in different lighting. Eight pictures of my eyes shifting. Eight pictures of my nervous smirk turning into a full-blown smile. Eight pictures stored in that man's spank-bank.

He didn't have to say anything of the sort. I just knew. And no wonder his wife had daggers for me. I steered clear of them for the rest of the day.

Feeling small, I roamed Kualoa Ranch—the next stop on our tour. Gawking at mountains once dressing the movie set of Jurassic Park, I wished to disappear inside the huge dinosaur prints scattered on the ground; it'd feel much safer in there.

Our island tour guide had noticed I was no longer part of a throuple. Sitting alone in Aunty Pat's Café, he came over and kept me company during lunch. I welcomed the presence of another human but dismissed his overt friendliness.

At various stops along the way, back to our respective hotels, the guide dared getting closer; boldly inserting himself into my personal bubble.

At the last tourist stop of the day, I stood in an antique shop deciding which mass-market paperback on the spinning rack was coming back to my room with me. He came up beside me, grabbed my elbow, leaned into me, and said, "I can give you a private tour tonight if you like."

What fucking hubris.

Wiggling my arm free, I knit my brows, and said, "No, thank you."

Leaving the antique shop with no book really pissed me off. I returned to the bus and sat with my arms folded.

Along our journey back to Waikiki, the perverted tour guide quizzed us on all the Hawaiian trivia we'd heard throughout the day.

Standing at the front of the bus, facing us, he asked, "Anyone remember the state fish of Hawaii?"

I piped up. "It's the humuhumunukunukuāpua'a!" Ha! I'd even pronounced it correctly.

He ignored me. "Anyone?"

I said it again. Louder. "Humuhumunukunukuāpua'a!"

He ignored me again.

An older woman on her thirty-fifth wedding anniversary muttered the state fish's odd name from the back of the bus.

"Right! The humuhumunukunukuāpua'a!"

He glared at me. I'd bruised his ego and he wanted to be sure I knew it. As further punishment, my hotel was the last stop. I was the last tourist to exit the bus.

Just before the door closed, the creeper said, "Last chance. You sure you don't want to join me on an after-hours tour tonight?"

Without looking back, I shouted, "I'm sure!" and walked toward my hotel's entrance. That couldn't have been his first time offering private tours, and he'd probably been successful in the past.

My gut instincts were spot on about that weasel, and I knew deep down there had to be more to my feelings than just a lucky hunch.

It was the feelings; I had these feelings about people that I couldn't articulate. I just knew that I knew what I knew. There was no other way to phrase it.

In the safety of my hotel room, I dropped my bag to the floor and fell on the bed. I heard a crumple. *Oh, the Myers-Briggs packet.* I conceded to finishing the test instead of starting the mysterious book I would have purchased had I not been manhandled by the firm grip of a pushy island-dweller.

I flipped to the most recent page I was on and continued answering questions.

4. You contemplate human existence and the meaning of life often. AGREE
5. You have no interest in philosophical discussions. DISAGREE
6. Time spent alone is more satisfying than time spent with others. AGREE

Upon finishing the test, I read through my diagnosis.

Introvert: a quiet, reticent person who prefers minimally stimulating environments. Often preoccupied with their own thoughts and feelings, they may feel drained after socializing, and prefer to recharge alone, mainly because their brains respond to dopamine differently than extroverts.

And on the flipside, extroverts are talkative, outgoing, and assertive. Sometimes attention-seeking, easily distracted, concerned with external things, and likely unwilling to spend much time alone.

Well, I'm definitely not an extrovert. I'm vacationing alone and perfectly content doing so.

I read through the packet again and lay on the bed, staring at the ceiling in deep thought—no, wait—in deep *feeling*. This novel information explained things about me that I'd always been stumped by. It might be why I didn't feel like I fit in at school, the Kingdom Hall, or even with my own family; why I cherished being alone, waiting for the trains; why I preferred books, animals, and nature to crowds of people.

I'd heard the word "introvert" several times, but it was usually said in a belittling tone—as if introversion was some sort of character flaw—like introverted people were just shy, incompetent, frustrated, socially awkward extroverts. But that didn't feel like me. I wasn't anti-social, just picky. I loved people; the right kinds of people; people I could be soul-social with.

And the feelings—I felt like I had some unspoken "knowing" coursing through my veins; for years I couldn't put my finger on it.

I felt centuries old and dark—like Dracula. I could see the whole existence of mankind from afar, understand nuances of human behavior, and still, connected with almost no one. Like Dracula—misunderstood, clogged, unsettled—I was able to feel the blood in people, boiling beneath the surface.

Poor Dracula. Year after year he's lonely, thirsty, forever stuck, and unable to escape the pain within. Missed human connections pass him by and he's left with vile pieces of people to feed on. That's not sustenance; it's bare-minimum survival. I snuggled into bed and fell asleep in Dracula's arms.

He gets me.

The next tourist activity on my itinerary was snorkeling in Hanauma Bay. With no husband nearby lulling me into a false sense of security, then ditching me to hit the reef as I bob alone in the Gulf of Mexico, I thought I could I confront my fear of water. I wanted to make friends with the ocean.

A shuttle bus carted eight tourists from Waikiki to Hanauma Bay. On the drive, I became the fourth in a group of three— one couple and one single gentleman—all in their late fifties, there for a business trip. The single guy, Eddie, had left his wife at the hotel, and I became her stand-in. Companionship-wise.

Snorkeling at Hanauma Bay was perfect. There was no boat bringing me to deep waters, expecting me to fend for myself. With snorkel gear on, each person was free to go as deep, or stay as shallow, as they liked. I had total agency.

Still nervous and scared of accidentally touching sensitive coral, I paired up with Eddie as suggested. Having someone to grab onto—if I accidentally swam too close to a sudden drop-off or near another bloodthirsty Barracuda—was absolutely necessary for me.

Eddie was a perfect gentleman. Not only did he hold my hand and bring me farther out to look at the sea turtles, but he wouldn't let me go until I said I was okay. Once I had my fill of being in the water (I'm talking minutes. I have an inexplicable fear of the ocean even though I love it), I flopped my way to shore.

Sitting safely on the beach with my AARP friends, I felt at ease. My body slackened in their presence. They were just the company I needed after being ogled via camera lens and accosted by a brazen tour guide. I felt like an average woman vacationing with friends.

Until the wife in our foursome suggested snapping a picture of me and Eddie.

We stood close—arm-in-arm, smiling with snorkel gear in hand—so that Eddie's wife could see the "sexy beach girl" he got to snorkel with. I didn't see what the woman snapping the photo saw, while my black tankini covered my growing Cosmo gut. But to her, I was a thirty-something sex symbol and she wanted Eddie's wife to know it for some reason.

What I noticed about myself over the course of those two days was the innate ability I had to read people. Regardless of anyone's intentions, or what they might have thought of me, I could feel it well before they had a chance to make it obvious. Whether sinister or benevolent, I could see plans formulating in their minds.

This would prove to be a useful tool my last night on Oahu. Well, sort of.

Sitting at Lulu's, looking out at Waikiki Beach, I jammed my Cosmo-drinking piehole with lilikoi stuffed French toast. My phone buzzed. Daren, a one-time-date-turned-friend back in D.C., had texted me.

He saw from my Myspace profile that I was on the island. So was he, playing roadie for a popular Top 40s band. They were performing on the island near my hotel. Did I want to be picked up by a limo, go to the show for free, then party with him and the band? *Yes, Daren. Yes, I do.*

At the Pipeline Café, Daren and the band buzzed about, setting the stage. While drinking at the bar, I stood in the eye of the club's storm watching people come in group by group.

By night's end, as the band's one-hit wonder pierced the air, I was barely able to stand. I don't remember leaving the bar and have no memory of how I wound up in a hotel room with Daren and the band.

Thank goodness my instincts about Daren were spot on and worth trusting; I'd drunk my intuition away, falling face first onto a queen-sized hotel bed.

The room spun. My vision was beyond blurred. I mumbled, "Oh, my god. I shouldn't've…drank…that much."

I heard Daren laugh from the other queen bed and felt the weight of someone on top of me, hands roaming, pretending to fuck me doggy style.

I heard Daren again. "No. Dude. Get off her."

"Why, you want to go first?"

"No," Daren said. "Leave her alone."

The intentions of the band were not nearly as noble as Daren's. The one-hit wonder lead singer peeled his body off mine, and said, "Well, in that case, we're going."

And they left.

The room fell silent. Although I was irresponsibly drunk, I knew well enough then that it could have gone really bad, really fast. I lay in utter shock, heart pounding, silently cursing myself for allowing my growing spider-senses to be muted by alcohol. I also knew enough to mumble two very important words to Daren.

"Thank you."

"Eh, those guys can be such pricks sometimes. Wanna see the pictures I took during the Japan tour?"

I could hear the excitement in his voice, and I knew I owed him more than a slurred "thank you." I rolled over and opened my eyes. The ceiling was moving.

"Sure," I said.

Daren kept me there until 5 a.m., showing me his favorite Japan photos. The city, the lights, all of it were streaks of neon but I humored him as best I could without puking.

Once I was sober enough to walk to my hotel, I left Daren's room after making tentative plans to grab dinner when we were both back in D.C.

Stumbling down Liliuokalani Avenue with my McDonald's Spam-and-sticky-white-rice breakfast-to-go, I looked forward to going home. I loved Oahu but longed for boring familiarity. I ached for my boys, the bit of solid routine I'd established for us, and a Bek that I knew.

Some places, situations, and people bring out versions of yourself you never knew before. Some bring out the ugly. Some, the clueless. Some, the angry. And some bring out the best parts of you. I'd met so many facets of myself—on this trip alone—it was hard knowing who the real Slim Shady was.

Though my chameleon muscles were useful—and I was grateful for their strength—left unchecked, to the detriment or suppression of my intuition, they had the power to betray me, leading me to my own peril.

I visited a local ABC store for cheap Hawaiian gifts and flew home to Maryland—curious which version of Bek I'd meet at the gate.

A Superpowered Cult

WITH EACH NEW experience, another version of me surfaced. Would I like her? Trust her? Allow her to make decisions? Connections? Or hide her, tucking her deep inside the crevices of her own familiar darkness?

Returning to my very predictable Spork-Bartok-and-Moron existence reeled me right back into fifty-hour work weeks, distracting me from introspective, existential questions. The personality test results were still on my mind, along with the strange things that happened in Hawaii.

Thanks to the busiest time of the year, I was scheduled for several all-day trainings at one government agency—teamed with an active, J-Dub interpreter. We hadn't worked together yet, and I hoped the Truth wouldn't wiggle its way into conversation.

The morning part of our assignment went well. We were each attentive, provided feedback when necessary, took notes and turns every twenty minutes. I held on to the hope that we could just talk shop when we broke for lunch.

Sitting at a small table, cafeteria-style lunches before us, she wasted no time getting personal.

"How's your family?" she asked, cutting up her salad.

Here it comes.

I'd forced the ugly parts of me so far down they were hard to retrieve, hard to remember sometimes. That's how I got by; I repressed the ugly, stuffing it deep into the shadows I lurked in at any mention of my childhood nucleus. Hidden, disfigured pieces wore Mallory faces; that name had sealed my fate.

Upon meeting me, most folks still "in" expected an above average interpreter and a spiritually strong J-Dub wrapped in a perfect, ready-for-Armageddon package. I wasn't either of those things, and there was no escape hatch in the lunch café.

"My family? They're good, I guess," I answered.

"I watched a recording of your brother's special talk. He's brilliant, amazing." She took a bite of her salad.

Heigh-ho! Heigh-ho! Into their shadows I go...*insert whistle*.

I smiled before taking a bite of my sandwich and said, "He is." I couldn't argue that; Mark was smart and a phenomenal ASL heritage user.

"Which sign language congregation do you go to?"

I felt my body twitch and I thought, *if I tell her the truth, the rest of the afternoon will be awkward. I'll have to tell my managers that she and I can no longer be teamed together, throwing a wrench into their schedule. If I lie, she'll learn the truth soon enough and my lie will make its way back to the agency.* A catch-22.

"I don't go to any." I looked down at my plate and waited.

"You're still *in* though, right?"

I sighed. "No. I'm not."

I avoided her heavy gaze, rearranging the contents of my sandwich.

From the corner of my eye, I saw her put her knife and fork down on her plate. She placed her napkin and drink on the tray, and said, "Then you understand why I have to do this."

She stood up and walked to another table, leaving me alone to throw my sandwich back together.

Tears welled. My appetite vanished. I felt as if I was back in third grade—heckled, pointed at, misunderstood, not seen as a real person. *I'm just the girl in a cult with the Deaf parents, nothing to see here, move along.*

I felt like shit back then for not being *part of the world,* like my classmates. And I felt like shit in that lunch café for not

40

being in the Truth, like my team. In or out, I was fucked. And the *Society* was still making sure of that.

•••

"Well, look who's back from her tropical getaway," Joel said, spinning in his leather chair, wearing a big smile.

I forced a smile, kicked off my shoes, and sat.

"Uh-oh… What happened?"

I told Joel about my trip, which was fantastic for the most part, aside from the horny photographer, the tour guide, and the slippery drunken slope I was on until Daren stepped in.

"Remember the cycle we talked about—only you can stop it."

I nodded. "Oh, and I finished this." I handed him the Myers-Briggs packet.

Flipping through the packet while scanning my answers, he snickered to himself once or twice. Closing it, he asked, "How do you feel about your personality determination?"

I shrugged. "I guess it all makes sense and explains things I kind of always knew but couldn't pinpoint, you know? I know I tend to be quiet and a bit withdrawn, but I'm not shy, and around certain people—"

"You're gregarious. You can light up a room. Which you do. I'm not at all surprised you had some unfavorable experiences in Hawaii."

"What do you mean? I didn't ask for any of that *or* welcome it."

"I'm not suggesting that you did but hear me out—you're a beautiful young lady who has experienced passionate love and deep loss. You're very open to the possibility of finding and keeping an unfathomable, drive-you-crazy type of love. You exude that and can easily pick up on others emitting the same type of energy—like a radar or radio waves, you can feel it. Am I wrong?"

41

I shook my head. *Nope. Not wrong.*

"And when those feelers, or antennae, are activated, people gravitate to you. You magnetize them. Most people hear the word introvert and think 'shy, awkward loners.' This is not always the case."

"Yeah, I read that in the packet."

"There's an odd superpower, for lack of a better term, that comes with this territory. And I knew it about you given the chameleon-suit sessions we've had."

That was more than I was prepared to take in. Introvert, I kind of knew. Superpower?

I shook my head, freeing myself from all the questions surrounding it and said, "Okay. Um, cool. Food for thought, I guess?"

"Yes. We can talk more about it in other sessions if you'd rather. Something tells me you'll figure it out before I get the chance, though. What else is on your mind? Your eyebrows are talking."

I smirked then said, "The J-Dub stuff won't go away. I just want to live my life, figure out *how* to live my life, without being burdened by this whole cult thing."

Joel rested his elbows on the arms of his chair and leaned forward, lacing his fingers. "That's the thing about cults, Reb— they're initially sunk in so deep, pieces continue to surface, and they'll cause PTSD, too. The pieces may subside over time, but I'm sorry, they may never entirely go away. Especially for such a deep feeler like yourself. This part of the cycle may not completely stop. What's bothering you?"

I told him about my recent work assignment, how my team had treated me once she learned I was *mentally diseased*.

He pursed his lips and shook his head. "I'm sorry."

"I felt a little better after emailing my team lead, telling him what happened. He's also an ex J-Dub, so I knew he'd get it."

"Oh, that's comforting."

"Yeah, he's great." I was silent for a moment, then said, "Just the same, though... Who does she think she is? Why did she feel it was okay to treat me or anyone else that way?"

"Mind control, Reb. You were there once, too."

"Leaving was the best thing I ever did."

"Good for you for getting out."

Yes. Good for me. But still. Being rejected by anyone crushes the spirit.

• • •

INSTEAD OF HOSTING the orphan Thanksgiving I'd once had with other homeless-for-the-holiday SLA misfits, I was invited to New York City for the Macy's Day Parade. My dear friend Jodi, her husband Tom, and their toddler, Ethan, were planning to insert themselves somewhere near Central Park West to watch oversized floats bounce and drift by.

Jodi had weaseled her way into my semi-hardened heart years ago with her straight brown hair, adorable freckles, and brown doe eyes—which were far from naïve. She's an old soul. The kind of person you feel so calm with, you could fall asleep. She has this way. She's real. Like warm apple pie, she's surrounded by a firm but soft crust with a sweetened center, making you feel at home.

With Jodi I could be me, like I once was with Jax and Kelly. And because she had seen so many hidden sides of me, it was hard to escape her omnipotent glare; she always saw right through me.

In New York City, I'd never experienced the rush of so many people, exuding so much excitement over a Snoopy Balloon. But there they were, awestruck. As was I. Snoopy, bobbling in the sky, wearing his "Flying Ace" outfit, sent a shiver down my spine.

It was nice to feel like a kid, if but for a moment. No mind-controlled interpreting teams to feel small around. No strange men grabbing at me. No childhood memories flooding to the surface. Just me, my best friend, and some balloons.

Fighting the Macy's Day crowd gave us all a ravenous appetite and led us straight to a nearby restaurant serving their Thanksgiving Day meal. With full bellies, we meandered through the obscure streets and alleys of New York City in search of the perfect fall photo.

Tom found it as little Ethan and I raced each other down a side street. Tom caught us in a moment where neither my nor Ethan's feet were touching the ground.

High on the ecstasy New York City offers, Ethan and I were forever suspended in time, racing toward our own versions of paradise.

Back inside the comfort of Jodi's house—tucked into a cozy atmosphere that only she could provide—we opened a bottle of wine and listened to the comedic vocal quips of The Jerky Boys.

"Do you have balloons? Those big, brown balloons?" Jodi mimicked.

I laughed so hard no sound came out.

"Uh-oh, Ethan. They're getting silly over there," Tom said from the living room, a puzzle piece in hand looking for its rightful home.

"I saw you...looking at your flip-phone while Tom drove through Times Square. Who was texting you?" Jodi whispered.

I tried to think of something clever to say. Nothing.

I stared at the last bit of wine with a notion to gulp it down and rest easy at the bottom of my glass—untouched by her bold veracity.

"Were you talking to the guy who can't spell?" She let a tiny smile escape her lips. She could rarely keep a straight face under the influence of alcohol; it was one of those childlike, yet grandmotherly, things I adored about her.

I sighed. "Caleb texted to wish me a Happy Thanksgiving."

"It's been months. Why is he texting you now?"

I shrugged.

"Well?" She raised her eyebrows and her wineglass.

I sighed again. "I texted back—"

"Bek, no! He had a girlfriend, didn't he?"

"*Had.* He said they're not together now."

"Bek..." Her eyes took this opportunity to burrow deep into my soul like an old woman, exposing my hidden desires, all with the innocence of a child. I wondered if she had the same type of superpower Joel said I had, the one that could read people. Because she knew. She always just knew.

And so did I.

"I know. I know." I shifted in my chair and poured more wine into my glass, knowing full well I shouldn't.

There was no way, even with our shared instinctual gift for clairvoyance, that she could understand the unique pain buried inside me; the pain of losing my family; losing Kelly; being rejected by an interpreting team who clearly idolized my family's Jehovah's Witness celebrity-like status. And worst of all—confronting the pain of certain childhood memories all alone, like Dracula.

She had Tom; they were high school sweethearts. Together they had Ethan, an intentional child, who adored them both. In that moment, I felt I had only them: a perfect little nucleus that I, some foreign mutant, had squirmed my way into.

"I know that you'll know what to do," she said.

I nodded and smiled; thankful she held such high hopes for me. But I could feel myself slipping. The belief that she had in me—in my ability to be a strong, independent woman—hung heavy in the air around me, sheltering me from my own plans to self-destruct. I knew I would let her down. I had already planned to. And again, she knew it.

45

Packed up, I was ready for my drive back to Silver Spring the next day.

Jodi stood before me, holding a bagged sandwich, and said, "For the road. A little more jelly than peanut butter, right?"

I hated leaving someone who knew me well enough to know my preferred peanut-butter-to-jelly ratio. I smiled, trying not to let her see tears well up in my eyes. She held the sandwich, and very significant parts of my life, with grace and tenderness. I didn't know how she did it, and I had no idea how I'd ever return the favor. What could I possibly give her other than friendship wrapped in chaos?

Driving along I-78, I thought hard about whether I'd allow Caleb back into the picture. Could I be the person Jodi thought I was—strong, independent, and capable? Or was I more the person I thought I was—weak, desperate, and alone with some inexplicable superpower I had no clue how to wield?

I was all of the above, thoughtlessly thrown into one bitter cocktail. A sloppy drink, capable of sour-flavored strength and twisted sagacity.

Behind the wheel I lost track of time, which was easy to do on the long stretch of gorgeous Pennsylvania highway I often took to and from New England.

Sometimes I didn't listen to anything but the quick birth and death of my own ideas. Thoughts danced while holding tiny daggers, scraping the insides of my brain. Then, once the whirlwind of meditation ceased, I was left with nothing but broken pieces of self-reflection, lodged into grey matter, mocking me.

And what about what Joel had said? That personality test chatter? How does that help me? Would knowing bits of my multifaceted personality help or hinder me? If I did possess an innate shrewdness, was it inherent? Did Mom and Dad have it? My brothers? Does this awareness have anything to do with being raised in the Deaf community? Or was it just part of me? Can I control it like a superhero?

Falling so deep into my own head often left me bewildered and oddly wanting more. The more I thought and thought, the more I felt I might understand myself and why I do what I do. I knew I was deeper than how I was behaving. I knew I had the power to stop the cycle but playing in the shallow end of the pool was easier.

I also couldn't allow myself to be some chick, hungry for the attention of a guy who was unable to adequately articulate his own lies because he lacked grammar sense. I wanted to fight tooth-and-nail, refusing to be that woman.

But at the time, I was that woman. The one often ignoring her own already-formed intuition, making excuses so she didn't suffer being alone.

I'd done that often with Dean. I loved him madly, and at one time wanted him so much that all logic slipped away on my trip down a shame spiral. I was so knotted, twisted, inside his hedonistic world that I repeatedly overlooked the abuse and exploitation. And like Joel had said, I was abused—plain and simple.

I'd also done the same with my own family. Growing up in such a constricted, compacted family unit—squeezed so tight I could barely budge an inch—only to be let loose in a world where boundaries were unclear to me, left me fucked.

Growing up, I knew well enough to say no to things I was instructed to reject. But, outside the bubble, left to my own devices, I didn't know shit. The intuitive superpower and the J-Dub instruction were battling, and just as it came time for full-out war, I was back at square one—excusing things I shouldn't, inviting in all the wrong people.

With memories of Dean on one end, my family on the other, and a grammar transgressor from New Mexico in the middle of my mind's eye, I decided that the ex-girlfriend-omission-of-truth and poor spelling seemed somewhat trivial. Nothing would compare to the abusive, controlling years as a J-Dub or my time with Dean. This guy couldn't possibly be any worse, could he?

I took a bite of Jodi's a-little-more-jelly-than-peanut-butter sandwich and called Caleb. His line rang as I passed signs for Allentown.

"Hi," Caleb said, "I wasn't sure I'd hear from you again."

"I wasn't sure I'd call."

"So...what made you call?"

"I guess I wanted to give you the benefit of the doubt."

What does that even mean? Giving someone the benefit of the doubt? Does doubt have benefits? Can you gift someone with that? Doubts do serve a purpose. I mean, I doubted my beliefs and that had served me well. Didn't it?

"Well, thank you. Have you thought any more about me flying out there to meet you?" He wasted no time pulling the bookmark free from the story we'd begun writing together earlier that year, making himself comfortable on a clean page in a new chapter.

The last bite of Jodi's sandwich stared at me from its crusted corner, oozing grape jelly and heckling my lack of self-worth. Jodi's voice came through the last bite: *I know that you'll know what to do.*

With my left thumb and forefinger holding the corner piece, my middle, ring, and pinky fingers tightly wrapped around the steering wheel, and my flip phone in the other hand against my right ear, the highway blurred in front of me. All I saw was that last bite and one important decision.

"Fly up," I said, tossing the last corner piece into my mouth.

● ● ●

"How was your holiday weekend?" Joel asked as I walked into his office.

"Good. I visited my friend Jodi in Connecticut, and we went to New York City for the Macy's parade."

"That sounds fun."

"It was."

I looked out the window at the clouds rolling in. It usually didn't get too cold in the D.C. Metro area during the late fall and winter, but it got cold enough. Nothing like New England, but the clouds came barreling in, bringing a visible cold front. Or maybe that was just me.

"Rebekah? You there?"

I turned my head slowly and met Joel's eye.

"I'm just thinking about all the things we've talked about, everything you've taught me this past year or so. I don't know how to juggle it all. What do I do with all this?"

"All what?"

"Well, when I first came here, I thought I'd just talk about my Deaf parented upbringing, figure out some shit about how I was raised, then dump all the guilt I felt about Kelly and our affair onto you; like, you could absolve my sins somehow, you know? But then I learned I was raised in a cult, an actual cult, an elitist club, and treated as a pawn. Then you tell me I was abused. Then I recall a childhood incident that I don't even want to *think* about. Then this weird personality superpower thing surfaces. And don't even get me started on my job; I'm beginning to resent it. I mean, what am I supposed to do with all this shit?"

Joel sat in silence. I looked at the clock and watched the minute go by slowly.

"Grow," he said.

"Grow? Get that from a friggin' fortune cookie?"

He chuckled, not at all offended. "No, I didn't. Listen, nothing you've presented me with during our sessions has been light. You're a multifaceted creature, raised and surrounded by layering complexities most people have not encountered, and frankly, would have no clue how to handle. Yet, you've soldiered on. You're fire, Rebekah. You're stronger than you realize and do have an innate *something* that could be more dangerous than you know.

"But you won't use it that way once you figure it out. And whether you see it or not, you've grown quite a bit without my two cents. Will you continue to make mistakes? Sure, that's how you grow. The thing I think most humans want to master is the art of forgiving themselves after galactic-sized lapses in judgment. And remember, you didn't grow up in a household freely forgiving those types of blunders, so how could you forgive yourself? You were punished with severity, shunned every time."

I sighed, taking in everything he'd just said, dissecting it, pulling out pieces, and storing them in separate files for future rumination.

"Will I know how to use this innate something? Will I use it correctly? Can I stop the cycle of abuse?"

"Just remember the little girl at the tracks; would she ask the same questions? Or would she trust that innate something without overthinking it?"

"What if my innate feeling steers me in the wrong direction? Like, I think that doing one thing is the right thing but it's not? I still struggle with that."

"Try to see it as it's happening, in slow motion. When you can see, in your mind's eye, the course of events playing out *before they do*, change your path. Like you're playing chess."

"What?" I was not very good at chess.

"Trust me. Or trust you, rather. You'll just know. You'll feel it. I have no doubt."

With that last piece of advice to ride on for the next week, I felt it best not to tell Joel about Caleb flying up. I didn't trust my own decision, and I didn't feel like getting into it.

I decided to test my gut during Caleb's visit to see if there was anything to this...*something*...Joel said I had.

●●●

YOU'LL JUST KNOW. You'll feel it, Joel had said. Whether or not my innate gut-checks knew what they were doing, Caleb was coming.

I told Kara.

"Really?" she asked, throwing Bartok's itty-bitty down the hallway.

"He says so. We shall see."

She pressed her lips together and nodded. "Be careful."

About a month later, I stood wringing my hands at the gate, waiting for Caleb to come forward with a swarm of strangers. For some reason, I doubted that he'd show up. This being the first online quasi-relationship I'd ever had, I questioned his desire to fly all the way from New Mexico just to meet me in Baltimore.

Then I saw him.

He was the last person to emerge from the crowd. Wearing a baggy t-shirt, jeans, some scruff, and a smile, he walked toward me holding his duffle bag.

I stood corrected; dumbstruck. He had flown in just for me.

I fidgeted while cracking my knuckles as the benefits of my doubt materialized before me in the form of one adorable New Mexican.

"You know, as a licensed massage therapist, I could go on about the damage you're doing to your knuckles and the extra work you're tasking me with as we get older." He smiled, stepped closer, his duffle bag fell to the floor, and he grabbed my hands to begin massaging them. "Lay off the popping or I'm going to have one hell of a time working these kinks out."

How could he already be so comfortable? We had *just* met and there he was, mapping out our future and the fate of my thirty-year-old-ASL-using fingers. It was difficult to stand guard. He was either that good or my instincts were passed the fuck out.

"Let's go home. I'm excited to meet the boys." He picked up his bag and held my hand as we walked toward the exit signs, making our way to the parking garage.

We spent days enamored with each other. It was nothing quite as strong as the connection I'd once shared with Kelly— I'd accepted that I likely wouldn't experience another Kelly connection; thus far Ben, Travis, and Caleb were real-life reminders. But Caleb was a fun distraction, and he came with a strange sense of comfort and relief.

Sex with Caleb was uninspiring, banal. Not terrible, but at the time, nothing more than an essential diversion from troubling memories.

She's Confused. She's Wet. It smells. It's over.

While I worked, Caleb kept house. The boys took to him quickly, which was pretty much in-character for them. All one had to do was give Moron cookies and throw Bartok's itty-bitty ball and they were in.

Our visit was going well until I noticed he had been dodging phone calls.

"Who keeps calling you?" I asked.

"No one important."

"Is it her? Your ex?"

Caleb half-laughed. "No. It's, um, a Navy recruiter."

"Oh. I'd forgotten about that. Is that still on?"

"I don't think so."

"Why?"

"I don't think we met by chance, Bek. I've never felt like this, never just hopped a plane to meet someone across the country before. I told you once and I meant it: you're my

52

reason. I don't want to join the service and risk missing out on what might be the best thing that's ever happened to me." He kissed my hands.

Either he felt it and meant it, or he was good. Real good. I fell hard. Right there in my basement living room.

"Can you do that? Not go? Didn't you take an oath?"

"I'm not technically in yet. I can do what I want. And I don't want to join now."

Regardless, he did owe his recruiter a conversation; there were certain procedures one had to follow to be excused from attending basic training. But Caleb was dead set against doing any of it. He dug his heels into Maryland soil and wouldn't let anything stop him from creating a life with me.

We were meant to be, he'd said.

He was just what I'd ached for. Someone making sacrifices for me; flying across the country; sacrificing duty to his grandfather and country. It took my breath away. I couldn't ignore it. I needed to believe I was worth a shit to someone.

Caleb flew home to face his recruiter as I excitedly planned an upcoming trip to the Land of Enchantment.

While I chaotically packed a carry-on, my conscience visited me from the depths of Kara's vocal cords.

"Beckalah, you know I don't mind staying with the boys, but are you sure about this guy? It's moving kind of fast, isn't it? Did he give up the Navy for you?"

"I know it seems fast, and it is. But I'm telling you, this is it. I feel so at ease with him." I was half-lying but certain that once we were together, my doubts would dissolve. "He doesn't put on any airs, what you see is what you get. I need someone to ground me, and he does. It's nice."

Something inside me jabbed; my body knew I was reaching for the unreachable.

"And the Navy?" she asked, raising an eyebrow.

"I had nothing to do with his decision. He said it was for me, but I didn't persuade him to do anything. I learned my lesson from trying to talk Kelly out of going to Memphis."

I was getting defensive, but for what I wasn't sure.

"Okay. We'll be here when you get back."

I flew out the door.

What just happened inside my body?

Cold Stone Crazy

FLYING OVER THE Sandia Mountains was like a dream. The White Mountains in NH felt like nothing compared to this majestic view. A deep purple sunset kissed the orange sky and fell with poise behind the mountains. Albuquerque's city lights twinkled with excitement. The sky rested elegantly, like a lightweight blanket, embracing the city in a warm hug.

I was indeed enchanted.

Caleb met me at the gate with open arms and we embarked upon a long weekend, smitten with each other.

While having dinner in a dimly lit, romantic restaurant—oblivious to the world outside—a light snow began to fall. We snuggled, watching from the restaurant's window as we made plans for Caleb to move in with me. We knew people would think we were crazy, and we didn't care. He was freed from previous Naval duties and had started packing boxes before I'd boarded the plane to go back to Maryland.

"He's moving in with you?" Kara asked, wide-eyed and thunderstruck.

"Yeah. It feels right."

I walked toward the bedroom; my boys followed. While Moron and Bartok sniffed my luggage, Kara did a little sniffing of her own.

"Hold on," she said, sitting on the edge of my bed. "This is huge. You and Kel didn't move in together and you dated for over two years, you uprooted your life for him. But this guy? C'mon, think."

"I have thought about it. That's all I've done. He's moving here as soon as he can."

My body started its tiny motor again. Every time I talked about Caleb, it felt like I was trying to convince everyone, including myself.

"Beckalah. You've known him a total of what, like, five months?"

Those facts were hard to ignore.

●●●

Sitting on Joel's couch, my ankle fidgeted. I was usually so at ease with him but not when I knew I'd have to come clean regarding major life changes I'd been especially quiet about.

Joel cocked his head, squinting with subtlety. "What aren't you telling me?"

"Um, a couple of things." I both loved and hated that he knew me as well as my closest friends did.

"Oh?"

"Remember the grammarless guy from New Mexico?"

"Yes," he said with caution.

"We talked sporadically even after his ex-girlfriend called and he's already flown here to visit and I just got back from a trip to New Mexico and—"

His eyes bugged.

I exhaled. "He's coming back here to move in with me."

It was like ripping off yet another Band-Aid.

"Wow. Okay. And how does your body feel about that?"

Though I'd told Joel very little about Caleb and me up to that point, he knew that I'd started noticing my body's reaction to things; how it often communicated what my head wouldn't. And he knew recent revelations about my superpower were sinking in.

Joel = voodoo psychologist.

"My body's been...aware? A bit on edge?" I said.

"And you're still going through with it despite your body's awareness?"

"Defenses are up, my body feels like it's battling a minor cold. But what if I'm imagining it? What if this really *is* love and I dismiss what could've been because I felt a sensation I couldn't explain?"

"Well, which is stronger, the love or the fearful sensation?"

"Fearful? Of what?"

"Being alone."

I sat looking for the little bird that usually flitted by Joel's window, but it wasn't there.

My body already knew the answer to Joel's questions, but I refused to let my mouth speak on its behalf. Though I'd been living my life cult-and-Kelly-free, the aftermath of abuse, shunning, and abandonment left me cold; I wanted someone to warm my icy edges. Joel knew that.

"I'm not sure," I said.

"You'll know. Pay attention. You'll feel it."

●●●

I DID KNOW. I did feel it. And I buried it down as far as I could; I was so tired of feeling everything all the time. Filtering other people's words and emotions while interpreting was more than enough to drain me and adding in my overly sensitive superpower left me exhausted.

I did all I could to ignore feeling and resolved to act—to *do*.

Caleb and I carried out our plans to move in together. He packed a Budget van then drove from New Mexico to Texas, and I booked a flight to Austin to meet him, his mother, and his grandparents. It was the first time since Carter that I'd be meeting a boyfriend's family and I was not as terrified.

I wanted to try *being* with Caleb. I wanted to let him in. I was so sick of thought stopping, second guessing, not knowing whether to trust my body, my mind, or my heart.

Swooping into the great state of Texas for the first time gave me chills. A positive indicator? I didn't know, but in the Lone Star state, it felt like there was plenty of room to *be*.

Austin was unlike any place I'd ever felt before, noticeably different from the Washington, D.C. Metro area. I'd spent about three years surrounded by big government secrets that I took an oath to keep to myself, and Austin—a very strange and enigmatic city—was a far cry from all the suits swarming in and around D.C. like locusts, flitting every which way, passing and vetoing bills, licking the boots of legislators.

Austinites were immersed in their own groove; it was the Haight-Ashbury of Texas. And little did I know, we were in Austin during South by Southwest (SXSW)—a funky week-long festival where people do what they want, when they want while celebrating film, music, and media.

Strolling the sick and twisted belly of Austin proper with Caleb and his family, we ventured down Sixth Street—also known as "Dirty Sixth"—and I hit sensory overload.

People surrounded me. The smell of weed filled the air. Folks staggered up and down barricaded streets, drinks in hand, dancing to live music playing on the corner of every block.

We passed a couple in their early twenties, sharing a joint between them, lounging on a sidewalk. They were just...there; not bothered and not bothering a soul. They wore glassy eyes, wide smiles, and the girl sat, leaned back, wearing a tube-top and a flowing hippy skirt hiked up to her knees. Her legs were spread open, her untamed bush waved hello.

Caleb's grandmother looked around, clutching her purse to her chest, and said, "I feel like I'm in the Devil's playground."

Later that night, we stumbled upon Katzen—a famous tattoo artist and ex-wife of Enigma, the sideshow performer—and she branded me and Caleb's mom with needle and ink.

Although I was in Austin, keeping it weird, I knew I'd soon be returning to D.C., keeping it covered. I'd started a tattoo collection the day I turned eighteen, and since then, I kept my secret love for the macabre, Marilyn Manson, serial killers, and needle therapy hidden in the dark corners of my soul and underneath my clothes.

The only person who'd had any objections about my tattoos (especially my back piece of Alice in Wonderland gripping a bloody knife), was Kelly—and he was in Memphis living life without me.

Caleb had no such misgivings. From Austin to Silver Spring, he only focused on two things: getting his license to practice massage therapy in Maryland and our future together. My choice to get another tattoo was last on his list of worries.

Once in Maryland, Caleb found a job at Cold Stone Creamery in downtown Silver Spring—a placeholder while he studied for Maryland's massage exam. He came home with a folder full of ice-cream flavor lists and silly songs to memorize for when customers dropped money in the tip jar.

"This is just 'til I pass the exam," he said, flipping through the packet of songs.

I could feel his contrived dignity collapsing, shrinking, in the air around me. A thirty-four-year-old man working at an ice-cream shop, when licensed to practice massage therapy, had to be a blow to his ego. I appreciated his willingness to work just the same.

Until a week later.

•••

Approaching the door to Joel's home office, my body sent and received all kinds of signals, shooting off in a million different directions. My anxiety worsened once I realized Joel would definitely notice.

"Hey, Rebekah," Joel said, spinning in his chair to face me.

"Hey," I said, sitting on the sofa, rigid and tense.

He looked at me, scrunching his eyebrows ever so slightly. "So, it's uh, been a week or so. How is living with Caleb?" He wasted no time getting to the heart of things; once he knew me well enough, he went right for the jugular.

I sighed and looked down.

"That good, huh?" he asked.

I remained silent and shook my head as a single tear judged me on its way down my cheek.

"What happened?"

I looked out the window. No bird today. I exhaled and said, "I caught him in a lie. Right to my face."

Joel sighed and I continued.

"Caleb started working at Cold Stone Creamery until he was able to pass Maryland's massage therapy exam." I hesitated, nervous to continue. "On days I work in the city, I park at the Wayne Avenue garage and ride the Metro into D.C. At the end of my day, I called Cold Stone to see if Caleb wanted a ride home after getting my car. Only, the girl who answered the phone said he didn't work there, and aside from his first day he hadn't been there all week."

Joel pressed his lips. "Mm-hmm."

"I asked him about it when he got home, asked him how work was and he said, 'Good.' He could've told me the truth, but he didn't. When I said I'd called to talk with him and was told he didn't work there, he lied again. He said whoever answered the phone was mistaken. Then I asked where he'd been going all week."

I stopped for a moment to gather my thoughts and check in with my shot nerves since it all had just happened two hours before I got to Joel's.

"Well? Where's he been going?" Joel asked, leaning forward.

"'Just around,' he said. He told me he couldn't face the fact he let his license lapse in New Mexico or that he ditched the Navy; he said he felt like a loser." My ankle started to twitch.

"Why do you suppose he lied?" Joel leaned back in his chair.

"He said he felt pressured to pay his share and I said, 'Don't bother. I've been paying my own rent, feeding myself, and changing fuses in the apartment on my own. I don't need your money.'"

I could feel my blood boil, bubble, and rise. Red blotches speckled my neck and chest. My cheeks flushed. I wanted to destroy a human life. I shot up and started pacing in front of Joel's bookshelf—the one housing apostate literature. To go back to that puzzling time would've been most welcomed.

He spun his chair around to watch me march in front of his library and asked, "What's happening?"

"He lied, like, three times in a matter of seconds; it happened just before I came here."

"I mean, what's happening inside you right now?"

I exhaled. Looking up to the ceiling, I said, "I'm livid! And I feel incredibly stupid because I fucking *knew*..." I felt my face scrunch, on the verge of an ugly cry.

"Rebekah, come sit." He leaned forward and patted the sofa twice then rolled his chair back a few inches.

I sat on the sofa and took a few deep breaths before he had the chance to suggest it. I felt like I had ants creeping all over me. That's the only way to describe how I feel when I'm lied to—my skin crawls and my body knows it before my brain does.

"I'm glad I caught you in this state—"

"What?"

"Just go with it," he said. He leaned forward, elbows on his knees, and his eyes bore into mine. "Close your eyes and try to remember another time you felt this. Another time your body

61

reacted before your brain knew what was happening, another time you knew that what you felt was justified."

"I don't want to."

"I think it'll help."

Resting my head on the back of his sofa, I closed my eyes, and within seconds I fell into a spinning vortex of memories. I landed in a classroom that came in just as clear as my 80s, turquoise sweater, teased bangs, and permed hair.

I'm sitting in the back row. The class is reading silently. I look up and catch my teacher's eye. I think he's about to scold me for my eyes not being where they're supposed to be—in the book. But instead, he looks at me and signs in ASL, "You pretty." I smile, shift uncomfortably in my seat, and continue reading.

I could feel my hands on either side of my legs, gripping Joel's sofa cushion. The air bolting from my lungs felt like tiny knives, scraping tissue on their way out.

Then I heard Joel ask, "Did you find it—another time you felt this?"

"Mm-hmm."

"Well?"

Eyes still closed to avoid his knowing stare, I said, "One of my teachers knew I had Deaf parents and liked practicing sign language with me. He did it in front of my classmates, knowing they were clueless. I felt special until he signed 'you're pretty' and 'you're cute.' It bothered me, but I smiled anyway."

"Did you tell anyone?"

"No."

"Why not?"

"I somehow knew he'd deny it."

"You *somehow knew*, huh?"

I nodded.

"What happened then?"

"I didn't meet his eye, didn't interact with him unless it was for classwork."

"How did that feel?"

I sat silent.

"C'mon. Focus on what you're feeling now and tell me if it mirrors anything you felt then," he said.

"I feel the same burning...blotchy...skin-crawling...I-wanna-jump-out-of-my-skin-and-find-a-parallel-universe feeling."

"What else?"

"The anxiety is replacing itself with some sort of rightness; like another version of me is taking over."

"A part of you that maybe *somehow knows*?"

"Yeah."

"Your train-track self," Joel said.

Oh, my god, yes. What would I do without my own Larry David reminding me of this shit?

"This is what will help you stop the cycle, Reb—confidence in yourself, confidence in your ability to know what you need. It doesn't need to be understood by anyone but you."

●●●

HOW QUICKLY CALEB'S falsehoods had made me forget my precious, penny-clutching friend. She was still deep inside, guiding me in her own special way.

I hushed her, told her I was okay, and she was safe to keep playing by the tracks; I'd be back with her soon enough.

As for Caleb, the sucker in me felt sorry for the sucker in him. The fact that he found a job almost immediately after his oral blunder and did everything within his power to help me forget the drama he brought with him from New Mexico, helped reboot our harried relationship. Throw in my ability to contort, all chameleon-like, and I was bending until almost broken.

63

In the upscale city of Chevy Chase, Maryland, Caleb found a massage gig at a salon and spa. The owners—an older Italian couple—gave the sad sack camping out in Caleb's big, hazel eyes a chance, with the understanding he'd get his license as soon as possible.

I knew he wasn't faking this job because I went to the spa to see for myself. Of course, I didn't trust him, but if someone else was willing to give him a chance, why shouldn't I?

He was trying so hard, I felt I owed him the benefit of the doubt again (even though that phrase continually baffles me). I had slammed doors on people so many times, I was dying to know what it was like to leave the door ajar, forgive wrongs, let someone in for once.

Mark's voice scolded me once again...

"You can say you 'never get what you want,'" Mark said. "But think about that statement. Isn't everything that happens a result of 'what you want?' By doing what you've done up until this point, you have *gotten what you want. Your problems aren't because you 'don't get what you want.' Your problem is your sense of loyalty—or lack thereof. You've not given yourself the opportunity to remain loyal to* anything *in your life. Not your husband, your family, Jehovah. When the going gets tough, you get going, in search of the next thing you 'want.' When are you going to try and stick with something, or someone, when things get hard?"*

Though Mark had referenced Carter and my choice to have an affair, I couldn't help but wonder if he was right. *But I can't try loyalty out on a liar, can I?*

Then, something inside me snapped. Like an unexpected chiropractic adjustment. My insides twisted, unwillingly, and my body took over for my brain once again.

I thought back to my last session with Joel, the exercise we did after I wore out the flooring by his bookshelf. After that session, I was much more aware of how my body responded to things. What's more, I couldn't get the Myers-Briggs test results out of my newly diagnosed, introvert-obsessed brain.

I wanted to tell Caleb that I still didn't trust him. I'd tried to, but I didn't. He'd killed all hope the day his ex-girlfriend called me, and I'd been lying to myself since then. I knew it. Kara knew it. Jodi knew it. Joel knew it. Hell, even Travis knew it when he looked at Caleb's Myspace page.

So, I silently made the decision to tell him we were done, I'd help him find a place of his own. Only…

There were these moments he could be incredibly sweet and tender; I fell for it every time.

And the cycle continues.

Lying in bed one night, Caleb asked, "So what do you want, you know, in life?"

I love questions that lead to wild conversations—ones that start with an innocent, random thought but have the potential to go anywhere. Fair-weather bullshit is of no interest to me; never has been, never will be.

So, I said, "I want to know what ninety-nine red balloons look like, gathered together in one spot."

I was half-joking about the balloons, but I'd been curious to see them all in one place, in their bouncy splendor, for years.

And then it happened—taking me by complete surprise.

After an exhausting day in U.S.-government-acronym land, I opened the door to my apartment and red balloons filled the living room, coming at me from all sides, reminding me of late-night pillow talks with Caleb.

The smell of sweet and sour sauce filled the apartment and, once I pushed aside a few balloons, I saw Caleb—down on bended knee, holding open a black velvet box. I looked at him and the simple, but stunning, solitaire diamond ring staring back at me.

"Rebekah, I've never felt this with anyone else. I've never felt so sure about being with someone. Please, marry me."

He looked up at me with such sincerity that I hurriedly stuffed all the doubts I had into a wooden box. I closed and locked it, dismissing the muffled screams demanding that I turn him down; I wanted them to sound miles away.

I smiled down at him and said yes.

It was the ninety-nine, rote luftballons Nena sang about; they'd gotten to me.

I spent the rest of the night counting them all. Several times. And each time, I came to the same number—ninety-nine. They were magnificent.

We ate homemade sweet and sour cabbage for dinner and snuggled into a restful night on the couch. Every so often, I'd glance down at the shimmering diamond staring back at me and smile.

It all happened so fast. I refused to acknowledge the gut-jabs and barely heard the muffled screams ordering me to run in the opposite direction.

I bled internally, forcing myself to ignore it all.

Kara and I made plans to dress up that following Saturday night and meet in the city for dinner, drinks, and dancing; she loved to salsa.

Stepping out of the Metro's street entrance I spotted her on the sidewalk in Adam's Morgan and ran up to her.

"Hey, sweetie!" she said.

Kara, standing above me at five-feet-eight-inches, stepped closer and threw her arms around my neck. Every time she drew me into a hug, she'd sneak her fingers into my armpits and tickle me until I thrashed.

"Stop it!" I said, laughing.

"Let's go, I'm starved," she said, releasing me from her grip.

We worked our way into a crowded, upscale D.C. restaurant and the smell of Mediterranean fare hit my olfactory system so hard my stomach groaned.

Waiting for our table, we stood at the bar, Cosmopolitans in hand.

Kara looked down at my fingers, wrapped around a martini glass, and said, "Oh, my god, that's an engagement ring."

I gushed. "Caleb asked me a few nights ago."

"Sweetie, I'm...happy for you..." Something in her voice told me otherwise.

"But...?" I said after her forced congratulatory remark.

She sighed and smiled, sipping her drink. I know her too well to dismiss that smirk.

"Are you sure? Doesn't something seem...I don't know..."

Off, I thought.

She was about to use the same word everyone else who'd met him was using. I looked down at my engaged finger, clutching a martini glass, and I thought, *yes, Kara, something is very off.*

We were interrupted by waitstaff leading us to our table. Setting my Cosmo down, I said, "I'm gonna go to the restroom, I'll be right back."

Staring at myself in the mirror, I looked for *her,* but she wasn't there. She'd been there before: after fights with Dean, when Dean and I had broken up, when I'd moved her to Silver Spring to be closer to Kelly. But tonight—nothing. She was nowhere to be found.

Has she given up on me?

I dabbed a tissue under my eyes to stop the tears before they had a chance to drag mascara down my cheeks. I put a huge, fake smile on, left the ladies' room and walked back to our table.

"I ordered the Mediterranean platter for two," Kara said as I sat down.

"Yum." I grabbed a piece of pita bread and dipped it in a bowl of hummus.

"I have some news, too," she said.

I sat on the edge of my seat; eyebrows raised.

She took a deep breath, exhaled, then said, "Okay, I'm just gonna say it—remember that SCUBA diving trip I took with my friend from Colorado?"

"Mm-hmm." I nodded, looking down at my ring—trying to feel good about saying yes to Caleb.

"Well, we slept together in Belize. We both agreed it was just part of the trip and that was that."

"Okay. I knew that. So?"

"Well, it's become something more and—"

"That's great, I know you kind of had a thing for him."

"Thanks." She blushed. "We've known each other for years. We hung out at all the Blue Grass festivals in Telluride; I told you all that." She waved her hand casually then said, "He's still in Colorado and, well, I decided to move back."

The platter for two was delivered, and as soon as it hit the table my appetite disappeared.

I looked down and sighed.

"Aw, sweetie, we'll stay in touch."

"I know. And I'm happy for you. I am, really. I'm just gonna miss you. I don't hang out with many people, you know that."

"Beckalah…" she said, tilting her head sympathetically.

I took a long pull from my Cosmo and pouted.

My D.C. crew was shrinking and all I had to show for it was an engagement ring and Caleb.

Weirder in Austin

IT WAS TIME for show-and-tell with Joel.

I cringed.

The shimmering solitaire diamond on my left hand glared at me. The little rock cackled and said, "You're engaged to a lying sack of shit. I'm not even a diamond, I'm cubic zirconia, bitch!"

It didn't matter what the ring's stone was. I was horrified by what it meant. It reminded me of my lonesome desperation and the fact that I, too, felt like a lying sack of shit.

I'd been lying to myself, the woman in the mirror (who'd been hiding), and my tiny, four-year-old train-track self. The liar in Caleb gave the liar in me permission to surface, and it was the first time I'd ever worn a chameleon suit to writhe for my own sake.

Hands resting on my thighs, I wiggled my digits, drawing attention to my betrothed finger.

"Well, *that's* new," Joel said, looking up from his datebook, eyeballing my hand. He flipped through a few pages and said, "You've also missed a session or two."

"I know. Sorry about that."

Joel looked at me and waited for an excused absence note to justify my own missed appointments.

"I guess I wasn't ready to tell you about the engagement. I was afraid of what you'd think," I said.

"Were you afraid of what I'd think or afraid of what you'd realize?"

I sought my mind for anything to defend my engagement and the upcoming move I'd told no one about. Coming up with nothing, I said, "Do you remember when I told you about my brother Mark and how he'd once said that I always got what I wanted?"

Joel leaned back in his chair, crossed his leg, and said, "Mm-hmm. Why?"

"I feel like he was challenging me to be loyal to someone or something, even if it was hard, even if I didn't really want to. I silently accepted his challenge and now I feel like I just need to follow through. I need to know I can be loyal, that I can stand by something or someone when the shit hits the fan, you know? I mean, I didn't do it for Carter and that still haunts me. Maybe I'm batshit to think a liar like Caleb deserves loyalty, and maybe that's harsh to say, I don't know. I just—"

Joel sighed before interrupting. "Listen, compulsive lying is a convoluted thing. It's sometimes a coping mechanism for low self-esteem or past trauma. That doesn't make it right or easier to accept, but given what you've told me about Caleb, and how much he's lied to you in such a short amount of time, I wouldn't be surprised if he's suffered some harsh blows himself, caught in his own abuse cycle."

"He has suffered. He lost both his sons—" I stopped myself. *His story, not mine.* "He has plenty of reasons to feel like shit. He *was* put upon. Shouldn't I try to be loyal to someone who seems to need it?"

"If that's what you feel you need to do. Just don't bend until you break. Be mindful of the cycle we talked about. Your cycle. Not his."

I sighed, looking down at the mysterious stone on my finger.

I could feel Joel trying to keep his cool, silently dismissing Caleb from his office chair. He tensed, just like my parents had during my first judicial committee hearing. Since he was my therapist, it was his job to keep his opinions in check. But our sessions and our relationship had been different.

Knowing it was difficult to hide things from Joel, I told him about some of Caleb's other little white lies. There had been a couple before we were engaged and a couple more afterward.

"Did you confront him about his 'little white lies?'" he asked.

I nodded. "Yes, I did. When I found a random number in his phone, I called it, and some chick answered. During our brief conversation, she said she was a new massage client of his and he'd asked her for her number. She also said she didn't know that Caleb was engaged when I told her who I was."

"And?"

"I thanked her, hung up, and threw Caleb's phone at him. Rubbing above his eye—where the phone struck—he said I was just paranoid, worried over nothing, and she was only a massage client; nothing more."

"And you don't believe him?"

I shook my head, not meeting Joel's eye.

"Okay. Do you suppose, maybe, Caleb's ex-girlfriend felt the same way when she found your number?"

Avoiding Joel's truth mirror, I stared at the ring again, trying to hold on to the good things I thought it meant—stability, a family, a home—all the things Carter tried to give me once, all the things the *Society* had taken from me.

Then I said, "He asked me to move to Texas with him, so we could start again, turn over a new leaf."

"And?"

"Three versions of me are duking it out, and no one seems to be winning."

• • •

CALEB PACKED UP a few of his belongings—which didn't amount to much—sent them ahead via USPS, flew into Austin, then made his way toward Comfort, Texas to stay with his grandparents.

I stayed in Maryland to tie up loose ends and transfer my job to Austin, which was easy to do when SLA's CEO merged with three other companies. There were offices all over the country, and once the merger paperwork had officially been signed, SLA wasn't the same. A lot of SLA folks either moved back to their home state (Kara), or simply quit, and I didn't want to stick around.

Not only were Kelly's ghosts still lingering, toying with the dead Sarlacc I used to care for, but now my scattered SLA family and their spirits loafed around D.C. monuments and historical landmarks.

Caleb leaving just before that Thanksgiving also ailed me; I was alone. Kara left and since SLA had changed drastically—in vibe and in company name—most folks had gone their own way. I felt orphaned once again.

Longing for the holiday sleepover I'd hosted for my mini-SLA family two years before, brought on discontent which gave way to a familiar cycle.

I drank alone, heavily.

Looking around my apartment—strong, homemade Cosmo in hand—I noticed that some of the bigger things Caleb left behind, for me to bring down to Texas, didn't complement my things; they didn't belong.

He took pride in being a Scorpio, born Year of the Dragon; there were colorful stuffed dragons everywhere. His blue, moon-sun-and-star-decorated bed set draped atop my queen mattress was nothing but a weak depiction of the universal spirituality he so desperately wished he possessed but didn't.

I stopped scrutinizing Caleb's things and waxed sad and pathetic with my vinyl collection.

I drank myself to tears, remembering when the hungry Sarlacc used to make me feel alive. Caleb was no Kelly; no one ever would be. I didn't expect anyone to fill those shoes.

Jesse flew down to spend a long weekend with me before my move to Austin, rescuing me from further self-destruction via vodka and triple sec.

"Are you absolutely sure about this?" Jesse asked, dropping his duffle bag onto the coffee table.

"Well, no, but I'm going to give it a shot."

"What's the work like in Austin?"

"I'm going to transfer with SLA's newly merged company and work in the VRS center until I get my name out there."

He sighed. "Okay. I'll be down after you move. You know that, don't you?"

"I know, and I love you for it."

He sat on the couch and dug through his bag, pulling out a DVD.

"Sweetie, I want to show you something." Jesse put a DVD in the player and sat on the couch to cuddle the boys.

"What's this?" I sat next to the three of them and covered up with a blanket.

"Some wise words I think you should hear."

A poorly filmed play began.

Three quarters into the movie, I understood why Jesse played it when a large Black man in drag, dressed like an old lady, sat back in a recliner, and said, "When someone shows you who they are, believe them."

I felt Jesse look at me.

"Did you hear what Madea just said? Should I play it again?" he asked, reaching for the remote.

"I heard it," I said, looking down at the ring.

"Sweetie, when I met him, I got the weirdest feeling. Just be careful, okay?" He sat closer and pulled me in for a crushing bear hug.

•••

I didn't like the thought of living in Austin, plucked from Maryland and Thursday evening dates with my Larry David lookalike.

Joel had been my voice of reason; held up the mirror I couldn't hold up for myself time and time again; introduced me to the evil, *mentally diseased,* apostate literature that freed me in so many ways; listened; advised; and saw me for who I was. He really was like an uncle to me, and I shuddered at the thought of not seeing him week after week.

"Uh-oh, her ankle's twitching," Joel said, chuckling at his own joke.

I grinned and "heh" was all I managed to get out.

"What is it?" he asked.

"What am I gonna do about therapy when I move?"

"You can find another therapist, that won't be a prob—"

"Start from scratch? At the beginning? With some stranger? And my job, like, I'm not thrilled about working full-time in a VRS center; I enjoy my D.C. assignments. I've come a long way from that scared, little New Hampshire girl who didn't think she'd fit in with CloseUp intellectuals."

"I'm sure you'll have new, interesting, and possibly weird experiences in Austin. As for therapy…" Joel shifted in his seat and hesitated, unsure if he would allow himself to say what I could almost see dangling from his lips. "Rebekah, I think you could take a break and still make decent choices."

I was beside myself. My jaw dropped, and my eyebrows jumped. He must've thought I was someone else because even I knew the choices I was making about Caleb didn't deserve free rein.

"Are you serious? Haven't you been listening to the sordid tales of all my colossal fuckups?" I said.

"Listen, the work we've done over the past year or so has been instrumental. You're a smart, caring, beautiful young woman with no need to feel bad about yourself. You have plenty of reasons to feel proud. You're stronger than you give yourself credit for.

"The Witness aspects of your life have been the root of many unfortunate experiences. The research you've done on your own—remember, I didn't do any of that—has led you to making several decisions by yourself. You're human; humans make mistakes. Chastising yourself for making what seems to be a bad choice, either with or for the wrong person, isn't necessary. Mistakes are all part of the human condition. Don't punish yourself so much."

"What about the other stuff I told you just before I went to Hawaii? And the introvert personality stuff? I'm just figuring all that out, who am I gonna talk to?"

Joel nodded. "The personality stuff, we've worked on a bit together—all the things you feel; the way your body responds to perceived threats; your chameleon suit; your ability to know things without clear reasons or any frame of reference; your innate something; your superpower? You'll come into all that on your own—it's taking shape, I can see it. And you need to tap into that to stop the cycle of abuse. You just have to trust it.

"As for what you told me before your trip, your childhood incident, you may feel the need to talk to someone about that, and by all means do so. Also, you can call or email me anytime. But, Rebekah, try a bit of a break. See how it feels to own your life, to be autonomous. Give yourself some credit. When do you leave for Austin?"

"In a couple of weeks."

"And Caleb? How has that been?"

"Fine," I said, glancing at the ring, knowing full-well the decision to move fifteen hundred miles away for a lukewarm, rushed, relationship-turned-engagement didn't sit well with my train-track self.

Joel leaned forward and said, "You don't want to do the wrong thing, and you think you're going to. I'll say this, it may sound cheesy but here it is, the best therapist lives in you."

"That *is* cheesy."

"But true. The extreme, precarious situations you've faced underscore time and time again your need for family and connection. Your fear of abandonment just exacerbates your separation anxiety. That's why you sometimes cling to people, and that's why you're so quick to suit up and change colors; you don't want to lose anyone since you've lost so many people close to you. Two words, Rebekah: trust yourself."

●●●

HERE GOES NOTHING...

My last few days in the D.C. Metro area were like a fog. A sad, heavy cloud followed me around. Saying goodbye to the few people still inside the old SLA circle was grueling. Some of them had been my family since day one.

Travis, too; he and I became such close friends during our established routine of Sunday night beers and *Family Guy*.

I took my boys on one last jaunt around the neighborhood and to our favorite place in Silver Spring—the Montgomery County Public Library. The librarians would always let the boys come in with me as I scanned the stacks for books to borrow. Afterward, I'd let the boys off their leashes, and they'd run around the park.

I'm so gonna miss this place.

Caleb flew into Baltimore to help Lysah, the boys, and I drive down to Austin.

On the road with Caleb, I noticed how my body reacted to him, to his presence, and how things around us unfolded. I watched closely as other people responded to him and, in turn, how he countered. I didn't like what I saw or felt. I made mental tally marks on Satan's side of the paper for him.

I did my best to shake it off because I looked forward to the distraction of Savannah, Georgia. I'd wanted to visit ever since reading, then watching, *Midnight in the Garden of Good and Evil.*

While on an evening ghost tour in Savannah's historic district, narratives of the slaves and what they endured were much scarier to me than their lingering ghosts.

The truth behind the establishment of this country is being brushed aside in most educational settings. But there, in old, haunted plantation homes, the truth was being set free via apparitions and ghost-tour guides.

I'd never been so scared. Spirits of abused slaves woefully lingered inside houses that I couldn't wait to get into, then out of—I loved every second of it. I wanted to stay, learn more, and fall in between the cracks of cobblestone streets, away from the masses I knew didn't, and would never, understand me. Caleb included.

But we had an open road to hit, good time to make. Making good time wasn't an issue once we hit Mississippi.

At a gas station in the middle of nowhere, surrounded by weeping willows and rusted gas pumps, I'd never wanted to leave a place so much. I could feel Mississippi's woeful history pass through me. I wanted to get back on the road and stay on it until we were long gone.

Caleb asked if I wanted to let the boys out for their potty break.

"Nope. Not here," I said, turning the volume up as "Baba O' Riley" started.

I looked out the passenger side window and felt the heavy stare of other gas patrons. I couldn't explain it, and didn't even want to try, but I didn't feel safe. Between the run-down store and the weeping willows all around us, I could feel that history was just going to keep repeating itself and I didn't want to be part of the lesson.

Trust yourself, Joel said.

Will do, I told him.

We were somewhere in east Texas when Lysah's underside made an ungodly screeching sound.

"Oh, my god! You're car's freaking out!" Caleb pulled off the highway and into a parking lot to inspect Lysah's belly, even though I told him I already knew what the problem was.

I looked around the shopping plaza he'd parked in and saw a hobby shop. Leaving Caleb on the ground perversely looking under the dress of my car, I went in to find a sales associate.

"Excuse me, do you have any plastic zip-ties?" I asked.

The associate handed me a few from behind the counter. "Will this do, sweetheart?"

"Yes, thank you!"

I joined Caleb on the ground, slid my body under Lysah, and secured her splashguard myself.

Caleb watched in disbelief. "How did you—"

"It's happened before. I know my car."

I finished rigging the ties, got out from under my car and hopped inside, ready to finish the last leg of our journey.

Trusting myself, like Joel had suggested, didn't seem as hard as I imagined. I mentally took note of Lysah's last-ditch effort to slow the trip down, rest, and head back to D.C.

The humidity of Austin hit me like nothing I'd ever felt before. D.C. was a mellow swamp compared to Austin's mugginess and it was barely April.

The apartment complex I moved into was trendy, filled with young, spirited people; beautiful hard-bodied and fit twenty-somethings surrounded me.

I went to that weird city in the body of a lonely alcoholic, wearing many a take-out meal. I felt so out of place in the new-to-me, elite apartment club. Even at HEB, a local Texas grocery store chain, I didn't feel nearly as beautiful as everyone else reaching for their organic produce.

I'd let my health fall by the wayside after Kelly and I ended, and it had slipped even more with Caleb by my side. I pinched my waist-chub, scolding myself for allowing one compulsive liar to get under my skin.

I resolved to hit the on-site gym to better my physical health and feel secure around my sexy, new neighbors.

Aside from familiarizing myself with my new neighborhood, Lysah and I explored Austin and its surrounding areas. I loved San Antonio flea markets in the Historic Market District and fell hard for all things Frida Kahlo.

There was something in the way she stared at me from both her paintings and self-portraits, something about the faraway look in her eyes. She knew beauty. She lived pain. She thrived in conflict but always managed to find a way back to herself.

Staring back at her, I swore she was looking right through me. If she could have spoken to me from beyond the grave, she would've said, "You know who you are. Stop hiding."

I left the Historic Market District with four Frida paintings. My favorite has always been *The Two Fridas.* I can relate. I was frequently running into—and up against—another version of myself that I had to answer to.

I hung Frida's art in the spacious living room of my new, trendy apartment. Between working full-time in a VRS booth, walking my boys around the apartment complex, and daring to use the gym's treadmill, Frida and I spent time together.

Much more than Caleb and I did since he hadn't officially moved into my chic apartment with me.

I was quite used to living alone and I still didn't trust him. Which I commended myself for because once again, Caleb allowed his massage license to lapse and took a job two and a half hours southwest of Austin at a home for troubled boys, living there during his workweek.

Letting his license lapse again, I could see that he was fighting against his own cycle.

Austin—ranked the friendliest city in the U.S. for dogs—was just swarming with dog parks, "yappy hours" at the apartment complex, and five-star veterinary clinics. I found gold when I found Bluebonnet Animal Hospital.

I dropped my boys off to have their annual check-up and, while walking around nearby, discovered my new church—Half-Price Books.

Unlike Borders, the books I'd found in the dark corners and tight nooks of Half-Price had been loved hard, had brought someone joy, then made it there to be assigned a new value and sold to the next bibliophile.

I was lost somewhere between "Religion & Philosophy" and "Self Help" when my phone buzzed. My boys were ready to be picked up and I hadn't chosen a book yet.

I scanned the shelves of the self-help section, looking for anything on introvert personality stuff. Finding nothing, I walked to the front of the store and spun the dollar rack. *Misery* by Stephen King. I grabbed Stephen's paperback, paid the tattooed cashier, and headed up the street to Bluebonnet.

"They were so good," the vet tech said, leading me into a room. "The doctor will be right in with them."

I heard the familiar pitter-patter of my boys come down the hallway. The door opened, and I saw Bartok and Moron wearing...bandanas?

"Hi, babies!" I shrieked, getting down on the floor. "What are you wearing?"

They wiggled their long bodies against me wearing "I love Texas" bandanas, looking like hairy, little sausage-bandits. The doctors and vet techs at Bluebonnet mastered the art of puppy love, spoiling my boys rotten.

"They were such good boys. I have some things to go over with you," the doctor said.

"Okay," I said from the floor, loving on my wieners.

"We gave the boys a routine exam upon arrival and also did some blood work."

"Thank you," I said, kissing their snouts, barely listening.

She sighed, then continued. "Moron has a certain strain of canine lymphoma."

I stopped smooching and looked up at her. "What?"

"There's a great specialist in Austin I'm referring you to. We can stop it from spreading if he starts his treatment now."

The tone of her voice pulled me toward the examination table.

"Like, dog cancer?" I asked, looking her in the eye.

She pursed her lips and nodded.

I took the referral and called right away.

That weekend Caleb and his grandma came to Austin for a visit. Grandma wanted to see my apartment and snuggle the boys. Moron's health report was the topic of conversation that weekend.

"We have an appointment with a specialist right by the VRS center next week, so hopefully that will get things started," I said.

"I don't think you should worry too much about it, he seems fine," Caleb said.

His grandma and I both turned our heads, looking at him in disbelief.

"Caleb! He's her baby. You remember how torn up Grandpa and I were when we lost Heidi, Hans, Gretel...all of them. Don't trivialize it," Grandma said.

Caleb's grandparents were serial dachshund owners; she was clearly unimpressed with his callous tone.

The weekend ended with a tense argument. Caleb said I was overly concerned with Moron, as if I had no right to put a loyal friend above his damaged ego.

Moron had his specialist appointment the following Monday and a plan was set in motion—he would receive doggy chemo every week at a whopping three hundred dollars per visit.

The cost of care for one of my best friends was nothing I even needed to think twice about. Living in Texas had been way more affordable than living in the D.C. area, or anywhere on the East coast. Financially, I was fine.

Emotionally, I was a fucking wreck. My boys were the only unconditionally loving, stable thing I'd had in my life. Anyone who knew me knew I loved them more than I had ever loved any human.

Caleb's grandmother called the next week, inviting me to Comfort to spend the weekend with her and Grandpa.

"Grandpa plans to do some gardening, he needs the boys' help digging out the weeds," she said.

"Oh, ha-ha. I'm sure the boys would be happy to help."

I drove two hours southwest to Comfort, and Grandma and I spent time having tea on the back deck while my boys dug Grandpa's weeds.

Grandma and I did a little digging of our own when she suggested we take a drive and go antiquing.

"You know, my dear," Grandma began, "I don't think Caleb meant to be so terse last weekend. I think his job is stressful."

"Oh? He doesn't talk about it much," I said, inspecting an old mason jar full of random, orphaned buttons—turning the jar upside-down then right-side up. The rattling of the buttons boomed in my ears, and I set them down.

"He doesn't say much to me or to Grandpa, but I know he's been, well…" She walked around a dusty shelf, paused, and distracted herself with a pile of lacey doilies. Inspecting each one carefully, she unfolded and refolded her way through the antiquated stack.

I walked toward her while listening to the old, hardwood floor creak beneath me. The shop was still. A faint, thrift-store odor—mothballs and old lady perfume—drifted by. I could feel Grandma's words dangling in the air, waiting.

"He's been what?" I asked.

A rusty bell above the door rang as someone walked in. The door closed. The ringing of the bell faded into the nooks and crannies of the antique shop.

She sighed, folding a white handkerchief with dainty, yellow flowers on it. "It's probably nothing, dear, and perhaps he just needs someone he works with to talk to but…"

"But what?"

Waiting for her reply, I looked past her and stared into the vintage space in front of us. Tiny dust particles of days gone by flitted before us in the sunlight coming through a window. I watched them gather and float with certainty—up, up, and away.

"Well," she began, "there was one night a couple of weeks back when someone he worked with picked him up from our house. The hour was very late. I didn't get a good look at the woman in the driver's seat, but—"

"Woman? What woman?"

"I don't know who she was dear, but she picked him up and they drove back to the ranch together. I only thought it odd because he wasn't scheduled to be back at work until the next evening."

I pressed my lips, nodded, and walked away so she couldn't see the tears welling in my eyes. Once again, my body knew what my head refused to acknowledge, what my heart was unwilling to accept.

In that moment, I wanted nothing more than to feel like one of those aged particles—floating toward a new life, in a small group of like-hearted fuzzies, headed for the warmth of the sun.

But I felt cold, and Grandma's hand felt like ice when she touched the back of my shoulder and said, "I don't think it's anything to worry about even if it was a bit odd." She smiled, trying to reassure me.

Back at the house, I learned the boys were a big help to Grandpa.

"They're terrific little burrowers," he said.

"They're filthy," Grandma said, eyeballing their dirty snouts and paws.

"Oh, they're fine," Grandpa said.

I settled into a quiet evening with Caleb's grandparents, making peace with the fact that some weekends Caleb would join us but not if he could pick up extra shifts. Which happened to be the case that weekend.

I was comfortable with them in his absence. Besides, I was a pro at finding disagreeable situations then using them to remind myself why I should never dismiss my superpower.

So, when Grandma talked me into attending her church service before heading back to Austin, I simply added that discomfort to my long list of why-did-I-do-that scenarios.

At church, I was able to hush my obvious irritation until the pastor, dressed head-to-toe in black leather, said, "If anyone here has the calling, and feels it deep within their heart, let them come forth."

I looked at Grandma, bewildered. She smiled big, scrunched her shoulders up by her ears, and said, "I love this part."

Three men wearing button-up shirts, jeans, and cowboy boots walked behind a curtain and wheeled out a small pool. A handful of people formed a line at the portable body of water, walked up a few steps, and got inside.

One by one, they were dunked by the pastor, also in the pool. In his leather. No questions, no quizzes, no bible studies.

Driving on I-10, I did my best to shake the memory of people being submerged in a pool on wheels while dressed in their Sunday best. I'd never seen anything like it.

And my brain worked overtime trying to understand why Caleb rode around with his coworker on a night he wasn't scheduled. When I thought back to the lies he had told over time, they were really starting to add up and count against him.

I knew long before then, Caleb's depth was about as papery as his skin; the New Mexico sun had made his external layers pliable, much like his character. He didn't know who he was and resorted to lying while spinning in his own cycle.

Remembering what Joel said about my train-track self, my superpower, and the fact I suffer from PTSD made it easier to pay attention to how my body responded to things. Deep down I just knew what I knew. I felt it. Hard.

Things between Caleb and I hadn't ever felt right, and I couldn't dismiss the feeling that this woman he worked with was more than just a coworker.

I got confirmation the next week while parked outside of People's Pharmacy on South Lamar Boulevard, waiting to pick up Moron's prescriptions.

My phone buzzed with a text from Caleb.

"I can't wait to kiss my new girlfriend!"

My throat closed. I couldn't breathe.

"What?" I texted back.

It felt like forever before he replied.

"Um, one of the kids grabbed my phone and sent that."

"Why would they do that?" I texted.

"I work with troubled boys. I'll call you later."

I sped home, on the verge of hyperventilating. I gave Moron his meds and paced the apartment, waiting for my phone to buzz.

I looked down at my Moron, drowsy, balled up in his crate, snuggling with blankets and stuffed toys while Bart slobbered over his itty-bitty.

An hour passed and I'd still not heard from Caleb. My panic worsened and I became someone unrecognizable.

I called his grandma.

"I think he's cheating on me," I said.

"Oh, dear. What makes you think so?" she asked.

"He texted me earlier today saying he 'couldn't wait to kiss his new girlfriend.' Do you think it could be the woman who picked him up late that night?"

I sighed into the phone, staring at the engagement ring on my finger, disgusted with myself.

"I don't know, dear. But Caleb? Cheat? There must be some mistake. That just can't be. Aren't things going well?"

"Grandma...I just don't know anymore."

And I didn't.

All I knew for sure was that just the memory of Kelly felt like a drug; I always wanted more, and with him, no chameleon suits had ever been necessary.

Caleb was more like a hangover; I felt like shit around him, but it didn't matter because I knew I would drink again.

Fool's Gold

I POURED MY last Caleb cocktail later that same evening.

I knew better than to believe anything he said. I knew we weren't getting married, and I cried when I accepted that truth. Not because I was losing Caleb—he could keep all the lies, inadequacies, and misused words he wanted—I grieved for myself and the fact I was still stuck inside my own cycle, spinning out.

I'd slipped in and out of numerous chameleon suits over the years. They proved beneficial whenever it came to protecting myself, but I was through with twisting my principles and stuffing them into a skin-tight suit for someone else's benefit. Especially a mediocre friend and lover.

I raised the Caleb cocktail to my lips and decided to make one daring move. I called his cell. I figured the more I pushed him, the faster he would crack, and the quicker we'd be over so I could get the hell out of Texas.

Caleb didn't answer. I called again, and again, and again, like a madwoman scorned with nothing left to lose. Still nothing.

That motherfucker.

Emboldened, I went to the bad place—I called his work number. He wasn't there, so I left a message with specific instructions for him to call his *fiancé* the minute he walked in. I watched the clock.

Five minutes.

Seventeen minutes.

Thirty-three minutes.

I called again. He still wasn't there.

Forty-four minutes.

Fifty-two minutes.

An hour.

I called again. Nothing.

An hour and twelve minutes.

An hour and a half.

I called again. Finally, Caleb answered.

"Why have you been calling here all day? I told you I would call you. The house manager wanted to know why a 'neurotic woman' kept calling here. You're going to get me in trouble."

"All you had to do was call me back and explain this 'new girlfriend' shit."

My body trembled.

"I told you, one of the kids sent that text," he said in a hushed growl.

"Well, I don't believe you! You lie, and I don't even think you can stop yourself from doing it."

"Oh, please. You just need to trust me."

"How the fuck can you expect trust when all you've done is lie? Trust is earned, Caleb."

"You've never even given me a chance—"

"Oh, my god, I've done nothing *but* give you chances! With your girlfriend in New Mexico, the ice-cream job, the massage client's number—"

"You're so disrespectful and confrontational. You're always usurping me!"

A tiny chuckle escaped my lips. "What? I'm always what-ing you?"

"Usurping me—you usurp my authority."

Mid-argument, with a cell phone in my hand, you better believe I walked right over to my bookshelf and grabbed the dictionary. I just had to know if "usurp" meant what I thought it did and, more importantly, if he was even using it correctly.

I flipped through the pocket dictionary Kelly had given me a couple of years before.

Usurp: to commit forcible or illegal seizure of an office, power, etc.

The fool meant to say "undermine."

"Are you still there?" he asked.

I'd forgotten I was on the phone with him while deep inside a word-wormhole.

"Yeah," I said, sighing.

"Rebekah..." he said, lowering his voice. "You're hard to get along with. You expect way too much. You're a dominator. You make me anxious, and this crap is a result of it."

"Domineering would've been a better word choice—"

"See how you are?" he asked with another growl.

"Okay, I'll give you that. But tell me why one of the boys grabbed your phone and sent that text?"

"As a prank. They're kids, here because they're *troubled.*"

"He should apologize, then. That's not the kind of joke you play on someone," I said.

"Fine. I'll call you back when he comes inside."

Click.

I went to the only place I felt I could when things didn't make sense—a bookstore. My new church, Half-Price Books, had so many comforting, old, used books; they centered me.

Standing in line—holding *Introvert Power* by Laurie Helgoe, another Stephen King novel, a reference guide on the healing power of gemstones (I was broadening my horizons), and a few vinyl records guaranteed to make me feel better—I heard some shocking news from the store's loudspeakers.

"The King of Pop has died at the age of fifty."

A few patrons and I stood in line, in disbelief, hugging our merchandise and listening intently. The announcement was followed by "Billie Jean."

89

I couldn't listen to "Billie Jean" and simply appreciate it for the song it was. Memories of me signing the song for Mom at age five—when it was released in 1983—at nine, thirteen, sixteen, and twenty-five came at me full force and I smiled.

Beautiful queen, movie show-off, who me? Floor, dance, round.

"I can take you right here," a cashier said, interrupting the ASL performance in my head.

I walked up to the register and placed my items on the counter, fighting tears for Michael Jackson, for Moron, for my mom, and for myself.

At home, I could see Moron's chemo had hit him hard. He lay in his crate, snuggled with old blankets, a stuffed pigeon, and a blank stare. There was nothing I could do for him. Almost harder than seeing Moron lethargic was trying to keep Bartok entertained—he wasn't sick and still wanted to go on long walks and hunt scorpions. When I gave in to Bartok's pleas, Moron could muster just enough strength to look up from the crate. It killed me.

While outside with Bartok, my phone buzzed. It was Caleb's grandma.

"Did you talk to Caleb?" she asked.

"Yes. He said one of the boys played a prank and sent the text."

"Do you think that's the truth?" she asked.

I knew she'd asked because she remembered that Caleb lied to her about staying in Maryland one weekend while he was in NH with me, moving Spork in with my parents. Why he lied about his whereabouts then remains a mystery.

"No. Caleb had the boy call and apologize personally," I said.

"And?"

"It was weird. When the kid called, I felt worse for him than I did for myself. His apology sounded rehearsed, forced. I hope Caleb didn't use a vulnerable kid to lie for him."

"Me too, dear." She sounded conflicted and disappointed.

I snuggled into a peaceful evening with Moron and Bart on the couch with my *Introvert Power* book.

The author said some things I sort of knew, which was comforting. Like, I concern myself with people and ideas, not idle gossip, and that might be why some gravitate toward me, like Joel said.

Introverts prefer spacious interactions with fewer people, we use mental health services more because we're not afraid to look inside—which made perfect sense since (until I'd moved) I was in Joel's office every Thursday evening—and too much input can make an introvert miss their mind. I felt that one.

My phone buzzed with a text from Caleb. He said he'd come to Austin on Friday (the next day) to clear the air surrounding his "new girlfriend" text.

"Fine," I texted back, setting my phone down, eager to keep reading.

With the entire day off from work, I busied myself to keep distracted. I spent the day caring for Moron, keeping Bartok entertained—while trying to avoid fire ants and scorpions—cleaning house, rearranging furniture, researching canine lymphoma at the apartment's business center, refinishing my coffee table, and sewing an old t-shirt quilt. Anything to keep myself occupied.

Once I ran out of things to concern myself with, I picked up the gemstone reference guide and learned some interesting facts, things I sort of knew but had no idea where I knew them from. Like, I knew Kelly was amber; he carried that radiance effortlessly. The book confirmed it.

I thought back to Kelly's warm glow, his amber waves, his golden silhouette, and the bronze outline of him dancing on my train tracks. I remembered that his presence had the power to soothe my phobias and silence my racing thoughts. A tear trickled down my cheek.

I flipped the page.

The next gem proved worthy of note. Iron pyrite, fool's gold. "Iron pyrite is showy and glistens—giving off the illusion of real gold. It's brittle, has black spots, and when struck against metal or another stone, it sparks."

Caleb. Totally. He'd been showy the whole time I'd known him, constantly trying to prove something. There wasn't any substance behind his long-winded monologues to nowhere, and I think he knew it.

He'd made a habit of feigning confidence at almost every opportunity. His insecurity burst through his dark veins, revealing his brokenness. His inadequacies and self-loathing oozed from his pores. Anytime he was confronted, sparks flew in a defensive rage, and he found creative ways to lay blame on me.

The book further stated that "according to some studies on pyrite, it can help one see through façades and manipulation, noticing a deeper meaning behind words and actions. It guards against negative vibrations—" *Hold on, wait a minute. That doesn't make sense. If Caleb is fool's gold and fool's gold also shields against negativity, then how could he be the very thing he is protecting me from?*

That was too much for me to think about. I put the book on my coffee table and watched day turn into night.

Still no word from Caleb.

I tuned in to KLRU, an Austin-based PBS channel, around 10 p.m. I fell asleep to a cooking show hosted by Jacques Pepin and woke around 1 a.m. to a comforting sound I knew and loved. Leonard Cohen—the man with the golden voice—unplugged.

I watched the entire special, cuddling Moron on the couch. Leonard sang "Famous Blue Raincoat," my absolute favorite. I'm not really attracted to old dudes, but he could sing the panties right off me.

Come 2 a.m., no Caleb. My body ached; I was tired, wide-awake, and nauseous. All at the same time. I knew he wasn't coming.

I wasn't broken over losing Caleb. Deep down, and even somewhere on the surface, I knew I was only missing out on his lies and perversion of the English language. It wasn't him I longed for. I longed to feel there was someone in my corner, unconditionally.

Then, I realized my longing was for Kelly, for amber, and I suddenly hated him for still being perched on a pedestal in my mind with a big grin, legs dangling, arms outstretched.

At 3 a.m., I felt a slight panic attack coming on. With Moron cuddled against my chest and Bart chillin' at my feet, I decided to squash the panic and sleep Caleb away, tears and all.

The next morning, I woke to the sound of Moron falling off the couch.

"Aw, buddy," I said as he whimpered.

He was weaker now and experiencing the worst part of his chemo treatments. I called the specialist.

"Unfortunately, this is to be expected. We're in the thick of it now. Just keep doing what you're doing—meds, treatment, love, and patience. I think we caught it early enough and we're making some progress."

"He had a nosebleed the other day. Is that part of it, too?" I pressed a cool, damp washcloth to Moron's head like he was a feverish baby while Bart licked his brother's face.

"Sometimes. His body is adjusting to the treatment. Why don't you bring him Monday instead of Wednesday?"

"Okay."

Click.

I couldn't be bothered to worry about Caleb even if I wanted to, which I didn't. The only thing concerning me was Moron's health and the fact that it forced us to stay in Austin for his treatment; I really wanted to get out of Texas.

For comfort, I turned to Justin Furstenfeld of Blue October, who sang about addiction, pain, love, loss, loneliness. He took my indescribable agony and strung poetry effortlessly, using desperate melodies whilst screaming. I screamed with him. In my apartment, in my car.

I spent days and nights with Justin at my ear, assuring me I wasn't alone. With every heartrending lullaby, Blue October got me through one of the absolute worst break-ups I'd ever experienced.

Again, it wasn't Caleb. It was the mind games, the lying, the cheating, being slowly and systematically driven out of my mind, and worst of all—believing it was somehow my fault.

Before Caleb, *Gaslight* had only been the title of an old Ingrid Bergman and Charles Boyer film I watched with my family; it was one of Mark's favorites. But after Caleb? It meant so much more.

While obsessively piecing our relationship together like a jigsaw—going over every detail, every lie, and every fucking sob story—I knew there was no way I was the first woman Caleb had done this to, and there was no way in hell I'd be the last. His "new girlfriend" would have her turn, no doubt.

I couldn't really talk to anyone about my engagement woes because I'd only been in Austin for three months. I had no friends, no network. The people I worked with were great, but I was too distracted to really connect with anyone.

A voice surfaced from deep within telling me to beat feet, run away, go home. *It's okay, Bek, people uproot themselves all the time.*

Later that week, Bartok and I picked up Moron from his treatment appointment. We stood waiting at the glass door. As Moron walked toward us, I was excited to see some pep in his step. Once he approached the glass, he and Bartok pawed at each other, waiting for someone with flesh and thumbs to open the door.

"We've made some progress. We're not in the clear, but his blood count is stabilizing and we're seeing significant change." It was the first time I'd ever seen this man smile, and I hated that I was about to wipe it off his face.

"I'm so glad," I said, hesitating. "Um, we're gonna be moving, and I need a referral, names of other specialists we can see."

He sighed, shaking his head. "I wouldn't recommend leaving right now. Moron needs this treatment."

I looked down at my furry sausage bandits. "I know, and I don't want him to miss out, but we can't stay."

"Well," he said as I watched him formulate an alternate plan, "if you stay a few more weeks, for the treatments he has left in this phase, we can buy some time before the next phase begins."

"I can do that. We're not leaving until the end of August."

"But you have to find someone who can pick up where we leave off. You can't waste any time."

"Okay."

The next few weeks happened quicker than I was ready for, but I didn't fight it—when the Universe pushes, I don't ask questions.

I sublet my trendy Austin apartment once the new tenant's background check had cleared with the leasing office. Then, I completed and sent paperwork to begin interpreting in my home state. Next, I reserved and paid for a five-by-eight U-Haul and attached it to Lysah's rear.

At my apartment, I packed the boys' things, my books, vinyl records, clothes, sewing machine, and other personal effects.

With the apartment complex's permission, I left behind a brand-new couch and an almost-fully-furnished, swanky one-bedroom where all the beautiful people lived.

No one saw us off. We just...left.

My first stop was to see Moron's specialist to get all the necessary documents for his transfer of care. I could see that the specialist was not only concerned about Moron, but that he'd miss him. And who could blame him? Everyone who met my boys loved them instantly.

"I'm really sorry you have to leave. Please be sure to find Moron another specialist as soon as possible," he said, petting Moron's head. "And update us on his progress."

"I will."

I had no idea what I was going to do once I got to NH; I just knew I needed to be there and regroup, reassess, rediscover something. Like a salmon swimming upstream with no plans to spawn.

Near Texarkana, Texas, a truck driver honked and flashed his lights at me, motioning for me to pull over. I ignored him and called a La Quinta on the Texas/Arkansas state line to make a reservation for the night.

On my left, I saw the trucker pass me. I'd read that some truckers try to convince unsuspecting women to pull over.

Keep going, pervert.

When I pulled into the hotel parking lot, glad to be almost out of Texas, I spotted the same trucker again. Leery, I parked on the other side of the lot, hoping he wouldn't recognize Lysah's bright exterior. As I got out of my car, he exited his rig and walked toward me.

"Howdy, ma'am. I didn't mean to startle you on the road, or here, but I noticed your chains were sparkin'," he said with a southern drawl, tipping his hat.

"What?" I asked, standing close to Lysah's rear, Bartok and Moron frantic in the backseat.

"The chains from your bumper to the U-Haul were draggin' on the freeway. They're not tight enough. Sparks were flyin' like fireworks," he said, pointing to the chains and the shoddy job I did of hitching the trailer to Lysah myself.

"Oh."

He went to his rig, fished out a tool, and came back. "May I?" he asked, eyebrows raised.

I nodded and he started tightening the chains around the hitch, securing it better than I had. I stood, embarrassed by my wrong assumption.

I heard Joel again… *People—non-Witnesses—can be well-intentioned without using fear, guilt, shame, or conditional love to manipulate you; not to say some won't but not everyone* will.

"There. That oughta do it," he said, standing.

"Thank you. I'm sorry I was stand-offish. You just kind of came out of nowhere and—"

"No worries, ma'am. Can't be too careful."

"Can I buy you dinner or repay you somehow?" I asked.

"Oh, no. That's not necessary." He tipped his hat and walked back to his rig. "Be safe, now."

After the trucker reminded me that some people can be inherently good, I checked in, dragged our things into the room, and plopped onto the bed.

Bartok gnawed at his itty-bitty, and for the first time in weeks, Moron amused himself with a stuffed pigeon.

Exhausted, I stared at the ceiling, preparing myself for the journey home.

Get to Aunt Kathy's in one piece.

Get Moron to a specialist.

Set myself up with work.

See Mom and Dad?

I wasn't ready to think about the last item on my list.

So, I logged onto Facebook via my Blackberry and there was a peculiar message in bold, waiting to be opened.

"Hey, bekah how r u? The General."

Bekah? No one calls me that. The General?

I clicked the profile picture to see who the General was. A stocky, dirty blond, Dave-Pirner-from-Soul-Asylum lookalike, minus the dreads, smiled back at me. I vaguely remembered his Dave Pirner look from high school.

I responded with, "Oh, my god, haven't seen you in forever, how's everything?" and other vacuous pleasantries, briefly mentioning my journey back to NH.

"Let me no when u come bac if ur close we'll get sum coffee or somethin'."

Ugh. He's a txt tlkr.

Almost immediately after logging off Facebook, I received a text from Asshat, my new nickname for Caleb.

"Where are you? You're not at your apartment," it said.

Oh, my fucking god.

It had been weeks, yes *weeks*, since Caleb planned to come to my apartment and clear the air of his bullshit lies, then didn't show.

I called him.

He answered and I laid right into him. "What makes you think you could just show up weeks after you said you would, and I'd be there waiting with bated breath?"

"I thought we'd make time to talk about everything after a cooling off period," he said, irritated.

"If that's what you wanted, you should have made that clear—and a day or two is sufficient, not three weeks! I know you're dating someone you work with. It doesn't take a genius to figure out you're with someone else now. So, go ahead and start lying to her."

"Rebekah, you make being in a relationship so hard! You have these...expectancies, which make me anxious. When I fall short of your visions of grandness, I get frantic and am forced to find comfort elsewhere."

Not only was he spewing more bullshit, but he was still blaming me for his poor choices.

"Dude! What'd you ask me to marry you for then, huh?"

"I thought—"

"Listen, when someone is caught lying and suspected of cheating, then doesn't show up to clear the air, I call that over. And you can do whatever you want with these *expectations* and *visions of grandeur*—I'm not even in Texas anymore."

"What?" The tone of his voice told me he couldn't believe I had left without seeing him.

"Yeah. I quit my job, packed my shit, and left. So, fuck you."

"Do you still have the ring?"

Shit. I did. I stared at the ring thinking, *a fool's diamond, definitely synthetic.* With everything that was going on, I didn't even think to take it off or find a way to get it to him.

"Yeah, I do," I said. "What do you want me to do with it?"

"I don't care, it's cubic zirconia anyway!"

"I knew it!" I shouted.

As I was about to hang up, he blurted one last shit statement.

"And another thing—you're so focused on that damn dog, you don't make room for anyone else. And you probably won't ever be able to."

I hung up.

That damn dog? Oh, my fucking god.

I lay on the bed and stared at the ceiling, angry with myself for moving to Texas for him. I *knew* he was untrustworthy, and I fucking ignored it. I repeatedly hushed every single gut-jab until I bled.

He knew exactly what he was doing the entire time. He intentionally undermined my sanity, gaslit me. Only he wasn't nearly as sophisticated as Charles Boyer while he was doing it.

So, why did he methodically drive me bonkers with lies upon lies? I don't know, but I tell you this: Asshat should count his lucky stars I didn't stick around because Ingrid Bergman I ain't; I was on my way to a very dark place. If I hadn't left Texas when I did, the world might have another Betty Broderick *Lifetime* docuseries in the queue.

Then, like a bolt of lightning, it hit me—Caleb's place in my life wasn't meant for us to build or share anything together. His purpose was to show me what fool's gold looked like close up; he'd vouchsafed plenty of opportunities for me to see through his façade, his manipulation.

I'd had this bionic radar imbedded into my core since my train-track days; Caleb had merely given me occasions to trust it. It was high time I started paying attention and listening to me and my intuition. I couldn't afford not to.

To distance myself from all thoughts of him and our vexing relation*shit*, I pulled the gemstone reference book out of my bag to distract myself. I flipped to a random page.

"Feldspar, moonstone. The stone of self-discovery and self-awareness has a force that aids in self-connection, releasing old energy and old patterns in an effort to move forward. Moonstone encourages a higher perspective, powerful for one's intuition. Its milky white hue shows off its glowing inner light, representing strength and inner growth."

I thought about me, not connecting to family, not connecting to a man I had been trying to make part of my own pack. It forced inner growth, self-connection, intuitively moving me forward. I could feel myself resisting old patterns, old cycles.

It seemed that intuitive moonstone brushing up against deceptive fool's gold ignited some sparks, forcing me to grow into myself and farther away from Asshat.

Well done, Feldspar.

I happened to be rolling through Memphis when the urge to get in touch with Kelly struck. At my next pitstop, I emailed him from my Blackberry. It felt safe. If he didn't want to talk to me, I could take the rejection in an email better than in a phone call or text.

Well, there was no rejection. Kel was as genuinely kind as he'd always been. I was shocked when he told me he was living in Massachusetts, and he nearly knocked the wind out of me when he suggested meeting up for lunch upon my return home.

I was astounded. First, the General got in touch, asking to get coffee. No biggie there; he was just an old friend from days I'd forgotten to remember. Then Asshat had texted, spinning more bullshit. Then Kelly suggested a lunch date.

Another text came in while driving through Virginia, and nothing prepared me for that one.

"Mom and Dad said you were moving home. Are you okay?"

It was Luke.

I texted back when I stopped for gas. "I'm okay."

"Just *come back* and we can be there for you."

I didn't respond to that message. I couldn't.

Luke's text was well-intentioned—he's my brother, still one half of me—but the message reeked of "us versus them," and it was clear that I was with "them." The heathens; the corrupt; the worldly. And it was *I* who needed an adjustment, not the Mallorys.

I knew if I "went back," my family would be there waiting with open arms, but I hated that their arms would remain folded until *I* did their steering committee's bidding.

I drove on, reminding myself that I wasn't going home for them. I was going home for me. I had no idea what was waiting for me there, where I'd work, or what I'd do. Something about that freedom, uncertainty, and empowerment felt kind of nice.

I decided to make another pitstop in Northern Virginia, near the D.C. line.

"Hey, baby girl!" I heard as I walked into Yvette's house—a close friend and coworker that had become a cross between a mother and a sister to me.

"Hey, Mama."

She pulled me into a comfortable hug. "The boys with you?"

"Of course."

"Well, bring those babies inside."

Bartok and Moron were no strangers to my previous SLA family. They'd come to every staff picnic and softball game. There weren't too many people who didn't love them.

After a walk with the boys around Yvette's neighborhood, we snuggled up on her sectional, and she wasted no time making me an offer, hard to refuse.

"I'm sorry it didn't work out for you down there, Monkey-pig."

A "Monkey-pig" was something Yvette had seen in a local newspaper comic that she felt described me perfectly—a curious creature, both inexplicable and cute.

I sighed. "You tried to tell me."

She responded using the sign for instinct.

I sighed and nodded.

"So, what now?" she asked.

"I'm going home. That's all I know right now."

"Home could be here, you know. My basement is set up like a studio apartment—it could be yours."

"I don't know. I really feel this pull to go home."

"At least think about it. You could stay here, easily get back on the schedule, and I could take care of you."

"I'll think about it."

After dinner and the boys' nighttime walk around the block, I rested my head on Yvette's lap and she stroked my hair. I liked the idea of her taking care of me; it felt like a long time since anyone had.

The next morning, I'd made a loose promise to consider moving into her basement studio to pick up where I'd left off in the D.C. area just four months prior. Those months with Asshat felt like years; his bullshit had aged me considerably.

I loaded the boys into my car and drove the final stretch of my trip home to NH. I'd be arriving just in time for my favorite season—fall.

There's nothing like a New England autumn. The summer leaves die beautifully in a wild array of colors, the air is crisp, the mosquitoes peter out, and apples are ready for picking. There's a melancholy calm that rests over the mountains and trees, and I was elated that I'd be home in time for NH to greet me with hot cocoa and a fleeced hoodie.

The last bits of NH summer were beginning to fade as I drove into Laconia.

My aunt Kathy owned a four-bedroom, two-bath New Englander off Union Avenue with plenty of room to spare, and I was welcomed to stay as long as I needed.

I texted my dad to let him know I was home and he quickly summoned me to meet him in Governor's Island, near Weirs Beach, at a house he was painting.

I zoomed by Kathy's with full force, U-Haul attached, excited to see my dad. I was shocked he was willing to see me at all. Maybe there'd been something in a recent *Watchtower* study permitting parents to love their wayward children.

Anytime the *Society* published literature instructing parents to either show love or distance toward their disfellowshipped children, it was followed. No questions asked.

The week I got home must've been a good week for the *mentally diseased*.

I pulled up to the small mansion Dad was painting. When he saw me in the driveway, he came down the ladder to meet me as I climbed out of Lysah.

Pulling me into a tight squeeze, he said, "Hullo, Bucky. Miss you."

I didn't bother responding; he wouldn't have heard me. I waited until he was through hugging before I backed up and signed, "Miss you, too."

"No like Texas, huh?" he signed with cracked, paint-stained hands.

I shook my head. "Everything mess up," I signed.

"Sorry," he said, walking to the window of Lysah's backseat. "Hullo, puppy!"

Everyone loved the boys. Everyone.

"You drive long way. Hungry? You me go get beach pizza," he signed, pointing toward Weirs Beach.

I couldn't believe I was talking to my dad, and he'd asked me out for pizza. I felt starstruck, like I was in the company of a major celebrity. Butterflies darted from my stomach to my chest, fluttering with intensity, and I wanted to release years of bottled tears on him. I wanted to cry on his shoulder, the place John Denver's sunshine lived.

Eating greasy boardwalk pizza, Dad said the same thing he always said, "Me, mom hope you come back truth."

I'm not really a fan of hyperbole but trust me—he *always* said this. And I *always* smiled and nodded.

I mean, what could I say to a man who's built his whole life around this one fictitious ideology? How do I tell an already broken man—holding onto his own childhood trauma and pain, spinning in his own cycle—that the thing he loves and believes to the death is a farce? I couldn't. I wouldn't. What right would I have?

As much as I abhor the *Society* and would love to see its demise, I cannot bring myself to further break this man.

Call it an unearned pass or call my parents undeserving if you will. I choose to call it: Bucky-still-loves-her-daddy-and-learned-how-to-forgive-in-order-to-live.

With Dad, I made another loose promise—as if in some kind of trance—to go to a meeting.

I drove to Kathy's, successfully backed the U-Haul into her driveway, (with the help of her neighbor guiding me) and unloaded the little life I'd brought back from Texas.

Good Follow Through

TWO WEEKS INTO our new life in NH and I didn't get Moron to a specialist quick enough. I failed as a wiener-mom. I had hoped the pep in his step bought us some time. But it didn't. He got sick again. I called every vet within a two-hour drive, even vets in Massachusetts, and no one could give him the treatment he needed.

I rushed him to an emergency vet where they made the very quick decision to give him a blood transfusion, and I didn't object. If I was willing to do that for him, surely, I would be willing to do it for myself.

Any J-Dub wringing their hands at the gates of paradise, waiting to get in, would see Jehovah's doors slam then lock shut once their concealed file showed they'd accepted a blood transfusion. Not me, though. And not my Moron.

A week later I brought Moron to the emergency vet again and was told, "He's so tired. Given his history, it may be time. I'm so sorry."

Bartok and I sat close to Moron as he went to sleep. A huge piece of me, and a huge piece of Bartok, died that day. Days turned into weeks as Bartok and I settled into our own hazy routine, barely holding ourselves together after losing Moron.

Somehow, I'd managed to set up a homey room at my aunt's and establish a sole proprietorship in the state of NH once I had my interpreting state license in hand.

Keeping myself busy allowed me to squash the hurt I felt over Moron's loss. Driving all around the Granite State, from assignment to assignment, I sometimes had Bartok in tow; he was brotherless, and I just couldn't leave him alone all day. Most gigs were less than an hour, and the crisp September air swept through Lysah's cracked windows for Bart, keeping him entertained while I hand-flapped.

Coming from an interview at a new VRS center in Concord, I got a text from the General.

"Hey, did you 4get abt me?" it read.

"Forget what?"

"Coffee at the Black Cat. Been waitn 4 u."

"Um, shit. That was today? I'm on my way."

"K lots has happnd since we tlkd last."

With everything going on, I must have forgotten that we'd set a date to meet for coffee.

I hopped in Lysah and headed to Laconia, though I really just wanted to go home, wherever that was. When I pulled up to the Black Cat, he was sitting at an outside table, smiling, with a glass of beer.

I stepped out of the car and tried like hell to remember this guy. We went to high school together for a brief time; he was there, I knew that much. I'd seen him sporadically over the years, bumping into him at Cumberland Farms when I worked there, and at the aerospace factory (L&S) when I worked there. He seemed to appear, then disappear often, but he rarely seemed changed. He was pretty chill, a bit of a flirt, a big joker, easy to be around.

I walked closer. From what I could see, he had lost his Dave Pirner-esque, teenage mystique and replaced it with a goatee and a Boston Red Sox ball cap. He wore a thick, plaid flannel, dirty jeans, and clear blue eyes. The cutest chin dimple I'd ever seen peeked out from behind his ubiquitous New England goatee.

"Hey, pull up a chai-ah. C'mon, sit down," he said in a thick N' Hampshah accent—all *ah*'s, no *r*'s.

"What's the rush?" I asked, walking closer to the table.

107

"You're wearin' heeled boots. You're lucky I'm sittin' down. How dare you." He smiled.

I sat down and ordered water. "I don't remember you being *that* short," I said.

"Well, height don't matter if you're layin' down." He laughed, winked, and sipped his beer. "When did you get back?"

I shook my head and half-giggled. "Um, end of August...ish?" I said, eyeballing his hands.

I have this thing with people's hands. I'm sure it has a lot to do with hands being a big part of my experience growing up; I was always looking at them, deciphering their movements.

Over the years, I'd found if I could be attracted to the hands, I could be attracted to the person. I wasn't planning on dating the General; I was mentally and emotionally barren. Just the same, I look at people's hands to see if they're worth looking at for longer periods of time.

The General's hands were nice, but it was clear he'd been nibbling at his thumbs like a starved zombie.

"And you're just gettin' 'round to seein' your friends now?" he asked.

It was the third week of September and, *are we even friends?*

"I've been going through some shit," I said.

"Me too. Want a beer?" he asked.

"Yeah, maybe I need a beer."

I ordered a beer, which I really don't care for, and we waxed tragedy for hours. It was remarkable that this person I barely knew, hadn't seen in years, opened up so quickly and vice versa, like we picked up where we'd once left off in another life. Some people are like that, and they almost feel like home.

That's how it was with the General.

I talked about Asshat and losing my beloved Moron, and he rambled on about his soon-to-be ex-wife.

"She started gettin' texts and flowers from some guy she worked with, and well, you know…" He shrugged and looked down.

I clinked my beer glass against his. "Man, I'm sorry. My ex-fiancé pulled some of the same shit. It's like, 'You don't wanna be with me anymore? Just tell me the fuckin' truth. I can take it.'"

"Yeah, what sucks is we have a house, two kids, two dogs, two cats, the whole thing." He gnawed at one of his thumbs.

"Shit. How old are your kids?"

"My daughter's ten and my son's six."

I felt my face twist into sad, pathetic shapes. "Aw, they're just babies."

"Yeah. I tried to make it work. We've been together eleven years, but we're gonna have to tell the kids we're splittin' up."

As we sat, lamenting over our respective situations, it felt like some cosmic force had gone through the trouble of pulling us toward each other. He was going through something very similar to what I had *just* gone through with Asshat, and what he told me about his wife's situation mirrored my cheating days with Carter.

It was easy for me to see things from his soon-to-be ex's vantage point, almost knowing what her next move would be, because I'd once done the same things to Carter.

I felt bad for the General. I felt bad for Carter. I felt bad for myself. I felt relieved that I didn't have any kids in the mix. Then I felt guilty for thinking my situation wasn't as bad as his.

I gave the General a hug before leaving the Black Cat, but when I backed away and saw the hurt in his eyes, I pulled him in for another one.

On my short drive to Kathy's, I thought about how funny life had been thus far. I hadn't come home to meet up with friends. I had come home to distance myself from anything resembling my old life, but my past had a way of finding me, and because of that, I knew I needed to spend time with my train-track self to get shit straightened out. I owed her that.

The following weekend, I drove a parallel line by the railroad tracks on I-93 South to meet Kel for lunch. I couldn't tell you what I wore or what I expected to happen, if anything, but Lysah took me to Massachusetts faster than I should've gone.

I wasn't sure whether to thank the Universe or tell it to fuck off because, the way I saw it, I'd come full circle—from NH with Carter to Silver Spring toward Kelly, to Austin for Asshat, then back to NH.

I hadn't seen Kelly since the Christmas break-up when I'd scooted him toward my couch and heard him sobbing in the dead of night. We'd talked sporadically after that, but I hadn't seen him. I knew if he still smelled like home, I was fucked.

I parked at a dead mall then walked inside. Sitting at the sandwich shop Kel had suggested, I waited anxiously. He came in a few minutes later, sporting his well-worn *Dudley Do Right* t-shirt and baggy shorts.

We were about to pick up where we'd left off.

His soft stubble and smile looked the same. "Did you order?" he asked.

"Not yet," I said. I stood, hugged him, and my heart raced as I inhaled his familiar scent without looking too obvious. "How are you?"

He slowly backed up, his dimples pierced his cheeks as he smiled and said, "Doing okay, I guess. Been really exhausted lately." He rubbed both palms over his face, inhaled, then sat.

"Oh? Why so tired?" I asked, sitting down.

"Well, I'm between teaching jobs right now. I've taught at three different schools in three years. I'm friggin' wasted."

I had to ask. "How the hell did you wind up in New England of all places?"

"Just following that student need." His dimples indented again when he asked, "So, how are you?"

"I don't know, fine?" I skimmed over why I had come home and what I was hoping to find.

"So, you're not really fine, then? It's okay. I've not been well, either."

The sandwich-maker brought the sandwiches we'd ordered and two bags of Cape Cod chips to our table.

"Are you just tired, or...?"

"After we broke up, I went to therapy," he said, taking a bite of his sandwich.

"I was in therapy, too."

"Joel?" Kel asked, opening his bag of Cape Cods.

"Yeah, I miss him. As an independent contractor, everything is out-of-pocket for me. So, no therapy right now. What's next for you?"

"I'm in a weird place at the moment." He looked down at his plate. His lip quivered. "I don't know what my next move will be. There's an opportunity in Michigan. I have an interview scheduled there. I may go back. We'll see."

Michigan? Any thoughts of resurrecting what we'd once had shriveled into themselves like the podlings from *The Dark Crystal* and died as soon as he said "Michigan."

I hadn't necessarily met up with Kelly to rekindle any embers, but not even being able to flirt with the idea, because he'd likely skip town anyway, left an unfillable hole. Much like the podlings—our essence was gone.

I remembered the exact moment my heart let him go—at the Memphis International Airport, arms overhead in the millimeter wave scanner. It felt like I was standing there all over again.

Even so, I wasn't at all prepared to hear that he struggled after our break-up. And I was totally shocked he was in *my* New England having lunch with me, ready to leave again.

The sound of Kelly laughing threw me.

I looked at him. "What's so funny?"

"Your cute sandwich routine—you're still rearranging and reassembling it as you eat."

I looked down and he was right. Without thinking about it, I had been taking a few bites, resting the sandwich on my plate, opening it, taking it apart, rearranging it, then taking a few more bites, over and over.

"I'm glad my odd, little neuroses still amuse you." I smiled, tight-lipped, with a mouthful of food.

After lunch we drove in tandem on the hunt for a bowling alley. We found one, parked, and I walked to my trunk to get my bowling bag.

"Ooh, big-time bowler now, eh?" Kelly said.

"Ha, hardly. Asshat got me fitted for a bowling ball and shoes for my birthday. He was the big-time bowler. Even though he's a shit, I'm not gonna toss a ball that's fit for my fingers or a decent pair of shoes."

We walked in, excited, only to discover that the alley was candlepin bowling. *I hate candlepin.*

"Well, that sucks. Maybe we'll try again sometime," he said.

"Yeah, if you're not in Michigan."

We stood in the parking lot of a bowling alley, in the middle of the afternoon, speechless. I knew this was it, probably the last time I would see him. I had silently prepared myself for that pain all afternoon.

Hugging him, taking in his unmistakable scent, I accepted it would be the last time I ever did. He kissed me on the cheek the same way he had when CloseUp ended, and his stubble felt the same—silky.

Lunch with Kel had been strangely anti-climactic. I loved seeing him, missed him, but our midday date felt so lifeless compared to the all-out frenzy we'd once experienced. I felt ruined, just like I'd predicted. No one would ever hold a candle to the way he made me feel or the uncontrollable fire that had once consumed us both. Kelly had left some big shoes to fill, and our time together already felt like eons ago.

Losing Kelly again didn't hit me until his lingering scent swiftly darted through my cracked window and found a home somewhere on I-93.

Though the closure was necessary for me, something told me we'd stay in touch; what we once had was just too special to forsake each other's existence completely. Even with that bit of reassurance to ride home with, I still cried.

I'd come home to get some footing, and part of that meant confronting all the things I'd run away from. Though I'd kept busy with settling myself, finding work, mourning Moron, keeping Bart amused, and lunching with men that I'd lost in some way, all I felt was sadness.

Having pizza on the boardwalk with my dad—while the sound of video arcade games filled that end-of-summer air—forced every Weirs Beach memory to bubble forth. And I realized then, I might never feel home again.

The feeling's sort of like this comforting, funereal sensation that totally consumes me. Sometimes it sits heavy, right in my chest, then shoots down on a nerve landing right behind my bellybutton. It transports me to another world, an alternate universe. Almost like I want to *go* home, but home is nowhere.

Home is the sound of a Black-capped Chickadee singing; it's the smell of boardwalk pizza at a beach I went to every summer growing up; it's the smell of chlorine surrounding me and my brother, Luke, as he stands in a shallow pool waiting to catch me after I come down the waterslide; it's the sound of my dad laughing as he throws me into the lake; it's wet sand between my fingers and toes while I make sandcastles; it's the smell of Mom's tanning lotion; it's feeling fireworks boom at the Weirs on Sunday nights, walking the boulevard with Mom; it's the sound of picture booth photos being taken with Mom during her wayward year; it's the sound of a tattoo needle buzzing over Stevie Nicks on the radio while working at the tat shop...

Being home was excruciating. Every day I passed lonely phantoms, gathered together for my sake. And it was more than mere homesickness. It was a heavy longing for safety and stability while straddling two worlds at once—one where everything's upended and another where I could almost feel rooted.

The ghosts of me and Kelly—lingering aimlessly in D.C.— had become the empty shadows of me and my family, me and Dean, and me and Carter, circling NH day in and day out.

Just like Dracula: centuries old, lonely, forever stuck, and thirsty for something but left with very little to feed on.

It was getting gorgeous in New England—the leaves were dying, and their death has always been colorful.

Bartok and I had a routine despite my emotional limbo. Work was picking up. Living with Kathy had been good. Sometimes my five-year-old cousin, Gianna, and I watched *Gummi Bear* DVDs together. Some nights were spent alone in my room, watching *I Love Lucy* reruns, snuggling Bart.

And some nights I fell back into drinking my emotional mess away; I could endure the sharp pangs of endometrial pain that usually took place after a few drinks. What was intolerable was standing beneath looming Mallory shadows, waiting for a connection that was unlikely to happen.

I left my aunt Kathy's (I never drank there), and I headed around the corner to my favorite drinking spot. As I drove, I swelled with gratitude; fellow Mobil Misfit Shari and I had sporadically kept in touch over the years.

Her brown eyes, Cabbage Patch Kid-like, caramel-colored hair, and coffee cream skin allowed us to pick up right where we'd left off, eight or nine years before.

Most nights, at Jay and Shari's, Jay cooked up something delicious while Shari tended their home bar. Walking into their apartment one night, I was surprised to see the General sitting at the table with a drink.

"Hey, what're you doing here?" I asked, putting my bag down.

"Havin' a drink. Bitchin'."

"Ah. It's not any better at home I take it?" I asked, sitting at the table with him.

"Nope." He shook his head and took a pull from his drink. "We told the kids. They thought we were joking. When they realized we weren't, they both lost it. Shit sucks right now."

"Man, I'm sorry."

One drink turned into many. It was dangerous to drink any concoction Shari mixed. She was notorious for making them strong and challenging you with a time limit. I could rarely meet her time limit. I was a sipper and no longer twenty-one.

Jay and Shari listened on as the General and I succumbed to another night of drunken bellyaching.

"I let my ex's new dude park his Jeep in my driveway," the General said, sipping his drink.

The three of us looked at him in disbelief.

"Why?" I asked.

He shrugged. "If he's gonna be around my kids, I want us to try and get along."

I wasn't prepared to see the General as more than just a guy I knew in high school and ran into over the years. Yet, there he sat, short in stature but bigger than anyone else in the room. Certainly, a bigger person than I.

"Wow," I said, unsure how to lift the heaviness in the air. "You, uh, wanna know some of the ridiculous shit Asshat said to me?" I said as my head swayed; the room was starting to spin. "He said…" I started laughing as the three of them looked at me, then to each other, and to me again, waiting.

"What? What did he say?" Shari asked, giggling.

"He said that I was always usurping him." I released an uncontrollable belly laugh, barely able to breathe as my face turned red.

Jay lit a cigarette and shook his head, smirking. "Idiot."

"I have to write this down. This is too funny." Shari grabbed a pen and sage colored notebook with four cartoon-character nuts on the cover. A nervous almond, a peanut with long hair, a happy acorn, and a worried cashew all stood next to each other, blissfully out of place. The caption under the legumes read, "All my friends are nuts."

"There's more," I said. "He once told me to *baroose*, B-A-R-O-O-S-E, his Myspace page."

All three looked at me, perplexed.

"What?" Shari asked.

I laughed and said, "He meant peruse."

"Oh, my god," Jay said, taking a drag.

"And sometimes he'd listen to Christian Rock while painting pictures of sunsets," I said, laughing as a snort came out.

"Oh, my god, Bekah," the General said, shaking his head.

"He thought his paintings were worth hundreds. I wouldn't have paid more than five bucks for one at a sidewalk sale," I snickered, waving my hand around.

Shari laughed while drunk scribbling in her notebook.

Before our evenings got too rowdy—sometimes we had drunken Bounce Ball races in the middle of the street at 3 a.m.—the General would call his kids to say goodnight.

This broad, stocky, deep-accented, seemingly-tough welder guy became someone else when he was on the phone with his daughter—she had him wrapped around her little finger.

"No way. I love you more," he'd say to her.

When his little boy's voice came on the line, the General's face would soften, and I'd wonder how he was managing to keep his shit together.

It was easy to feel sympathy for the General and his kids, but hard for me to feel any for his ex. And I *did* try because, the way I saw it, she and I were spitting images of each other, having one major thing in common: I had done something similar to Carter.

The General's ex, Cassie, became a mirror—one I didn't like looking into. Hearing him talk about what she'd done only reminded me of what I had done, and I hated remembering who I once was.

"Hey, wanna go bowling?" the General texted one day.

"Sure, I have my own ball and shoes."

"Shit. Are you like a pro bowler?"

"No. They were a gift."

My dad, however, was a pro bowler with a Deaf league years ago. He'd have been nothing but proud to see me waltz into Funspot, the largest arcade in the world, with my own bowling bag on a random Monday night.

"There she is. Miss pro bowler herself," the General said, lacing up his bowling shoes.

I smiled and shook my head. "I'm not a pro."

After a couple of strings, we stepped into the bar for a drink.

"You're not half bad," the General said.

"Thanks. You've got good follow through."

We sat in awkward silence with our drinks.

"I remember you talkin' about sign language way back in high school. I always thought you'd do somethin' with it, and you are. Good for you," he said, sipping his rum and Coke.

I barely recalled the General from high school, or bumping into him over the years, and he remembered something I'd told him ages ago. But what he didn't know was, although I was indeed doing something I'd briefly mentioned way-back-when, I was struggling.

117

I was surrounded by homeless words, floating in mid-air, every day. No auditory commas, semicolons, or parenthetical statements; no cadence whatsoever. Just a sad string of words looking for a place to make sense. I was stressed because it was up to me to pull them from thin air, derive some meaning, and put them in their rightful place, using proper affect in a timely manner.

It was the timing that got to me.

In my *Introvert Power* book, I'd learned that it took some introverts longer to process things, sometimes days. Add that to the overwhelming amount of input, making me miss my mind, and it was no mystery why interpreting exhausted me. Needing to be minutes ahead while interpreting—with catlike predictive skills and sharp, split-second quickness to voice what others said or felt—left me weary.

That's not to say all introverts should rethink their career choice due to information overload and slower processing times, but this introvert was definitely struggling to keep up.

I missed my own head, my own words, my own timeline, like, all the time. Every day, little by little, my spirit felt like it was being sucked dry. Burnt out from uttering other people's words, filtering other people's emotions—with barely enough time to process my own—I'd grown bitter.

Do my brothers feel like this? Wish I could ask them.

"You remember me saying that?" I asked.

"Yep."

I felt my face wince like I'd just tasted lemon.

The General noticed, then said, "What's that face for?"

"Huh?"

A look of pure consternation fell upon his face. His eyes widened. Then he said, "You secretly hate it, don't you?"

I smirked while giving him side-eye, wondering if I could possibly explain how it felt to be born, and deeply immersed, into a subculture many people scoff at thinking, *oh, those poor*

118

Deaf people. While others fight tooth-and-nail to squeeze their way in, giving me stink-eye because I'd been "blessed with the language and culture since birth." An impossible position—caught between Scylla and Charybdis.

The Deaf community has always been home to me; those are my people. Collectively, they've given me trust, love, stories (my god, the best stories), and a skill worthy of livelihood. But at times I felt I owed them pieces of me I'd never see again while my own boundaries and overtaxed mind blurred into the distance.

I looked at the General and simply said, "No, not hate. I'm just burnt out, I think."

He nodded and smiled.

I ignored his smile, revealing two more dimples. I'm a sucker for dimples—Jax, Dean, Kelly, and Asshat all had them. *I don't have the energy to ward off another dimpled man and this fool has three.*

The conversation lulled.

"So, what's your, um, favorite holiday?" he asked, reaching for a topic.

I chuckled. "Did you just meet me? I'm not big on holidays."

"Oh, that's right. You were a Jehovah," he reminded himself.

There's that phrase again—*a Jehovah.* I hated it. I thought it was just ignorant elementary school kids who used it. Well, ignorant adults use it too.

"If I had to choose one—"

"I'll bet yours is the same as mine," he said.

"It'd be Thanksgiving."

"Yep, mine, too. My birthday is a week before Thanksgiving. It's always been my favorite."

The General's coy smile suggested he may be interested in more than just friendship and being around him wasn't at all unpleasant. Still, I resolved to keep him farther than arms-length.

I was in no position to get involved with anyone. I didn't want to keep spinning inside the cycle of abuse. And my mind was preoccupied with connecting to my younger self.

It was time to visit the tracks again.

An Asylum of Loons

IT WAS ALMOST Halloween, the perfect time to dance with my demons.

I stood on the railroad sleepers in Northfield and looked out at the tracks fading into the horizon. The maple trees on either side of the tracks clung to their last living leaves. Bright red, vibrant orange, and soft golden-apple yellow lined the path toward the back of my childhood home. The leaves that had already sacrificed themselves to the gods of autumn crunched as I walked. The sound of their final moments was comforting.

I looked ahead to where the rails veer right around a corner and heard Jax and Rene's coquettish laughter coming from the next town over. I shook my head and freed my ears from past betrayal.

At the back of the house, close to the rusty, wired fence, I stood and waited. I wasn't sure if she'd come out, and if she did, how would it go this time?

I looked to my immediate right when I heard a rustling in the woods.

She looked different, older, tired, and well beyond her years. Her uncombed hair was down, her bangs were in her eyes. She wore royal blue corduroy pants, a white turtleneck with tiny strawberries all over it, a magnetic Care Bear belt, and a light purple Members Only knockoff jacket.

She walked toward me, pushed the wired fence down, stepped over it, and dug a few pennies from her pocket. She handed me one then laid hers down on the rail in silence.

I stood above her, looking down, nonplussed. I set my penny on the rail and followed her back over the fence to the log-sofa.

We crouched down and waited in silence.

We waited and waited.

I turned my head to face her and saw tears trickle down her cheeks. She ignored me, stubbornly looking ahead, waiting for the Pullmans.

She sniffled quietly.

We squatted there for what seemed like years.

Finally, I asked, "What's wrong?"

"Something happened," she said, "something bad, and now I can't go to McDonald's because of it."

I looked out at the tracks, lost inside a whirling sensation in my chest. *Yeah, something happened, all right.*

There were lots of somethings that had happened, and I knew exactly which something she was talking about. She's not going to McDonald's because of the incident.

A boy Mom babysat, a bit older, had talked us into "playing doctor" in the closet and we were caught with our pants down.

I looked ahead, unmoving.

A foreign part of me—and I think most humans—believes it's quote-unquote normal to be intrigued by sex, exploring body parts at a young age. Maybe in some ways it is common.

But how far is too far? Just how much exploration will leave damning effects on years to come? Was that why I was so reckless with my body? Reckless with sex? Did it all start in the closet? I'd always thought it started with Dean, but maybe it didn't. Which came first, the curious doctor or the insatiable man?

What could I possibly say to her? I knew all too well what was coming—all she was about to endure. How would I bring that up? And if I did, would that change the path she was on?

I looked at her again, unsure what to say or do. She was stoic. I didn't need to ask her about what happened. Of course, I knew, and I suddenly remembered it all...

They'd grown bored playing with Yoda, Vader, Artoo, and Luke on the Dagobah System.

They found themselves on the floor of her bedroom closet, door closed, pants down, facing each other in the dark.

With her legs spread, the way he'd told her to do, he scooted closer to her and rubbed his tiny pecker between her legs.

She winced in disgust, shouted "No!"

He ignored her, peed on her, then told her she was going to have babies.

She screamed. She didn't want to have babies, especially not with him.

Minutes later, Mom opened the closet door, shrieking in horror, demanding that he get away from her. Mom scooped her up and carried her away, rescuing her from further humiliation.

"It wasn't even my idea and I still got in trouble," she said, looking at the tracks. "I don't want to see him, but I probably will."

Unfortunately, you will, I thought, *because—*

"He goes to our meetings sometimes," she said.

"I know it wasn't your idea, and you know..." I thought hard before continuing. I wanted to be sure I should say what I was about to say—it could potentially change the course of her life. And maybe, as part of some predestined trajectory, she was meant to have these experiences for some reason, as horrid as they were. "You don't ever have to do anything you don't want to do," I told her.

She looked at me like I was the seven-headed beast of all false religion and her face told me that she truly believed she didn't have any choice, any free will. The look on her face gave

123

me a chill—I was literally beside myself. I felt high and hard yet couldn't feel my body at all. Could she feel hers?

I looked into her eyes and saw that she was already losing her light.

Eyes lose their light with years. Something changes between the ball and socket, and then, the light dims. Her luminescence had already started fading. The colors were dulling, and the dreams of my train-track self had now become the worries of my adulthood.

Who were each of us before the light weakened? Before the daydreams, the fantasies, the pomegranate of ideas spilling from our minds were lost among unfortunate experiences?

Dad bellowed from the back door. "Bucky!"

She sighed and looked down at the sleeves of her lilac jacket. She lost herself in thought, running her dirty fingernail across the grooves of her jacket's filthy wrist cuffs. She looked ahead to the tracks and sniffled; the Pullmans hadn't come through yet.

"Bucky!" Dad yelled again.

"Will you save my pennies after they're squished and bring them by another day?" she asked.

"Of course, we're penny sisters."

She slowly stood then labored along the foot trail, through the woods to the backyard where, between the trees, I could see Dad standing on the back porch.

He signed, "Time ready meeting."

And she signed, "Don't want."

And so it begins.

Passing bodies of water on my way home, I could hear loons screaming in the distance. I'd read somewhere that their hauntingly beautiful cry was a way for an asylum (flock) of loons to find their mates, announce their arrival, locate their chicks, and sometimes, it's a duet sung between pairs.

I rolled my window down to hear their undulating wails and wondered if the loons ever found what they were looking for.

My Blackberry buzzed with an out-of-the-blue text from the General, killing my Loon Love Affair.

"I don't wanna stay in the friend zone," it said.

My mind wasn't at all prepared, or in any space whatsoever, to grasp that phrase. I'd spent years familiarizing myself with government acronyms, surrounded by D.C. professionals, and the term "friend zone" meant nothing to me. Not to mention, I was one hundred percent distracted by the encounter I'd just had with *me.*

Annoyed and on edge I texted, "Huh?"

My phone buzzed again.

"I don't wanna jus b friends with u. I like u."

He's text talking again. And no. I can't. I won't. I don't want to. I'm in no place for anything other than friendship.

I didn't text back; what could I say? What? Would I tell him that I'd just stood at the tracks behind my childhood home and recalled a harrowing memory in detail, inviting the rest to come flooding through? A memory that forced me down a shame spiral? A memory tangled up in reimagining all the reckless, serial dick-sucking-and-fucking I'd done?

Anything more than friendship meant knowing glances, touching, intimacy—in both body and mind. The thought of that suddenly turned my stomach and saliva grew in a pond under my tongue. What had I just told myself? *You don't ever have to do anything you don't want to do.* My train-track self had spoken; case closed.

"Ur killin' me," the General texted twenty minutes later.

By then I was at Kathy's, on the couch, sitting in a pool of my own sweat. I realized that I didn't want to lose his friendship, but I was in no way interested in a romantic relationship with *anyone.* Getting involved now would only screw us both up. I stopped the conversation from going any further.

"I like you, too, but I can't get involved right now. I'm fucked up from Asshat and other shit. Dented. You're still dealing with your ex and new family dynamic. You're gonna have to stay in the friend zone."

"I'll wait."

"For what?" I asked.

"4 u 2 b ready. I plan 2 woo u."

"You may be waiting a long time."

"That's fine. Still on 4 bowling Monday?"

Something inside me trusted him—I was getting better at paying attention to my intuition, my superpower. Regardless of his plan to woo me, my plan was to keep him at a safe distance. Neither of us deserved to be a rebound for the other.

"Yeah," I responded. "Monday."

Monday, I arrived at Funspot with bowling ball, shoes, and a crockpot full of my vegetarian chili; the General and I had inadvertently joined a bowling league and it was potluck night.

Between frames and bites of chili in disposable Dixie bowls, our conversation by evening's end called for a drink at the bar.

"Some people who worship God are dangerous," the General said, tipping the bartender, walking toward the bar's leather sofa tucked into a dark corner.

"I agree, kind of," I said, carefully balancing a Cosmo.

"Kind of?" He smirked, revealing his dimples as he sat.

"Well, I don't think my parents are dangerous. Although, I think their steering committee is fucking lethal." I bent down and set my to-the-brim drink on the table carefully.

He bobbed his head in agreement. "Okay, I'll give you that. I don't know much about Jehovahs; they seem friendly and all but..."

"But what?" I asked, sitting beside him.

"Well, what does it say about a person who gives their love to a force that ignores the world's pain? If God is all powerful, can't it see the child abuse before it happens?"

"One would think," I said, realizing the child abuse he spoke of involved his own kids and what they'd been experiencing since he and his wife split. I let my little penny sister hang out in the ether with his kids, hoping all of them could soothe each other in some way.

"And it does nothing to stop it. Nothing at all." He sipped his drink and stared out at the bowling alley.

As a J-Dub, we were repeatedly told Jehovah loves the world and everyone in it so much that he's waiting for each person to seek him out, so he doesn't need to destroy such a multitude of people. Meanwhile, what makes the human experience unbearable down here doesn't really affect him up there. He's just...waiting.

I thought about the dangerous ones, the ol' GB, the evil soul suckers, the psychic vampires. Taking your dreams, your love, your hope, your spirit and stealing it. No, wait. They don't steal it; they convince you to give it away. For free. And while you're handing over pieces of yourself, they're planning the next bit of nonsense to sell you. Then once you're sucked in, they take your most precious commodity: time. Your time, your energy, your youth, your intellect now belongs to them, and they write twaddle with it, leaving you in a puddle of your own waste.

I shook free from my own thought-hole and said, "You're preachin' to the choir. I take it you weren't raised in any type of religious environment?"

I sank into the corner of the sofa.

He shook his head. "My mom sent me to Sunday school for like a year. Some parts weren't that bad—arts and craft-type shit—then we moved, and I just stopped going. I think she just wanted Sundays to herself cuz she didn't really push it."

I bobbed my head.

"Hey, what're you doing for Thanksgiving?"

I shrugged. "I dunno, probably nothing."

"You should come to my mom's; she really goes all out."

I nearly spit out the last sip of my Cosmo. "What? Go to your *mother's* for a major holiday?"

"Relax, I know I'm friend-zoned." His cheeks indented again. "She'd be happy to have you—besides, she says she knows who you are."

Knows me?

I peeked at her Facebook photo and could honestly say I didn't recognize the woman. But I wasn't about to shrug being invited to an all-out Thanksgiving meal with the General at his mom's, no strings attached.

I pulled into Loretta's driveway and the General's truck was already there.

On the back deck, a woman with blonde, shoulder-length hair and glasses stood—cigarette in hand, elbows resting on the railing.

The General walked past her to meet me in the driveway.

I had barely closed my car door before she said, in a heavy N' Hampshah accent that I assumed the General got from her, "You look just like yah fath-ah."

"I—what?" I skipped past anything that resembled a proper greeting. "My father?"

"Yeah. Deaf guy, right?"

"Yeah."

"He and your mother used to come into Community Action when I worked there, and I'd help 'em with their finances. You were little then. I used to set you up in the corner with toys."

Suspended in time, I saw life, death, everything in between. In this woman's driveway, I found rough, misplaced shards of my life; some of the pieces I'd been looking for had come full circle. And those missing bits rested comfortably in Loretta's eyes.

She continued, "They started comin' by the house, leaving their Jehovah magazines. They'd start talkin' 'bout the bible, but somehow we always got 'round to talkin' 'bout our kids. Your parents are good people."

Time's passing resumed when Loretta complimented my parents; it drove a knife right into my heart. Knowing that they're good people, not at all dangerous, made being in NH and having almost no relationship with them harder. I smiled at her, the General walked me up the stairs, and the three of us went inside.

Loretta's place was warm and inviting. The kitchen walls were blood red, which I especially liked. A kitchen island separated it from the living room/dining room area, which were somewhat combined. There was a TV set in the corner, between two walls with large windows, and a dining room table in front of it. The black-ironed woodstove was on the opposite side of the room, blazing. I hadn't been anywhere with a woodstove since I'd left my childhood home. I wanted to cry.

"Have a seat," the General said, gesturing to one of the four chairs around the table.

I sat, took my coat off, and smiled awkwardly at the General as he sat next to me.

"Should I fix myself a plate?" I whispered, forgetting how family Thanksgivings play out; the last family Thanksgiving I remembered was spent with Carter right before I'd been reinstated as a J-Dub.

"I got it, kid. You relax," Loretta said, fixing me a plate.

I turned to the General, "You're not eating?"

"I did. Before you came."

Loretta handed me a plate with a little bit of everything then sat at the table, holding an unopened can of Bud Light and a

129

neon pink straw. She and the General smiled at me while I self-consciously began to cut my food.

"It looks and smells delicious. Thank you," I said.

"You're welcome. I feel like I need to warn you, kid," Loretta said.

"Oh?" I asked, satisfying my mouth-water with a forkful of mashed potatoes.

"Yeah. There're a few things you need to know about my son," she said, cracking her beer open. "Number one—he can be a dink, just roll with it; whatever it is will blow over. Number two—he cheats while playin' board games—"

"Mom, I play to win," the General said.

"You. Cheat. And you don't even let your own kids win a game of *Sorry*," she said, slipping her straw inside the can's opening.

"The game's called *Sorry* for a reason. I want them to earn the win, Mother; how can they feel a sense of accomplishment if I let them win?"

My cheeks—full of gravy-drenched mashed potatoes—and my gaze shifted between them, and I smiled.

Of course, Loretta asked about my parents. And I, of course, said as far as I knew they were doing well. I noticed that with time, I was learning how to maneuver my way around that question without my emotions getting the best of me.

Leaving Loretta's with a full belly had felt...okay? Around Aunt Kathy, Gianna, the General, Jay, Shari, and now Loretta, my superpower felt dormant. I thought there was something wrong with me, and I could feel myself rebelling against my quiescent intuition.

It's usually activated. Is it, like, broken or something?

The more I thought back to sessions with Joel, and the research I'd done on my own personality determination, I figured that my superpower was probably relieved.

My overactive intuition was on ninety-seven percent of the time. Likely because I'd often been in precarious situations; my keen sixth sense was usually tasked with letting me know there was potential danger. And perhaps I didn't feel it jab because there was no immediate threat.

With Asshat out of the picture, my sensitive radar had had a break from on-edge activity; my defenses were lax.

It was strange to think of myself as anything except broken, but it felt like I was coming together. Elegantly. I've never felt there was anything elegant or graceful about me. Ever. I'm quite the opposite—brooding, harsh, and dented. But maybe the process of coming into myself was about as elegant as it got.

Though I was in the thick of some shitty memories, being home started to feel good, like my superpower had led me there.

I'd gotten to NH just in time to enjoy my favorite season, I had the best wiener dog, a place in Aunt Kathy's family unit, a group of friends, a budding sole proprietorship, and a spot on a bowling league.

I wasn't broken. Just timeworn. And old. In human years I was thirty-two. In soul years I still felt like Dracula.

A little less around the General, with him my armor was down, and I was intrigued. He had a way.

"Woohoo! Another strike," the General said, strutting back toward the alley chairs.

"One more and you could've had a turkey," I said, high fiving him.

The General walked to the bar, turned to me, and signed, "Champagne."

I nodded, walking toward the bar. "Picking up some ASL, I see."

"I've been looking up some stuff online."

And unsolicited.

On the leather sofa with a glass of bubbly, celebrating an almost-turkey, I studied the General—looking for something to dislike. If I looked hard enough, at anyone, I could usually find it and finding it helped me justify my singlehood.

His hoodie was tattered and torn. His jeans were ragged with oil stains. His ball cap frayed along the edges. He smelled of stale cigarettes and metal. His thumbs, calloused, nibbled to the bone. His coloring was pasty white. He had faint circles under his eyes. His stubble was unkempt. His pencil-thin, pink lips stretched sideways into a dopey grin. And I wanted to honk the springy bulb of his nose.

"Why do you always wear a ball cap? What're you hiding under there?" I asked, looking for unattractiveness.

He sighed, clinging to a coy smile and took off the hat. "Cuz my hairline is receding. I've been losing my hair since I was eighteen."

He had a budding ring around his scalp; the front of his hairline was in a race to find the back of his head. The hair he did have was thinning.

While forcing myself to put all these unfavorable pieces of him together, the General was still dimpled (my weakness), sincere, trustworthy; he had some of the ingredients that successfully cooked up an old soul.

"Eh, it's not so bad," I said.

"What you see is what you get," he said.

I stared past his face, lost somewhere between scattered bits of him that intrigued me and one recent revelation.

"Bekah?" He waved his hand in front of my face.

"Sorry, I..." I hesitated to speak then decided, *why not?* "Eh, I guess there's no harm telling you that I peeked at Asshat's Facebook recently and, judging by the pictures he just posted, he and the coworker he dumped me for in Texas got married."

"Oof," he said, scrunching his face.

132

"Yeah. Get this—they had a beach wedding in Galveston. At the very same venue I had been researching for me and him just before everything happened. I mean, they've barely been together for four months! And now married? It won't last."

I shook my head and looked into the flute of cheap, bowling alley champagne, watching tiny bubbles dance around.

"How do you know?" he asked.

I shrugged. "Just do."

Thinking about Asshat again reminded me that he was, by far, the worst relationship I'd ever had. His actual gaslighting had driven me to doubting my train-track self. Which, to me, made him nothing more than a cowardly man-child.

"I'd love a Joel chat right about now," I muttered to myself.

"Joel?"

"My therapist," I said, returning my focus to the General's dimples.

"Therapist? Why pay someone to tell you things that you already know?"

"What makes you so sure I already know things?"

"Everything anyone needs is right inside 'em; you just gotta look."

How can he be so friggin' confident, so himself? How did he become suddenly irresistible to me?

When the General walked me to my car, an awkward silence surrounded us; my attraction to him was now unavoidable.

I started my car and Billy Joel's "Just the Way You Are" blared from the speakers.

"Ooh, I love Billy Joel," he said.

"You do? You don't strike me as the Billy Joel type." I closed the door and leaned on it, waiting for my car to warm up.

He took a step toward me. "I don't?"

"Nah. You seem more like a Nickelback type of guy."

"Oh, fuck you." He smiled and stepped closer. Looking me in the eyes, he asked, "Is this okay?"

I wasn't sure. So, I showed him both palms, to keep him at bay, and he walked into them; they were now on his chest. I took a deep breath, inhaling stale cigarette smoke.

He leaned in closer, gently pressing his thin, pencil lips on mine. I didn't stop him.

The flood of sexual energy between us was surprisingly overwhelming. This five-foot-three, balding, wan, unkempt welder kissed me so passionately that my anxiety became tranquility. My open palms relaxed, found the lapel of his jacket, and pulled him closer.

His hands gripped my waist then creeped up my back, moving around front. His fingers boldly went under my shirt, under my bra, skin on skin.

The General had quickly made it to second base.

I gently pushed him away. "I gotta get home to Bart."

"Okay." He smiled then asked, "Shit, was that okay?"

"Yeah. We're good." I hopped in my car, smiled at him, and drove away.

The loons' abrupt fall departure left behind a harsh silence. I missed them. Their night wails had kept me company, and the stillness was unnerving.

It had been a couple of weeks since I'd seen the General. I sank into the holiday season, yielding to its uninvited glee.

Christmas Eve was days away.

My little cousin and I watched the snowflakes fall from my bedroom window while I played old vinyl records. The crackle of the needle hitting wax was so soothing; I could spin there forever.

Leonard Cohen's "Famous Blue Raincoat" was a groove my needle found repeatedly. I wasn't above moving the tone arm back to the beginning, once the song ended, to play it again. It was the perfect winter song, wrapping me in a slow-moving, lugubrious melody.

I moved the tone arm to the beginning for the seventh time.

"Again?" Gianna asked.

"Again," I said. "And don't touch the needle."

"My fingers want to touch it," Gianna said, grinning, playing with her fingers in order to stop herself.

"No, child." *She's lucky she's cute.*

Bright headlights moved from the middle to the top of my room, then froze on the ceiling, spotlighting my melancholia, interrupting Leonard's concert.

"Someone's here!" Gianna jumped up and ran to the back door.

I followed her.

It was the General.

I opened the door and asked, "What're you doing here?"

He kicked snow off the soles of his Chippewas then stepped inside and took them off.

"Well, I need to tell you something," he said.

"You could've called or text—"

"This ain't that kind of conversation."

"Oh. Okay, come in."

We walked through the kitchen, living room, then into my bedroom. Along the way, I left Gianna in the living room with Kathy who was doing a crossword on the couch.

Bartok, of course, followed me.

"What are you listening to?" he asked.

"Leonard Cohen."

"Never heard of him."

"He's Canadian."

"Ah, maybe that's why."

"What's up? You didn't come here to talk about a Canadian folk singer—"

"Maybe I did." He smiled and his cheeks indented.

"What couldn't we talk about on the phone?"

"Well, first of all—where you been? Avoiding me? The kiss freak you out?"

I sighed. "No, I've just been…" I shrugged. "This is my first winter home, I'm kinda…" I shrugged again.

I didn't want to tell him that I'd been spinning out like a madwoman since our Funspot kiss.

"It's okay. I'm still waiting. I was just wondering." He took his ball cap off and rubbed the top of his stubbly melon. "I got a text from a friend earlier tonight who needed my help."

I sat on the edge of my bed, listening.

"She said she was stuck cuz of the storm and needed a ride. So, I hopped in my truck and went to go pick her up."

"That's nice of you, it's really coming down out there," I said, looking out the window; there must have been about eight inches of snow already accumulated.

"Yeah. Halfway to get her she texted a bunch of times and called, only I didn't get the messages until I was in a service area. She started talkin' about movin' in with me and all kinds of shit. I thought I was just giving her a ride somewhere, then all of a sudden we're dating and she's movin' in with me. There was no way in hell I was gonna pick her up and bring her to my house."

"Oh. Wow. So, what happened?"

"I came here instead." He laughed and sat next to me on the edge of my bed.

"Why are you telling me this?"

"Cuz, I felt wicked guilty."

"But why?"

"Well, I thought I was just giving her a ride until she had us friggin' livin' together. I didn't want to have anything to do with her after that. Plus…I kinda want to see where this goes." He pointed to me, to himself, then to me again. I'd seen that invisible line before. "I don't wanna mess anything up before it starts," he said, leaning into me.

136

"Quite confident, aren't you?" I said.

He shrugged, smiled, and said, "I don't know if you know this but I'm kind of a big deal."

I shoulder-checked him and laughed. "Oh, my god."

I was taken aback by his honesty and also a bit relieved. His plan to rescue a snowed-in, tricky temptress—one he thought was just a friend—quickly morphed into him rescuing me from my tried-and-true methods of wintery self-destruction.

Looking into his blue eyes, three dimples staring back at me, I realized what we had the potential to be.

When two people get together, they create a mirror. While holding up shattered pieces of themselves, they check to see if all their respective cracks and busted pieces of self, combined, can forge a whole person. Sometimes they can and sometimes they can't.

I wanted to see if we could.

"So, what now?" he asked.

I looked at him, kissed him softly on his little, pink pencil-lips, and said, "Lie down."

He leaned back on the bed, grinning ear-to-ear.

"Not for what you think, asshole," I said.

I turned off the light so only the glow from my turntable illuminated the room. I moved the tone arm to start "Famous Blue Raincoat" again. I shifted my body on top of his, one leg on either side of his waist, and sat on the spot between his stomach and groin.

He cocked his head in curiosity, and I said, "Shh. Just listen."

The soothing crackle interrupted the room's silence once the needle scraped its way across the record, and the somber tones began again. Leonard's deep, enigmatic voice pulled me in for the eighth time that night.

The General lay unmoving like I knew he would.

The way I saw it, if he was willing to put in the time and wait, I wanted him to know the bits of stained, busted mirror he was getting. Jagged pieces and all.

The Cold Empty

AFTER WEEKS OF inseparability, the General invited me to his house on a kid-free night.

He lived in a white, four-bedroom, two-story cape with a two-car garage and a screened-in back porch, overlooking his backyard. A metal swing set rested near a chain link fence, separating his yard from a neighbor's.

Walking in through the back door, I tripped over little shoes scattered around a wired shoe rack. The tone of the house hit me immediately; I almost backtracked. It felt vacant. I could see the air.

As I scanned the kitchen, my eyes found the only appealing quality—the gorgeous, stained pine cabinets to my left.

The kitchen was roomy but had little counter space. The stove stood alone, directly across from the back entrance, and a thirty-two-gallon garbage can was set beside it, filled to the brim.

On my right was the dining room table, littered with kid drawings, homework, clutter. Beyond that—scads of papers, unopened mail, and random items were haphazardly stuffed inside (and around) an open, mini secretary's desk against a wall. Next to the desk, a three-drawer plastic storage cart rested with a coffeemaker perched on top.

"Want a drink?" he asked, walking to the fridge. "I've got handles in the freezer. Stoli and Sprite?"

"Yeah, sure."

"Go sit in the living room, I'll be right in."

I stepped through the kitchen toward the living room and stopped. I whipped my head to the right and noticed the bathroom door, open. Next to the bathroom was a mostly closed door that gave me willies.

I went into the living room.

Sitting on the blue, plaid, lint-littered couch—feeling a bit uneasy—I looked over the room.

A large TV set was on my left, surrounded by an expensive gaming system. The front door/mudroom was between the TV and a closed door which I assumed was a bedroom.

A stained pine, banister staircase was directly in front of me, and a cushioned chair to my right was near the living room's entrance.

I studied the room again.

The soon-to-be ex's things were everywhere; her presence lingered. Packed boxes with her name written on them ate useable space in the living room. Family portraits still dressed the walls.

Desperation, chaos, abandonment, loss, and betrayal circled the house—I couldn't feel much else.

The General came in with drink in hand.

Yes, I thought, *I'd like to feel something else.*

After a few quick gulps, I looked to the General and smiled. "Wow. Want another one?"

I nodded. "Can I use your bathroom?"

"Yeah, it's right through the kitchen."

I stood up and stepped into the kitchen. At the fridge behind me, I heard the General drop more ice into my glass.

I passed the freestanding stove and stopped in front of the bathroom. Glancing to my right, I remembered that the door to the mystery room was ajar. I pushed it. The door stopped; something was blocking it. I pushed again and opened the door to see complete and utter turmoil in the form of packed totes, boxes, clothes thrown everywhere, upturned furniture, and useless bric-a-brac.

Ahh. This *is where the chill is coming from. Trapped behind a closed door, it's still passing through the entire house.*

The General came up beside me, handing me a refilled glass.

"She hasn't cleared out all of her shit yet."

I grabbed the drink and shook off the screams coming from Cassie's abandoned things. I closed the door, turned, walked toward the living room, then stopped at the refrigerator.

I looked at the pictures covering the fridge, held up by local business magnets. The picture of one sweet face surrounded by blond hair and freckles jumped out at me.

"This your son?"

"Yep. That's Maximus. Max."

"You've got an old soul in that one."

Max's essence came through that photo in turquoise waves. He looked timid, often on-edge, but sure of himself just the same, and obviously perspicacious. I could tell by his eyes.

Perusing the fridge, I saw a newspaper clipping with a photo of students looking at an exhibit on a field trip. I noticed one girl's face, perplexed. She was in deep thought, tugging at her bottom lip.

"That's your daughter, right there," I said, pointing to the mischievous lip-puller.

"Yeah, that's Stormy. How'd you know?"

"She looks like you," I said, peering at him from the corner of my eye. "Like trouble."

The General took a pull from his drink and nodded. "Don't I know it."

I walked back into the living room.

"Find the bathroom?" he asked, following me.

I sat on the couch and sipped my drink. "I didn't really need it."

He looked at me and tilted his head.

I shook my head and said, "It's nothing."

A dog's whine came from behind the closed door across from the couch. I looked at him with crumpled brows.

"Oh, Joey and Squints are in there. I'll let 'em out."

"You keep them locked up?" I asked disapprovingly.

King Bart had a crate—a doggy bedroom—for his blankets, itty-bitties, and other toys. He was able to go in and out at will, but locked up? No, he was never locked up; he wouldn't stand for it.

"You sure you wanna meet 'em? They're rowdy."

I nodded.

I followed the General into the bedroom off the living room, which was recently his and Cassie's. It was small and dusty. My eyes were instantly drawn to the painting that hung above their bed—a creepy, naked baby, smiling.

The General caught me scowling and said, "Cassie put that there; she said it was good luck."

"Luck for what? Didn't you tell me you had a vasectomy after Max was born?"

He closed his eyes and shook his head. "Yeah, I don't know," he muttered to me and to himself.

I surveyed the room and noticed a three-tiered, plastic shelf next to the bed, plagued with candles of desperation, reeking of a last-ditch effort to save what was left of their marriage. The General didn't say that; the candles did.

The air in the bedroom was thick. Old ghosts, once in love, circled above the bed in mourning.

Inside an oversized dog crate, a big brown, energetic boxer, Joey, and a black and tan, miniature-pinscher mix, Squints, snuggled.

As soon as the General opened its door, they shot out, going through the bedroom and into the living room. They bounced from the sofa to the cushioned chair, playing Hot Lava.

"Look how happy they are! Why keep them crated, beyond crate-training?"

They leapt in big circles, eyes wide, mouths open, tongues flapping.

"Cass—"

I sighed then said, "Why have fur-kids just to keep them locked away? If they're family, they're *family*. Bart and Moron were crate-trained, and once they were fully house-trained, they could be trusted out and about even when I wasn't home."

The General nodded.

To shake off the hollow loneliness I felt circling the house, where every creature there was undoubtedly love starved, I made the General watch one of my favorite new releases—*Away We Go.*

Allowing myself to get swept away by the quirkiness of the couple, the evening progressed enough for the General to make it past second base.

I blamed the strong drinks, the movie, the soundtrack, and something in his blue eyes; something about being with him that night just felt right.

The cold empty drifting through the house didn't feel right. The literal house dust, unsettled, didn't feel right. But laying with him—unarmed, fully exposed—felt safe. It relaxed me in a way I'd never felt before, not even with Kelly; with Kel, I was constantly looking over my shoulder while Jehovah wagged his finger at me.

Not at the General's; I had nowhere to be and no one tugging at my sleeve.

I dozed off on his chest to the sound of his voice, drifting away to a place where trust wasn't even a second thought and real intimacy wasn't just a fantasy.

I startled myself awake around 2 a.m. *Family Guy* reruns were playing, and the General snored with his arms wrapped around me. I looked toward the end of the bed and saw Joey cuddling Squints on top of the comforter.

I gotta get home to Bart.

I wiggled out from under the General's grip, and he woke up.

"Where ya goin'?" he mumbled.

"Home. To Bart."

"Oh. You can't stay?"

"No, sorry. I'll call you."

"Hang on, I'll walk you to the door." He got dressed and staggered to the back door with me. "Lemme know when you get home, okay?"

"Okay." I kissed him and met up with Lysah in his driveway.

While driving, I caught myself humming "Strangers in the Night" by Frank Sinatra. I couldn't figure out why the song was suddenly stuck in my head. I hummed it the whole ride home until I remembered the General had doo-wopped the song aloud just before entering my Holy of Holies.

The air hung thick and sad at Kathy's; she and her husband were separating, and Gianna and I were wedged somewhere between *Gummi Bear* reruns and unbearable tension.

Even Leonard couldn't carry me away on the wings of his golden voice.

Bart and I started spending more time at the General's Cold Empty on kid-free nights. I wasn't ready to meet his kids and I didn't want to yet. I wasn't prepared for the expectations radiating from the eyes of a ten- and six-year-old. His kids knew of me—that was it. My plan was to keep it that way for as long as possible.

I meant what I'd once told Joel—cult life had left too big a scar. I couldn't be trusted to influence children, biologically mine or not. In most families, promises are often made too easily, then shit falls apart. Kith and kin: not my jam.

After I'd had an argument with my aunt one night, I called the General in tears, looking for a distraction.

"Come over," he suggested, little voices in the background.

"Don't you have your kids tonight?" I sniffled.

"Yeah, they're goin' to bed soon. Grab Bart and come over."

I love kids, I do. I'd worked in elementary schools, day cares, and even had a nanny gig for a year when Dean and I were together; kids love me.

Coloring books, make-believe, arts and crafts, learning to read, riding bikes, playing outside...I'm great with kids. Other people's kids. For short stints.

Gianna and I were buds until I felt like I'd inadvertently become a surrogate parent once my uncle had left. When responsibility, discipline, and daily hygiene coaching replaced spontaneity, imagination, and *Gummi Bears,* that's when her unspoken expectation started following me around.

So, as long as the General's little cherubs were out of sight and expectation free, then—and only then—would I go to the Cold Empty.

It was close to 10 p.m. when Bart, a splitting headache, and I made it to the General's house. I was met in the driveway and covertly ushered inside. I hurried Bart toward the bedroom and closed the door.

The kids knew I was there; I heard them whispering at the top of the stairs. The boy's presence emitted a heavy sadness that tumbled down the steps, found its way under the bedroom door, and spun around me. Not the girl, though. She was unusual. Her mischief curiously pulled at its lip, then leisurely descended the stairs to linger outside the door.

"Max, Stormy... Mind your business and go to bed," the General said, walking past the staircase toward the bedroom door.

Voices tittered and feet scampered, finding their way into twin beds. I wondered if they, too, felt the void or saw the air lingering in the Cold Empty.

I lay on the bed and rolled over as the General opened the door. I faced the wall, spooning my furry wiener. Joey and Squints were welcomed at the foot of the bed; that's as close as King Bart would let them get.

"Gonna tell me what happened?" he asked, climbing into bed.

I remained silent. I pulled Bartok closer and rubbed my foot affectionately toward Joey and Squints; dogs run the only family pack I'd ever come close to understanding.

The next morning, I woke to the smell of coffee and no dogs. *Where's my pack?*

I sat up, anxiously looking around the room. Seconds later, the General opened the door and three very excited dogs barreled in behind him.

"Hi, Bart!" I whispered, relieved to see my fluffy wiener.

I still did not want to meet any children. I was content to let the General and his offspring go about their morning routine without me.

He wasn't.

"Come out and meet the kids."

"No." I smiled flirtatiously, trying to ensure I got my way.

"C'mon. They know you're in here."

"This is not ideal. Me, coming out of the room their mother occupied not too long ago. It's...ick. It's too much. Probably for them, too."

I'd been canoodling the General and snuggling Cassie's abandoned dogs in their old bed. And I was expected to meet her kids then send them off to school?

"Relax. They're super easy going. They just want to say hi."

I should have known better than to come to the Cold Empty on a night he had his kids. I felt like he'd put me in an awkward situation on the sly. Tricked.

"Fine." Giving in, I threw on my hoodie and pajama pants.

I reached for the doorknob; "Once in a Lifetime" by Talking Heads came to mind. That was not my beautiful house. Those were not my beautiful kids. And their mother was not my beautiful ex-wife.

Stormy sat on the couch, hugging an American Girl doll. She looked up at me, smiled, and said, "Hi, Bekah. Thank you for the shirt."

I'd recently gone shopping with the General and picked out cute clothes for Stormy. She was wearing what I assumed she knew I'd chosen.

"You're welcome."

I smiled and sat next to Stormy on the couch. She talked a blue streak about her doll, Felicity, and the Revolutionary War. When she ran out of historical American Girl doll facts, an awkward silence befell the room.

I turned to my pack of one.

"Bart can do tricks. Wanna see?"

I summoned my furry sausage and threw his itty-bitty. He brought it back and nudged it toward me with his nose. I ignored the nudge, then proceeded to point to various spots on the floor with my socked big toe. He picked up the ball and put it wherever I pointed. This was a game we played often.

"He's smart," she said, giggling.

"And that's not all. Watch this."

Whenever I felt especially devious, I'd torture Bart with my own tricks. I covered his itty-bitty with my foot to hide it. Then he did what he always does—he stared, cooed, and grumbled. When he couldn't take anymore, he'd pull the sock off my foot to uncover his hidden itty-bitty.

"That's how I get him to take my socks off for me," I said.

Stormy laughed and it filled the room. I looked at her as she smiled down at Bartok. She had the General's crystal blue eyes, sandy blonde hair, freckles, and the General's cute, bulb nose.

Maximus was withdrawn and kept himself hidden on this particular morning. He sat on the floor in the corner of the living room, playing a handheld game. Occasionally, he'd look up at me and smile.

The General scooped him up, brought him over to me on the couch, and hung him upside-down. "C'mon, say 'hi' to Bekah."

Hanging upside-down, Max looked away from his game for a second, giggled, and said, "Look at my eyelashes."

This kid was just as confident in his way with women as his father. Max looked like Stormy, except smaller and blonder. He also had freckles and a bulb nose, but his eyes were green, and his lashes were longer than most I'd seen.

Little did I know upon meeting Max, with his intense green eyes and luscious lashes, that he'd unintentionally break my heart a thousand times more than Kelly ever had.

The General put him down and said, "Okay, guys, let's go. I'm driving you to school today. Bekah, there's coffee if you want some."

The three of them shuffled outside to the General's truck, leaving me inside with all the dogs and a full pot of coffee while Cassie's things screamed from a disheveled room.

I was standing in the doorway to her mausoleum, coffee in hand, when the General returned.

"I gotta get her shit out of here," he said, standing next to me with a fresh mug of coffee.

"You're not going to work today?" I asked.

"No. You?"

"No, I've gotta figure out what I'm gonna do—I don't feel comfortable at my aunt's right now. Too much going on there that has little to do with me."

"In the truck, Stormy asked why you don't just move in with us."

"Move in with you?" I nearly spit out my coffee.

"You could. If you wanted to."

I'd barely started getting comfortable with the idea of seeing the General as more than a friend. I'd *just* met his kids. I scanned Cassie's room again; clothes, half-packed boxes, and bric-a-brac looked to me for a decision.

In that moment, I accepted that I may never find a home or a family I fit into. Home was this elusive notion that often came in waves, bringing scents and clips from my past. No human could ever give me that.

I wanted my own space, and I knew most NH landlords didn't rent pet-friendly apartments; I'd rather have lived in a car than without Bartok.

I weighed my options and thought that maybe I could stay temporarily; until I found a studio, or something.

Toying with such a life-altering decision without running it by Joel felt weird. I had the urge to tell the General, "Before this goes any further, I gotta call my therapist."

And how would that come off? A grown-ass woman unable to make a decision on her own. Joel told me before I'd moved to Austin to "own my life, be autonomous, give myself some credit." I needed to start doing that.

Then I had an itch to visit the tracks and see if that helped. And how would that sound? "Thanks for the offer, but I gotta ask my mini-me what she thinks. I'll get back to you."

You're daft, Bek. Make a fucking decision already.

I walked to the kitchen table and sat. I looked at all the mail and unfinished homework scattered about the table. *Nothing here is mine but the clothes on my back, Lysah, and my dog. My dog...*

I stood up and walked into the living room. King Bart was perched atop the back of a couch cushion looking out the

149

window, Joey and Squints were snuggled on a cushion below him. He seemed content. Could I be?

My hidden superpower already knew the answer to all my questions; I was just prolonging the inevitable.

I walked back into the kitchen, put my coffee mug on the table, and before heading into the bathroom said, "Maybe Stormy's right."

Bart's Favorite Place

I MOVED IN and very quickly rearranged the Cold Empty to my liking. The kids were spending that weekend with Cassie which gave us more time to get settled sans their excited and confused energy.

At this time, my brother Jesse was still "out." With intentions to screen the General, he drove up to NH. In the absence of children, Jesse, the General, and I loosened after a few drinks.

"Like him," Jesse signed to me, smiling.

I nodded, signing "Good heart."

"Oh, no! That's not fair, you talkin' about me when I'm right he-ah," the General said. His accent always got thicker with alcohol.

"That's what you get—only knowing the signs for beer and champagne," I said.

"Unfortunately, I'm on call at the hospital. So, if I have to go, I'm gonna have to just go, regardless of what time it is," Jesse said.

"Do you wanna sober up in the vinyl room?" I asked.

"The vinyl room?"

"C'mere, I'll show you."

Stoli and Sprite in hand, I led Jesse through the living room into what was the General and Cassie's old bedroom. I turned on the light and proudly looked at the transformed room.

"Nice," Jesse said.

To the right of the door, against the wall, was a neatly made twin bed. Across the room was an antique, wooden chest filled with vinyl. Next to that, on a side table I'd rescued from the screaming room off the kitchen, my record player sat.

Jesse walked over to the chest and said, "Was this Mom's?"

"Yeah, she gave it to me years ago."

Jesse lifted a record from the chest. "This looks interesting."

"Oh, that's a record the General got for me. Wanna hear it?"

"Sure, sweetie." Jesse sat on the bed, waiting.

I put the record on, moving the arm to my and the General's song, and handed Jesse the album sleeve.

"The Airborne Toxic Event? I don't think I've heard—"

As soon as the violins started, he stopped speaking.

I was then lifted above the room, suspended by a sudden yearning. The room filled with a passionate longing, born of the aching all humans feel but don't talk about.

"Wow," Jesse said, with a faraway look in his eyes.

"Yeah."

"I think I will lie down for a bit." He kicked off his shoes and swung his legs around to lie on a twin bed that barely held his linebacker body.

"Okay," I smiled. "But the General...he's good?"

"He is, sweetie."

"I'll let you rest. Want me to turn this off?" I pointed to the record player.

"No, it's nice. You can leave it on."

I turned off the light and closed the door.

In our transformed bedroom (previously Cassie's cemetery-of-junk), the General sat on a new queen bed, side tables on either side, holding a Halloween-themed popcorn tin, wearing a mischievous grin.

The tin was filled with items we'd picked up one Saturday at a porn shop. And boy, did we pick the wrong night to pull out our tin-of-toys, but when alcohol and sex-play meet, there can be no stopping the horniest of people.

"Wanna play?" he asked, pulling off the lid, wiggling his brows.

I nodded.

The General was curious, fun, up for anything, and sex with him wasn't nearly as awkward as losing my virginity to Red the Mullet Boy ages ago. It wasn't filled with the passion of a *Lifetime* movie like it had been with Kel. It wasn't perfunctory like it had been with Carter and Asshat. And it didn't compel me to scrub my forehead clean with steel wool, trying to free myself from memories of sexual humiliation.

Together, we'd stumbled upon intimacy, trust, safety...and adventure.

The General sat me on the bed's edge, and I closed my eyes as requested. I heard him stumble into the door, laughing.

"Keep your eyes shut," he said, "I'm not ready yet."

Sounds of leather creaking filled the air.

"Okay, I'm ready," he said.

I opened my eyes and cackled once I saw him. He was naked, wearing nothing but assless, black-leather chaps.

"You like that?" he asked, slapping his own ass.

I bent over laughing.

"Go ahead, laugh at the naked guy. I don't feel insecure at all," he said. Then he caught himself in the full-length mirror. "Oh, god. What are you doing with me?"

I pawed through the tin, pulling out a strap-on. I put it on, according to the directions on the box, but something didn't feel right.

"Shit, it's too tight," I said.

"It's that cute booty you've got."

"You sound relieved that it doesn't fit. I'm using it anyway. Bend over."

I pushed him over and he fell face first into a pile of pillows.

"Whuu abah looff?" he asked, his face shoved into pillows, leather-chapped ass in the air.

153

"No lube for you!" I spit into my hand and rubbed the little plastic wiener.

I didn't hurt the General...much. I followed his muffled cues of "eaffy doff it," lost myself, and then something unearthly came over me.

Buildup of the anxiety, disorientation, and uncertainty I'd felt being back in NH—along with childhood memories I was trying to understand—came together all at once, exploding with frenzied, hushed gasps and moans. Like I'd climaxed my troubles away, if but for a moment.

I stopped, looked up to the ceiling, and exhaled.

The General turned his head to look at me. "Wow."

I removed the constricting strap-on; it was on so tight it had left indents on my hips. I flung it across the room, and it hit the wall. I pushed the General down and rolled him over. I knelt between his legs and wrapped my mouth around him.

It had been a long time since I'd done that simply because I wanted to. I didn't do it because I felt coerced or was trying to keep a failing marriage, or previous engagement, together. I did it because I wanted to. And that felt different.

The General's breath began to quicken just as I was gaining momentum, and the door flew open. The glow of a cell phone screen spotlighted my performance. Naked and knelt over the General's crotch, cock in hand, I stopped and swung my head to face the door.

"I got a call from the hospital. I have to go," Jesse said.

I'd totally forgotten he was there, occupying the room on the other side of the Cold Empty.

"Um, okay," I said looking away from him, mortified.

"Nice to meet you, Jesse. We'll catch up soon," the General said.

The door closed, we heard Jesse leave, and I buried my head in my hands. "Oh, my god."

"These chaps are chafing me," the General said, shifting on the bed.

Stormy and Max came back to the Cold Empty that following Monday after school.

Max had a soul that was much older than six, he was soft but wary. It didn't take but a few seconds for anyone to see the hurt and worry in his eyes; he knew more than he let on.

Stormy knew things as well, only she spun her agony next to mischief. And behind her resilience, her eyes also danced wildly with worry; she was penetrable.

They were both surprisingly amenable to my presence; our personalities fused together seamlessly as the weeks went on.

"Did a wet, naked boy just streak through the kitchen?" I asked, holding a bath towel.

"Uh, maybe?" the General said, scrubbing the dinner dishes. "Hey, do you want a drink?"

"God, yes," I said, walking through the kitchen, living room, then up the stairs. Bart followed, curious. "Max. Will you come dry off, please?" I heard him giggling from behind a closed door. "Bartok wants to see you..." I knew he'd come out for Bart.

The door opened.

"Bubsy!" Max screamed, looking down at Bart.

I scooped Max up in the bath towel before he saw me coming. "Ha! Gotcha."

He giggled, grabbed the towel, and started drying himself off.

"Get your jammies on and come down for dessert."

"Okay."

Stormy and Max's nightly routine was well-established: homework, TV, dinner, clean-up, showers, dessert, bedtime stories. Stormy was usually in the shower when I came back downstairs to collect my alcoholic beverage and sit with the General.

I sipped my stoli and Sprite.

"Good?" he asked.

"Yes, thank you. I thought you weren't much of a drinker, but you always seem to have liquor on hand."

The General took off his Red Sox cap and rubbed his head. He took a sip of his rum and Coke then said, "We have until the end of the month. I got another foreclosure letter."

I couldn't say I wasn't relieved to be leaving the Cold Empty, but still, I expressed concern and said, "Why didn't you tell me sooner?"

"Cuz it's not your home; not for you to worry about. I tried to work with the bank, did everything they told me, but we have to go."

"Will Cassie want the house for her and the kids?"

He took a pull from his drink and shook his head. "No. She and I already tossed that idea around."

Stormy stood outside the bathroom door, wrapped in a towel. "We're moving?"

The General sighed and muttered "shit" just loud enough so that I heard him. "Yeah, we have to. Sorry, babe."

She went upstairs.

Driving to the Cold Empty on my way back from a gig, with Bartok in the passenger's seat, I found the perfect place. A sign outside a grey duplex advertised: LARGE THREE-BEDROOM, GARAGE, PETS ALLOWED. This was it, our place to start anew.

Except it was in Laconia.

Not only would that disrupt shared custody, but depending on how things worked out, the kids may need to be registered in a new school.

"Let's do it. It's closer to my job, and the bank is takin' the house—we have to leave," the General said, scrubbing dinner dishes. "I never really liked it here anyway," he continued, lost in his own voiced thoughts. "She did. This is where she grew up. We moved here for her. The custody paperwork will have to change but Laconia's not too far; she can see them on weekends, vacations, whenever she wants. I'm obviously not gonna keep her from 'em but being out of Milton would be nice."

I wondered if there'd be a nasty custody battle, if witnessing a campy *Lifetime* movie court case would be a chapter in my life. But Cassie didn't object to the General wanting custody and said she'd take the kids on weekends.

This means...shit. I don't know how to "mom."

All at once, the relationship I didn't have with my own mother hit me square in the jaw. All the parenting I'd received growing up—the good, the dysfunctional, the cult-ridden doctrines, the conditional love, the control, the abuse, the neglect, and the abandonment—flooded my senses, sending me into sheer panic.

I didn't want my childhood experiences—the ones I didn't feel remotely close to healing—seeping through the armor I'd built, recklessly attacking kids who weren't mine. I knew I had no right, but I was afraid that it would happen anyway.

The real reason—the sneaky, underlying reason—I hadn't had any children wasn't because I was with the wrong person, because of my ghastly bouts with endometriosis, or because I would someday be able to have perfect children in the *New System* forever. It was because deep inside, swirling around in my restless bloodstream, I was terrified that the cycle of abuse my family had started would continue.

The good parts—painting the new place every color of the rainbow, reading bedtime stories, playing with dolls, arts and crafts, riding bikes, family walks, helping with homework, even meeting with teachers, and being a shoulder to cry on—

157

felt good. I felt more like a fun, extended family member than the dreaded, wicked stepmother.

Along with the good comes the bad.

I could tell by their sad, little faces that only seeing their mother two weekends a month baffled them. Our new home was bright and colorful, but their hearts were dark almost every time they returned from their weekend visits.

Max had full-out meltdowns one could set their watch to. Every other Sunday through Tuesday night—several times a night—he'd wake us from a sound sleep, sobbing, and say, "I love you" while hugging us. The General would tuck him back in and he'd come into our room an hour later to repeat the same scenario.

Every other Sunday, Stormy came back to the apartment increasingly obstinate—headstrong over the littlest things. Though volatile, she was still lovable, of course.

Being a full-time stepparent was incredibly confusing to me. I struggled with knowing when to say something and when to let the General handle things without my two cents. Parenting was not my jam. I sucked at it.

The day before Easter Sunday, the first holiday I celebrated with the kids, I found the General stuffing candy and dollar bills into plastic, pastel-colored eggs.

"What're you doing?" I asked.

"Getting the eggs ready for the kids' baskets. I'm meeting Cassie early to pick them up tomorrow," he said.

"Then what? Do you go to church? Wear the big hat? Have a ham?"

He laughed. "No. I just hide these around the house and the kids look for them on Easter Sunday."

"Then what?"

He shrugged. "They eat their candy and then, you know, do whatever."

"Do they know you hide them?"

"No. We'll tell them it's the Easter Bunny."

I scratched my head. "Why?"

"Cuz he's the Easter Bunny, it's his job."

The tradition, although meaningful for some, lacked depth for me. *Why not just* give *them the candy and be done with it?*

Either way, I found myself hiding eggs in the nooks of the couch, behind lamps, in the toaster oven, in the fridge, and any other place we could think of.

The next morning, the lies I'd agreed to tell took on a life of their own.

"Look at all my eggs, Bekah! The Easter Bunny left me a lot this year," Max said, showing me his basket.

"He did, I saw him." *No, you didn't, Rebekah.*

"You did?" Stormy asked.

The General looked at me and his eyes informed me that what I'd said wasn't part of the lie. I ignored his glare.

"Um, yeah. He and Mrs. Bunny were here last night. They made a mess."

The General facepalmed while mumbling, "Oh, dear Lord."

"A mess?" Max asked.

I was in it now and couldn't stop. "Yeah. They were all over the place last night, drunk, fighting over where to put the eggs. They were so loud, friggin' woke me up."

"Drunk?" Stormy asked.

"Okay, let's get ready. We're going to Mémère's for Sunday dinner," the General said.

The kids scooted to their rooms to get ready.

The General looked at me and said, "Drunk Easter Bunny and his wife?" He shook his head. "You're lucky you're cute."

I smiled and shrugged. "What're we having at your mom's?"

"Ham."

Holiday traditions hold no meaning for me. The most we'd done while I was growing up was go to the Kingdom Hall on a very specific date, at sundown, and pass a plate of unleavened bread and glass of red wine up and down every aisle.

There was no bunny. No candy. No fancy hat. No ham.

Naturally, when my birthday rolled around, the kids and the General wanted to go all out, which made me quite anxious. Rewiring my brain to accept that I deserved a day set aside for myself was a foreign concept. I didn't want to do it. I didn't want gifts or a party. And I certainly didn't want all eyes on me.

So, I arranged for us to board the Mount Washington cruise ship for a scenic tour around Lake Winnipesaukee—grazing the buffet, partying with strangers.

For me, the best gift has always been the gift of experience. So, when Stormy asked the Deejay to play Michael Jackson, "because 'Human Nature' is one of Bekah's favorite songs," that experience was gift enough for me.

Stormy saved up these random moments where she made me feel like I hung the moon. And Max often melted into an adorable ball of love, burying himself in my embrace. I was completely in love with them both.

But none of that mattered once my own Cold Empty found me at our new apartment to reclaim pieces of me...and Bartok.

After a lake excursion at the Weirs, where he chased his itty-bitty relentlessly, Bart stopped eating. He stopped playing. He stopped jumping on the table when no one was looking to eat leftovers from our plates. He stopped standing, he stopped walking, then his face sagged. It came on almost overnight.

The local vet said he did all he could, which wasn't much. The care my boys had received in NH was not even close to the level of care they got in Austin.

The General left work and rushed to the vet's once I texted and told him Bart was slipping away and the vet suggested euthanasia.

The vet's office was butted up against the same lake I often brought Bartok to; he'd spend hours fetching his itty-bitty after I threw it into the water. Carter and I had thrown it together; Aunt Kathy and Gianna; Kelly; the General; and most recently, the kids.

While sitting outside next to the water, Bart's favorite place, I held him in my arms and the General held us both. I squeezed him tight as he took his last breath and went limp.

I carried Bart into the vet's office and a vet tech tried to take him from me. I screamed, refusing to let him go. The General calmed me so she could take my limp boy away, and I crawled on the floor of their lobby, into their bathroom, sobbing. I vomited, hyperventilated, dry-heaved. With nothing left, the General carried me out to his truck and we left my car there overnight.

I stayed in bed, nursing broken sleep and an empty stomach.

The kids would peek into the bedroom from the hallway anytime the door opened. I ignored them. Loretta drove over to sit on the edge of our bed and talk small. I stared at the wall.

"Bart and Moron are together now," the General said while we lay in bed. "I can see them running next to each other and hear 'The Boys are Back in Town' playing."

To this day, that image, coupled with Thin Lizzy's song, is how I see my boys. Running off into the horizon, shoulder-checking each other and finding trouble up around the bend.

After Bartok died, I lost my job.

The VRS center I contracted with, part-time, closed without warning. Our center manager hadn't even seen it coming. One day, our key cards didn't work, and we were instructed to call the district manager about our severance packages.

When I called, she told me I could reapply to another center (two hours away) in six months. I told her their VRS company could kiss my ass and hung up.

And voila! My life resembled a bad country song. Everything that made me who I was had been stripped away. I even had to trade in Lysah, my freedom ride, for a Toyota just before we moved to Laconia because she was barely able to make it around the block due to all the towing she'd done over the years.

I looked around our apartment. I looked at the General, the kids, Squints. Nothing looked familiar. Who I was before them was starting to fade. Moron was gone. Bartok. Lysah.

I realized I'd been squeezing myself into their mold while the one I started reshaping for myself was vanishing. I felt like an outsider looking in. One wiener-less, holiday-celebrating, Toyota Corolla-driving, unemployed imposter.

Perfection

I HAD TO get out. My new life didn't feel like mine.

The General drove me to the Manchester airport just before his bi-weekly kid drop-off date with Cassie. I was heading to D.C. for a two-week working vacation; my employee file was still active with the scattered remains of SLA, and there was more than enough work for anyone still holding their security clearance.

I needed steady income. I needed to get in touch with me again, a me I recognized. The last place I was me—without them, without anyone—was D.C.

I bounced between Yvette's in Northern Virginia and my friend Kym's in Maryland, working all over the D.C. Metro area. I got in touch with old friends and made appearances at several happy hours.

While visiting my favorite D.C. monuments, I thought hard. I thought about the General, his kids, and where I fit into their family portrait, if at all.

The hardest thing had been losing my boys. Spending eleven years with them, they easily became my pack, my world. I've still not recovered from their loss.

The train tracks and I had been making peace, the need to go there was decreasing on its own. There were times I'd been able to breathe, centering myself, feeling what was right and what wasn't. That same feeling had led me to surrendering to the General and his kids.

But still, I felt like I'd lost a major piece of myself by living among their marital and custodial turmoil; like I was merely a placeholder for when Cassie wasn't around, a last-minute stand-in. I was glad I didn't have any kids. With anyone. Then I wondered, *maybe I could leave it all and come back here?*

No. I couldn't.

The four of us had so much in common we needed each other. All of us—left by people who were supposed to be there no matter what. All of us—hurting and shifting through our own confusing agony.

Those kids loved me. And I loved them; the General, too. Though he hadn't once uttered the words 'I love you,' I knew he did.

My phone buzzed as I hopped in my rental. I fished it out of my bag. It was a text from Stormy that simply read, "Bekah..." followed by a sad face. I asked what was wrong. She said she missed me, and Max was still having his night terrors; he screamed my name at night. I told her I'd be back in another week. She said her dad wasn't the same without me around.

They do love me, in their own way.

After a busy two weeks in D.C., I was ready to go back to NH. Though Bart-less, I was comforted by the thought that my small family was eagerly awaiting my return.

Surprisingly enough, I'd talked my dad into getting me from the airport since the General was still working when I landed.

"Your boyfriend let you go meeting?" Dad asked, driving I-93 North.

I nodded then signed, "If I want, yes."

"Think you go?"

I shrugged, remembering the day I'd made a loose promise to my dad over pizza at the Weirs. Why couldn't we ever just be father and daughter? Why did every-fucking-thing hinge on whether I show up to a non-taxpaying building and nod my head in tacit compliance?

I love my father, and will until my last breath, but I couldn't wait to get out of that car.

Stormy and Max came home from school, and I was flooded with hugs and random stick drawings of me in an airplane, waving from the window as it took off. Under the doodle was a caption: "someone went to D.C. and I am sad."

They told me about their two-week stint with "grumpy dad."

"He was no good at helping me get ready for school picture day; I hope they come out good," Stormy said.

"I'm sure they'll come out fine," I said.

Once the General got home, I was shocked by how weeks without him had felt like years. Excited, he scooped me up and carried me into the bedroom.

"Where are you two going?" Max asked.

"We're gonna nap for a little while. Bekah's tired from her flight. Do your homework!"

He threw me on the bed, closed the door, and came at me with a devilish grin.

"But I have another picture for her," Max said from the other side of the bedroom door.

"We'll be out in a bit," the General said.

The apartment we rented was an old, stacked duplex— creaky floors, dresser drawers built into closet walls, rounded walls along the corners of the house, vintage brass doorknobs. The doors had shifted over the years, along with the house, causing cracks to appear down all the doors in the apartment. The biggest crack, the one you could see right through, was in our bedroom door.

Max, seven at the time, was beside himself when told to wait for us to resurface from our "nap." And once we did, he let his father have it.

"Dad," Max said, stomping after his father into the kitchen.

"What, buddy?" the General asked, starting a pot of coffee.

"I saw you."

"Saw me what?"

"Not let Bekah sleep!"

"Huh?"

"I saw you through the crack in the door. You were naked butt dancing all over her!" Max was pissed.

I closed my lips together to avoid laughing.

Max put his little arms around my waist and squeezed. "Do you need another nap?" he asked, batting his long lashes.

"Maybe. Let's go watch TV. Bring your drawing stuff."

As old reruns of *Punky Brewster* on Netflix DVDs played on, crayons, paper, pencils, and doodles of the four of us with Squints (Joey had moved to literal greener pastures, happy to have more acreage to exhaust himself on) covered our new lift-top coffee table.

Seeing the kids' doodles of me, as part of their family, was a new sensation. Especially since earlier that same day my father reminded me what I needed to do to be welcomed back into my original nucleus. In either direction, the word "family" still just didn't find its way into my core.

It wasn't them; it was me.

In bed that night, with Squints at my feet, while playing with a silly band Stormy had given me, the General asked, "Think we oughta move away?"

"We've been here barely a year, why?"

He sighed. "For the kids. Cassie rarely sees them and I'm not too fond of the new guy she's dating."

I tried to mask my inner panic. As much as I didn't enjoy the mirror Cassie held up—reminding me of what I'd done to Carter once upon a time—she was the kids' mother and them being closer to her took a load off me.

"That sounds like a lot," I said, pulling the silly band up and letting it slap my wrist repeatedly.

"I know but think of the fun we could have. I've been here my whole life. And your VRS center is closed. Wouldn't it be

166

nice to have something steady rather than scrounging for work like you have been?"

That did sound appealing.

He brought the subject up again a week later.

"Maybe we try Austin? Didn't you like it there?" he asked as we sat on the porch for our evening mixed drinks.

"Yeah. It's a great city. It's also a sore spot for me. Because Asshat," I said, sipping my raspberry stoli and Sprite.

"It'd be different this time." He smiled, flaunting all three of his dimples.

My liquid courage had been activated. I looked at him and said, "We've been dating for a while now, living together, and I'm playing part-time mom now. Though, I'm not one hundred percent certain you, um, love me... Do you?"

I sipped my drink, avoiding eye contact.

"You're not sure?" he asked.

"Well, you've never told me," I said.

He looked at me and smiled. He took a sip of his rum and Coke, looked out across the street, and around the yard, then nodded to himself before speaking.

"Remember when you slipped in the shower?" he asked.

I nodded.

"What did I do the next day?" he asked.

"You installed a bar in the shower, so I'd have something to grab if I slipped again."

"Who made sure you ate after Bart died?"

"You," I said softly, mentally redressing my Bartok wound.

"And who rubbed alcohol wipes all over your back when the bedbugs on our recent San Francisco getaway mistook you for a meal?"

"You promised you'd never mention those nasty vultures again," I said, wagging my finger at him.

"I could force the words, but none of the phrases I've come up with would be enough to tell you that I do care for you, I wanna be with you, and, yeah, I *luve* you."

Luve (LOO-V) was our thing.

Luve was an accident.

While living at the Cold Empty, I'd spent all day entertaining the kids on a teacher/workshop day while the General was at work.

Max wanted to text his father and I let him do it from my phone. When he misspelled "love" and typed "luve," I showed him the correct spelling.

Max, being the old soul that he was, simply said, "Well, I like *luve* better. It means so much more."

It was so goddamn sticky-sweet it stuck. And from that day forward, it was a word only the four of us would use; it was just ours. A special word for the unique affection we shared.

And it did mean *so much more.*

Taking in our Norman Rockwell neighborhood, I breathed in the General's words—dancing with the crisp autumn air of October—and fixed the moment to my memory. I pressed it into me, packing it deep within my cells so they'd never forget.

Cyrano de Bergerac the General was not; he was a man of few words and many deeds. He wasn't one for grand romantic gestures, poems, or amorous monologues—but I knew I could trust him. I knew that if he loved me, and saw a need, he'd fill it. Case closed.

"Okay. So, you love me," I said, not meeting his eye.

"Yeah. I just say it differently."

The superpower I'd come to heavily rely upon nudged me into sending resumes and appearing for on-screen interviews via videophone.

I could envision myself moving almost across the country with a man who was willing to show those closest to him how much he could luve. He carried a calmness that made me feel safe. I could rest. Breathe. Enjoy being, without the worry that he was secretly up to something. With the General, what you saw really was what you got.

A few months and a few phone interviews later, we were packing for a flight to visit Austin.

Loretta had come to stay at our duplex and watch the kids because if they'd stayed with Cassie they would have missed school.

On the plane back from our week in Austin, I slipped *Johnny Got His Gun* into my carry-on bag and grabbed a pad of paper and pen. I started drafting our to-do list, mapping out our finances. When I'd grown increasingly frustrated with all the details staring at me, the General took the pad and pen from me.

"I'm great with lists. I love checking things off once they're done."

We effortlessly balanced each other out.

He was the thinker, structuring things in his mind, making sense of them, then carefully planning each practical step. He loved instruction manuals (shoot me) and tinkering with things that could potentially solve problems—e.g., the bar he installed in the shower.

I was the feeler; he knew about my superpower and trusted my hunches. There were times I was right about things and people. It often left him wondering how I knew what I knew, and when my sixth sense matured into an odd perspicacity (some folks were just so transparent to me), he realized he'd never fully understand it.

Most things involving the combination of the General and I had been seamless. From our budding relationship, living with the kids—which had its challenges, but worked—to finding jobs, and an apartment in Austin.

The all-knowing Universe had thumped us both upside the head and pushed us toward each other and in a new direction. I wasn't at all shocked when the same Universe told me to visit the tracks before leaving for Austin.

The end of March came. The last snow of a harsh New England winter had melted away. The tracks were caked with the mud and slush of an early spring. The comforting squelch beneath my feet meant I was alone.

Stepping on the sleepers between the rails, I could no longer remember why I once thought of jumping into the rushing waters below the trestle. I didn't hear Jax and Rene's laughter veering off toward Canterbury. Kelly's amber silhouette had stopped dancing on the tracks. It was finally quiet.

I stood at the tracks behind my parents' house and waited for her. Tree branches above me were starting to bud. The air smelled like wet earth. In the distance, I heard a woodpecker jamming its face into dead wood.

I inhaled, exhaled, and in that breath, I knew that she wasn't coming—she didn't need to. I felt her drifting away before I'd even started walking. The truth was, she didn't need to carry my hurt anymore; it was my turn to carry hers.

I turned and walked back to my car, parked at the corner store. As I left, instead of turning toward Laconia, I veered right, then right again. I felt the car vibrate going over the train tracks in the road, turned left, and headed to my parents' house.

I parked at the edge of the driveway and looked to where my old wooden swing used to be. There was a two-by-four nailed between two trees, and the frayed remnants of two thick barn ropes still hung from it. Now, not only were the ropes worn, but the wooden seat once fixed to them was long gone.

I stepped out of the car.

On my way to the front door, I passed the memory of Mark and Luke using a two-man saw to cut down a tree for wood to make a fort. The tree had fallen right across the driveway where I sat, just a few feet away from them, playing the game *Perfection*. When the timer ran out, the board shot up, shapes flew everywhere, and the tree crashed down in front of me.

What were they thinking?

I'll tell you what they were thinking—that they didn't want dinner that night because they didn't get it. Dad had tossed a couple packages of Hostess Ding Dongs at them and told them to "Go rye affa bed, no pop-a-bie show."

I was drawn to the rock-walled culvert in the front yard. I walked on the grass, remembering when Melissa, Otillie, me, and our bikinied barbie dolls spent days sunbathing in a thriving jungle, surrounded by ferns and a rushing brook we pretended was a waterfall.

I looked to the front door and walked closer, wondering if Mom and Dad still used that entrance because the bricks had been pushed up out of the ground, creating bubbled mounds of soil and wide spaces between the bricks.

I rang the doorbell.

Through the window, I saw the strobe light flash and Mom and Dad come down the stairs.

When the door opened, I saw into the split entryway. It was sullen. The house missed the constant steps of my, Mark, and Luke's—sometimes Johnny and Jesse's—feet all hours of the day and night.

Those stairs had hailed many an excited stomp. After Bible book studies hosted in our basement, my father would invite everyone upstairs to the kitchen for coffee and Entenmann's.

"Come upstairs. We have coffee, cake. We associate," he'd say.

Our house was rarely empty.

And now, it exuded a sadness. Invisible ghouls swiftly flew throughout the house, looking for life to latch onto. When I told Mom and Dad we were moving to Austin, the specters of loneliness howled.

My mom asked for a forwarding address, for emergencies, and my dad asked me to *please* get in touch with elders in Texas, you know, in case I got the urge to *come back.*

I'd go back and bask in my family's love if what we agreed to worship was an intense love for dogs, fall foliage, *I Love Lucy* marathons, the classy, vintage aesthetic of the 50s, homemade Italian dinners, whatever.

But asking me to *come back* and kowtow to a deceitful, fearmongering, religious organization? No way. I'm sorry, I just couldn't. I just can't.

Austinopoly

COMING FROM THE tail end of a New England winter to an April heatwave in Texas shocked me. Again.

Thankfully, almost every apartment complex in Austin had a swimming pool; ours had five. Along with a movie theater, gym, walking trails, monthly resident happy hours, monthly neighborhood taco breakfasts, and an after-school kid's club for latchkey children—we were all set.

Or so I thought.

On move-in day, horror took hold. Even with all the boxes placed in the appropriate rooms for the ease of unpacking, our new three-bedroom apartment was a wreck.

To me, nothing was ever going to feel right, and my god, what was I doing there? The General and I had been together a year and six months, and I was now a full-time stepmom? In Texas?

I felt dizzy.

I heard the General talking to me, but he sounded like he was underwater. My eyes flickered, looking around the living room at all the things haphazardly in it.

I staggered to a door leading to our second-floor balcony, opened it, and stood outside for some fresh air. But it wasn't fresh. It was humid, sticky, heavy as a bull's shit-mound. I leaned onto the railing and looked around. A *view of the parking lot. Sexy.*

The General led me back inside.

"Sit down, I'll get you some wat-ah," his endearing accent said.

I sat at the only thing I recognized—my vintage, seafoam, Formica diner set. It was my favorite thing. I'd found it at an antique shop in Laconia for two hundred dollars. The General thought it was priced too high, but when I told him it was a vintage, mid-century antique, he agreed it was pretty jazzy. The weathered tag on the underside of the table showed the set was from the '50s, made in Maine. I loved it so much. It was very me.

I came to when the glass of water was set before me. "Thank you, I don't know what's wrong with me."

"Maybe ovah-heated. Let's do what we can today then go to Uncle Billy's for dinner. My brother is gonna meet us there."

Uncle Billy's was an outdoor restaurant serving anyone and everyone, even dogs. I had to hand it to Austin for being the most dog-friendly city I'd ever been to.

The General's younger half-brother had already been living in North Austin for a few years upon our arrival, as did his other half-brother and family near San Antonio. We had a unit forming; it was nice for the kids to have family around.

I was dazed when we got to Uncle Billy's, and the General had started acting weird, saying we had to wait in the car before getting a table. As far as I knew, the restaurant was a laid-back watering hole, no reservations needed.

"Why can't we just head in?" I asked.

"Yeah, Dad," Stormy said.

The General checked his phone, waited another minute, then said, "Okay, now we can go."

"Finally," Max said.

Walking toward the hostess standing in front of the outdoor section, I spotted someone behind her that my heart knew right away.

I ran, jumped onto him, threw my arms around his neck, swung my legs around his waist, squeezed and screamed. Cried. Everyone outside turned to look at us.

I kissed his face with tears streaming down my cheeks and said, "What are you doing here?"

Jesse laughed and said, "The General flew me down cuz he knew you'd be homesick."

I turned and saw the General behind us, smiling. I slid off Jesse's monstrous frame and hugged the General. "Thank you so much."

He luves me.

Jesse stayed the weekend on an air-mattress he'd purchased at the store just before meeting us at Uncle Billy's. He helped unpack and organize, then flew back to Boston that Sunday.

"I'll be back down again soon," he said while hugging me at the airport's drop-off area.

Even with lots left to distract myself with—a new job to start that Monday, the constant company of a man who really did love me, and two kids to keep up with—Jesse had left a painful void in my chest. Something was stirring inside him; I could feel it. I knew what he was about to do, and it petrified me.

Living with the kids now twenty-four seven, I wondered why people had children. I think when people spawn versions of themselves—whether intentional or not—they have some time to adjust to the idea of little people wreaking havoc on their general well-being. I think parents eventually accept it because, first of all, they have little choice in the matter, and second, part of them is ecstatic to see their past selves inside these tiny people.

That was not my experience.

Stormy's presence was loud. Though she wasn't biologically mine, she mirrored all the awkwardness of my own childhood. Things I thought I'd left far behind, she brought back instantly with pre-teen angst.

Her anxiety activated my anxiety, unconsciously hushing my intuition. When our uneasiness combined, it swarmed the apartment, spinning uninterrupted, leaving everyone (even Squints) exhausted.

Factor in Max's fear of abandonment, his need to please—which had him wound so tight he was like a couch coil about to spring from underneath the cushion—and very little could calm him.

We had been in Texas for a few weeks and, as was custom, Cassie called the kids around 7:30 p.m. to say goodnight.

Dripping wet, with a towel wrapped around him, Max sat on the closed toilet seat sobbing into Stormy's glittery, pink cell phone. He and Cassie had been exchanging I love you's until Max lost it.

I couldn't stomach it. I knelt beside Max, hugged him, and gently pried the phone away, giving it back to Stormy. It was too much for him, which was too much for me. I could feel his anguish, curling itself around me, gripping ruthlessly.

The General was fortunate to be more of a thinker than a feeler.

Max didn't understand why we moved, or why he wouldn't see his mother until summer vacation. He tightened his hold around my neck and bellowed, "Dad moved us far away on purpose!"

I wanted to take the heartache away from his little, old soul.

When I'd met Cassie the year before—beyond her perfectly styled, shoulder-length, curly brown hair, brown eyes, and pretty smile—it only took me seconds to feel a longstanding, unnamed sorrow, coursing through her veins, unattended. She exuded the same energy I did once Carter and I ended things. And instead of giving her grief a name, she allowed blame to take its place. Just like I had.

Only, her grief affected Stormy, Max, and the relationship they had with the General, which broke my heart. The kids

176

were caught in the middle of a battle they had no chance of winning.

Again, I silently thanked my lucky stars that Carter and I hadn't had any children.

Once settled into a manageable work and school routine, a month and a half later, we sent Stormy and Max on a nonstop flight from Austin to Boston to visit Cassie and her new boyfriend for the summer. They weren't nervous at all and hopped on a JetBlue flight, as unaccompanied minors, without one modicum of fear.

After leaving the airport, we stopped at our new favorite spot in town, Opa, a Greek coffee and wine bar.

In a dark corner, on a small leather couch, we drank our quiet, newfound kid-absence away. After a few drinks and a few rounds of the game Austinopoly, which the General was winning—games with him weren't much fun, his mother was right—his cell phone rang.

He pulled his phone out of his pocket. It was Stormy.

"They must have landed in Boston. Jeez, we've been here a while," he said, noticing the time on his Android.

The flow of drinks, coupled with the satisfaction of owning Austin on a game board, had thrown us into a time warp.

I looked at my phone for the time.

"Jeezum Crow," I muttered to myself; it was 9 p.m. central time and their flight was getting into Boston at 10 p.m. eastern time.

He answered his phone and said, "Hello?" then, "Uh-huh," "Spongebob, huh?" "That sounds fun," and finally, "Yeah, she's right here, let me put you on speaker."

"Hi Bekah!" Stormy and Max shouted.

"Hi, I miss you guys already," I said. "How was the flight?"

"Good. We watched TV and the flight attendants checked on us a lot," Stormy said. "We're in the car with Mum now."

177

"Oh, good. I'm glad the flight was—"

"Guess what?" Max said.

"What, buddy?" the General asked.

"Mom's pregnant!" Max said.

I could hear a wide grin on his little, freckled face.

The General and I sat in the dark corner of Opa, stunned. Austinopoly stared back at us and suddenly my martini glass was half-empty. We didn't say a word. What could we say?

Then Stormy said, "Ooh, awkward silence."

Max giggled.

Finally, the General broke our silence. "I'm glad you guys are excited about it."

I exhaled. I had no clue I was holding my breath until that moment. I reached for my glass and gulped what was left, then motioned for the waitress to bring another round.

"Yeah. Mom got us each a 'Big Brother' and 'Big Sister' shirt," Stormy said.

Before I had a chance to stop my lips from separating with sound, the words were already out into the ether.

"Stormy, you're already a big sister to Max." I looked at the General wide-eyed.

Shit. Bio Mom-one, Wicked Stepmom-zero.

"But now I'll be an even *bigger* sister," she replied, unfazed by my ill-timed truth.

"That's true," the General said, "I'm glad you guys got there safely. We'll talk soon. We luve you."

"Luve you," I said.

"We luve you, too," they said and hung up.

The waitress came back with our drinks.

"Oh, god, thank you," I said to her.

The General stared down at Austinopoly's gameboard and told the Congress Bridge bats, SXSW, Eeyore's Birthday Party, and Austin's never ending traffic jam, "I had the vasectomy because, after Max, we both agreed no more kids. It doesn't bother me that she didn't want more with me, or that she's having another. It bothers me that, no matter what happens now, she always makes me feel like the bad guy."

A month later I had my own flight to catch to Atlanta for my first Registry of Interpreters for the Deaf (RID) conference. The best part of Atlanta was Jesse. He'd met up with me at the conference and we shared a hotel room together all week.

Atlanta was odd, quirky. I had more fun riding MARTA—the public transit system—looking for the dark underbelly of the city than I did attending any of the workshops. I didn't feel I'd gain much from the conference besides a trip to Atlanta, time with Jesse, and CEUs keeping my certification active.

There are so many interpreters with massive amounts of skill, loving what they do every day. Many go on to get their master's and PhD's, write dissertations on the nuances of language, how to effectively team on the job, ethics, language acquisition and language deprivation.

Very little of it interests me. I don't know if I ever felt like a real interpreter. Truthfully, I hadn't felt like one since SLA had merged.

Long gone were the days of interpreting at CloseUp for a Kennedy, at the Democratic National Convention, for Obama's Disability Inaugural Ball, and sharing a stage with both John Waters and The Steve Miller Band. Those days felt like a distant memory; a distant version of who I once was.

Since leaving the D.C. interpreting crowd behind, I was simply Rebekah—just a CODA who figured out how to cling to her parents via interpreting. I'd made a decent living while using a language and culture I couldn't share with the parents who *gave them to me* because the ol' GB instructed them to see me as symbolically dead.

Every time my hands went up, they wept silently.

Although I had a great time in Atlanta with Jesse, and fun catching up with former SLA folks, something didn't feel right, and it was emanating from my brother.

When Jesse had come to Austin, just three months before our Atlanta trip, he'd briefly mentioned he was toying with the idea of "going back," and I ignored him, not wanting it to be true. But deep down I knew it before he'd said it.

The faint trails of anxiety coming off Jesse's body in wavy lines told me that's what he was going to do.

Being back in Austin, I could feel a few roots taking hold, pulling me toward the earth's surface.

I moseyed through the airport and stopped at Maudie's Breakfast Taco Stand. The smell of potato, egg and cheese wrapped in a warm flour tortilla welcomed me home and sent my salivary glands into overdrive.

A warm feeling surrounded me, wrapping me in the comfort and safety of Austin. It was then that I knew I could unclench and allow a place to feel like mine. I didn't expect it, but Austin became mine.

And when I saw the General standing in the non-secure area, holding a cardboard sign with stick figures of us drawn on it, I knew he, too, was mine.

He started running to me. My steps quickened, and when I got closer, I threw my arms around his neck. He picked me up, squeezed tight, then set me down, kissing my mouth and face over and over.

"Wow. Miss me?" This was a new side of him.

"Mm-hmm," he said, indenting his dimples. "Squints is in the car. Let's go."

He handed me a bouquet of flowers and grabbed my carry-on bag.

In the car, I looked at the stick doodles. The General drew me with long dark hair, arms outstretched, and a suitcase next

180

to me. He drew himself bald with a ballcap on his head, arms outstretched and a dog next to him. Both stick figures had tiny hearts above their heads and big smiles fixed to their faces.

The rest of our summer was spent in a lovesick haze; we had the chance to get to know each other all over again. Of course, we missed the kids, but kid-free summer was a blast.

We got to know Austin and its surrounding areas. We met up for happy hours after work and took long drives with Squints, eyeballing deep, beautiful crevices in Hill Country. We drove south to San Marcos—so I could get acquainted with a university I'd be working with part-time—and wound up in a bar, serving as props in a Blue October video shoot. Their song "The Chills" was being filmed in a small, seedy bar, and if you look close enough, you might see us fist pumping.

The summer flew by, and suddenly it was time to collect two kids from the Austin-Bergstrom International airport (ABIA).

We waited at the gate, on edge. I watched people exit the plane onto the jetway. None of those faces belonged to Stormy or Max. I panicked, wondering if Cassie decided to keep them. Then I saw a flight attendant come around the corner with them.

"There they are!" I screeched.

I waved like a lunatic. Max dropped his wheeled carry-on and bolted toward us. Stormy kept cool, strutting in a new outfit, picking up Max's abandoned luggage on her way.

Max leapt into my arms, and I squeezed, inhaling the boy-smell from his little, blond head. His big green eyes and sweet, eight-year-old voice had made a home in some of the dark corners, the aching places, of my heart. Having him in my life made me feel like a better person.

"Hey, Miss Sassy Pants," the General said, hugging Stormy.

Making our way toward ABIA's exit, we stopped at Maudie's on our way out. Clutching my bag of breakfast tacos, with two excited kids by my side, I thought, *I'm home now.*

Both kids squealed with delight when they saw that we'd decorated their bedrooms with all their favorite things.

For Max—a Nintendo Super Mario themed bed set, Mario posters, colorful shelving units, and new clothes were set before him.

For Stormy—posters of Cody Simpson, Zac Efron, and Justin Bieber (much like the *BOP* magazine photos of Kirk Cameron, Ralph Macchio, and Michael J. Fox I once had) were tacked on her walls. Fresh, funky clothes were draped across her brand-new black, white, and purple zebra-striped bed set.

I knew deep down that home to them would always be with their mother, but I wanted them to know they also had a home with us. With me.

Later that night, Stormy called for me from her bedroom.

"Be right back," I said to the General as I jumped out of bed and shot into her room.

She was curled up in bed, staring at the wall. I sat down and looked at her.

"I feel weird," she said. "I don't even know why. I just feel weird."

You and me both, sister.

"Bekah!" Max bellowed from the next room.

"You can go see what he needs. He had some night terrors at Mum's."

Stormy had been Max's protector since day one. Folks were only allowed to get close to him after her say-so.

I stood up and said, "Want me to come back and read some American Girl stories? Or maybe Dad can?"

"Not Dad. I don't wanna talk about my boobs with him."

I laughed while walking into Max's room and turned on his light. "What's up, kid?"

"Will you please read to me?" he asked, hugging the tattered remnants of an afghan Cassie had crocheted for him before he was born.

"What were we reading before you left for the summer?" I asked, eyeing his bookshelf.

"*The Velveteen Rabbit*," he said.

I grabbed the book and looked for a familiar spot.

The General walked in. "Whatcha doin'?"

I held up the book and sat on Max's bed. The General sat at the edge of the bed to listen. Then Stormy walked in. Then, in wobbled Squints whom I'd nicknamed "Squibble de Bibbles" after an ear infection rendered him unstable on all fours.

We huddled together in Max's room as I read *The Velveteen Rabbit*—the touching story of a rabbit who was loved so hard he became real.

Just like us: four loners, thrown together, in desperate need of some intense love to make us feel real.

My little misfit family was almost enough to help me forget things that commonly made me feel out of place.

Almost.

A Melodious Exorcism

WALKING THROUGH THE university's quad on my way to interpret a class, I noticed two clean-cut, well-dressed young men standing at a booth. I walked closer then froze, staring at them until I heard garbled voices.

"Hello?" one of them said to me.

"Are you okay?" the other asked.

I ignored them and looked at their exhibit, heart pounding in my ears.

Their booth paraded a variety of literature and a portable DVD player that scrolled through a slideshow of disgustingly happy people, belonging to every single race and ethnicity, surrounded by animals—wild and domestic—and enough fresh food to feed the entire world.

My eyes focused, confirming what I already knew—they were J-Dubs. But what the hell were they doing on a college campus? I (along with many J-Dubs of my generation) wasn't allowed to attend college; it would have only caused me to think, reason, and subsequently question the doctrines I had been force-fed since birth.

"What are you doing here?" I asked point blank, eyebrows furiously knit, arms akimbo.

"Excuse me?" one of the young men asked. No suit, no tie—just a pair of khakis and a white shirt—obviously trying to fit in on campus.

"Aren't you Jehovah's Witnesses?" I asked.

"Yes," the other guy said, wearing the same casual business attire; he wore navy blue pants.

"Then what the fuck are you doing here?"

I could feel my nostrils filling with air, flaring, then releasing steamed hatred.

"Spreading the good news," Mr. Khaki said.

In one hot breath I said, "But Witnesses don't attend college and you're on a college campus, it doesn't make sense for you to be here, you don't belong here."

"We have permission to be here, and for what it's worth, I have my bachelor's in mechanical engineering," said Mr. Navy Blue.

Bachelor's? They're allowed to go to college now?

"If you have a college degree, then why are you wasting it on solicitation?"

"We don't see it as a waste," Mr. Navy Blue said, speaking for them both.

"So, you gonna use that bachelor's for a quick, two-day build on a flimsy, new Kingdom Hall? Huh?" I asked.

Witnesses pride themselves on their two-day Kingdom Hall projects, bragging that because of Jehovah's holy spirit they can build a brand-new Hall in two days with the help of every able-bodied man, woman, and child, regardless of skill or qualifications.

During a meeting Carter had attended with me, the double doors separating the main hall from the lobby came off their hinges and fell to the floor with a loud boom. Everyone at the Hall gasped and turned to see what the ruckus was. Carter looked at me, grinned, and whispered, "Two days, huh?"

I pressed further.

"Since you're allowed to attend college, why not broaden your knowledge base elsewhere?" I asked, my voice getting louder by the second.

"How do you mean?" Mr. Khaki asked.

185

"If you're so sure Witnesses have the Truth, why not read *Crisis of Conscience* by Ray Franz? It would only strengthen your convictions."

I knew suggesting that they read apostate literature wasn't something they'd entertain, but I posed the question anyway, eager to hear their reply.

They both laughed and Mr. Khaki regurgitated a rehearsed line of reasoning. "Why would I date other women if I was already married to *the one*?"

I rolled my eyes and asked, "Afraid to read it? Afraid you'd have doubts?"

"Not at all. I just don't entertain the *mentally diseased*."

"I take it you've read it?" Mr. Navy Blue asked.

"I have." My voice, now loud enough for the students passing by to hear, drew in a small crowd.

"Are *you* disfellowshipped?" Mr. Khaki asked.

"I am, and glad to be!"

Mr. Khaki and Mr. Navy Blue shared a glance then nodded, silently reinforcing their beliefs to one another. It pissed me off so much an ogre from the depths of hell sprang forth.

Using my mouth as its megaphone, the fiend shouted, "Don't entertain these fools! Jehovah's Witnesses shun family! It's a cult! Go to class!"

Most of the students high fived me, laughing as they walked through the quad, and a few stopped to see the spectacle I had created.

"This right here is the reason we shun the *mentally diseased.* See how she's causing a scene, working against Jehovah's Holy Spirit?" Mr. Khaki said, pointing at me, a sardonic grin fixed to his smug face.

Remembering the account of Jesus—arguing with a group of headstrong Pharisees—I pushed over part of their display, laughed maniacally as their tracts and magazines flew around the quad, and walked on.

Working against Jehovah's Holy Spirit? There's no Holy Spirit to work against. The ol' GB's divinely inspired direction is a farce; they're not at all infallible, so who do J-Dubs think is steering their friggin' ship? Hadn't they considered that the reason they see those who have left the Truth as *mentally diseased* is because once *we*—the dis-eased—are cast out, we're driven to loneliness, decision-overload, and galactic-sized fuck ups? We act out in anger because their magic carpet of false promises has been yanked out from under us, stealing away our families. They fulfill their own bullshit prophecies by treating us poorly, and as a result, we appear off. Well, dammit, we *are* dis-eased. It was their own doing, their own self-fulfilled prophecy. Like, duh.

I arrived in class a few minutes late.

"Sorry. Late," I signed to the Deaf student.

"Class not yet start. You fine," she signed back.

"Are you okay? Your face is beet-red. You're shaking," my team whispered.

"Fine," I signed to him.

"Want me to start?" he asked.

"Nah, I'm okay. I'll start."

I stood at the front of the room and began working.

I pushed it down, deep into the pit of my nauseous stomach and interpreted better than I had all semester. I was amped. Ready for battle. But also conflicted because it seemed when my hands went up, all they wanted to do was cry; used again for anyone and everyone except the two people I wanted to show them to the most.

And those douchey J-Dubs in the quad, worming their way into my quotidian campus life, exacerbated my preexisting struggles. Them, ridiculing me in front of their booth, calling me *mentally diseased* was too much. What pissed me off more than anything was they reminded me that my trauma was rooted deep. Unyielding. Relentless.

The nightly ritual of dinner, dessert, showers, and bedtime stories were especially difficult for me that night. My head was elsewhere, and the kids only got half-a-Bekah.

Once they were in bed, I made a big bowl of stove-popped popcorn, doused it in ranch-flavored seasoning, and shoved handful after handful into my mouth while sitting on our second-floor balcony, watching the comings-and-goings of the parking lot.

The General came out and asked, "Bad day?"

I looked up at him and rolled my eyes while stuffing popcorn into my mouth.

"What happened?" he asked, sitting down.

I told him all about the clean-cut douchebags, counting time while peddling salvation on campus, and broke out into hives. I started shaking, stuttering. I threw a handful of popcorn into the air and watched it fall to the ground.

The General laughed. "Why are you taking it out on your popcorn?"

"Would you rather I took it out on you?"

"You couldn't throw me off the balcony if you tried," he said, laughing.

Max came to the balcony door and opened it. "Bekah?"

I looked over at my tiny, blond angel and softened. "Why you up?"

"I saw some popcorn fly by my window and—"

I laughed, amazed at how one little kid could shift my world within seconds.

"I'm sorry, lemme tuck you in," I said, standing up, handing my bowl of popcorn-ammo to the General.

Tucking Max in, I explained that I'd just had a bad day and wasn't upset with anyone. Or the popcorn. Then Stormy came into Max's room, rubbing her eyes.

"What's going on?" she asked.

"Bekah had a bad day at work," Max said.

She walked closer and gave me a hug. "Luve you," she said, walking back to her room.

I kissed Max and shut off the light. As I was closing the door he said, "Luve you."

"Luve you, too."

How on earth could I ever explain to kids who weren't all mine, that their stepmom was kind of fucked? How could I tell them that, at the time, they were looking to damaged goods for love and guidance?

You don't tell kids that. You power through, hoping that your own sharp pieces of busted mirror don't slice them. Unfortunately, if kids get too close, as little cherubs often do, there's a good chance they'll bleed, too.

J-Dubs fucking with me, I could tolerate. But when that shit unintentionally affected my kids—like I knew it eventually would—that was more than enough to have me frothing at the mouth in the ol' GB's direction, and there was no way I was about to let Mr. Khaki and Mr. Navy Blue exist on my turf, promoting poorly written, misogynistic crap.

I called the student affairs office and explained that J-Dubs proselytizing in the quad contradicted everything that J-Dubs supposedly stand for, and it was wrong for them to be on campus at all.

The student affairs office felt asking the Witnesses to leave would have infringed on their freedom of speech. I found it ironic that Mr. Khaki and Mr. Navy Blue freely used a right they didn't even support other people fighting for.

They were in the quad every day spreading more venomous hate disguised as God's love while their presence lingered in the air around me.

Concerning myself with school drama, homework, chores, dinner, showers, and bedtime stories was most welcomed; the

General, Stormy, and Max had become my respite. Only, when the apartment got quiet, my thoughts got rowdy. I tried my best to dispel my own anguish, but the General could usually see right through it.

"Those guys still on campus?" the General asked while I mindlessly flipped channels after the kids were in bed.

"Yeah. Why?"

"You haven't been yourself since the day you saw them," he said.

"Sorry. It's just... That part of my life is hard to get over, or through, or whatever," I said, waving my hand dismissively.

"Maybe you'd feel better if you got some shit out instead of pushing it down."

I remembered Joel telling me that the cult stuff had been initially sunk in so deep, it might never entirely go away.

"There's no point talking about it cuz every time I do, it feels like no one understands what it's like. I haven't met too many people out there who have experienced what I have."

"I'm sure there are other ex-witnesses around," he said.

"There are."

"There it is, then; try a meetup or something."

"There it isn't. There are other ex J-Dubs, yes. Other CODAs, yes. Find me one person that's both. One who had to interpret meetings and while going door-to-door," I said, hating labels.

He sat and creased his eyebrows into his dimpled, think-y face.

"We're like unicorn," I added.

Hearing myself say that out loud made me feel hopelessly lonesome. Adding my CODA-ness to my ex J-Dub-ness equated to what I imagined unicorns (and again, Dracula) felt like— lonely, rare, misunderstood.

Although many folks have had similar struggles, to varying degrees, my plight always felt like it couldn't be got. I felt there wasn't anyone I could talk to or even sit quietly with. No one who understood, no one else that felt the turmoil constantly bubbling just beneath the surface of seeming okay.

At best, all I could do was give jagged snippets, and pieces of my unique life, in hopes that somehow, somewhere, someone would get me.

I hadn't found anyone that could hold up that particular mirror.

The General knew about the estranged relationship I had with the Mallorys. To be supportive and help me get through days of passing Mr. Khaki and Mr. Navy Blue's booth in the quad, he'd email weekly questions about my life, my feelings, my experiences, and one-by-one I answered them all.

We never spoke about it at home, in front of the kids, or allowed these conversations to hinder our everyday. They were private, kept on their own shelf, solely for the purpose of me releasing some heavy shit. They rested in my journals, on my laptop, on printed email exchanges, and stuffed into worn-out folders. Little did I know they'd become anything more.

But at the time, it didn't feel like enough.

I searched for some type of ex J-Dub community on social media. I found so many groups—for both the hearing and Deaf. And very *un*surprisingly, a lot of the Deaf folks who'd left the Witness organization recognized my eyebrows and last name.

Upon joining those groups, I received many "I knew your brothers!" messages and I'd think, *well, of course you did.* Some messages were followed up with, "I didn't even know they had a sister." *Thanks for rubbing salt in* that *wound.*

I grew tired of talking about my family with strangers.

I scrolled through pictures in various groups, almost ready to ditch the idea altogether, until one group of folks stood out from the rest—a snarky band of New England misfits, sitting around a Smurf cake at a barbecue. In that group was none other than Kyria Abrahams, the author of *I'm Perfect, You're Doomed.* I was starstruck. I'd read her book a few years before and loved that she was now within reach. I friended her on Facebook and one other fella that would have a major impact on me—Gregorio Smith.

This beautiful man was producing, directing, and editing his own documentary, *Truth Be Told,* on Jehovah's Witnesses and the very real business of religion.

In one group, Gregorio asked that anyone able to translate languages show themselves (translating means manipulating written words; interpreting means manipulating words in midair, spoken or signed). His documentary trailer was ready, all it needed were captions in as many languages as possible.

He asked me if English captions would be acceptable to the Deaf community. I told him they'd be great for the Deaf folks who were bilingual, but not all Deaf people are comfortable with the English language (my parents are prime examples). It'd be best to have a person in the bottom right-hand corner of the trailer, interpreting in a box like they did in the 70s and 80s.

He thanked me, then asked a question I wasn't expecting. "Will you be that person interpreting in a little box?"

My parents are Deaf, and I'd been hand-flapping for years. But translating the text, writing a glossed ASL version on paper, then interpreting the trailer for everyone to see, would be better suited for…someone else.

"Wouldn't someone else be better?" I asked.

"No. You," Gregorio said. "Use your iPhone, interpret the trailer, and just send it to me. I'll take care of all video magic."

I spent days watching the trailer over and over, gritting my teeth. The documentary itself didn't upset me. Gregorio had done a remarkable job. But he'd also produced a film exposing everything I'd known, and felt, since I was a kid; it stirred my veins.

My angst found an escape route through my hands, and I interpreted one take then reviewed it. My face wore plenty of contempt, but the contempt didn't properly convey the pain.

I did it again. Then again.

I was fueled with so much hatred. I thought about Mr. Khaki and Mr. Navy Blue calling me *mentally diseased* in the quad. I thought about the D.C. team who'd left me sitting alone in a government cafeteria after learning that I was "out." I thought about my innocent, four-year-old, train-track self riding that assembly line of indoctrination—forcefully stamped with fear, indecision, shame, and rejection.

In order to effectively interpret Gregorio's trailer, I needed to soothe the ache while keeping the emotion raw.

I needed exorcism living inside melody.

I needed Michael.

Music makes time travel possible. For me, Michael Jackson could always bring me home. Back to a time in my life I felt safe. Understood. *Not* alone. From interpreting "Billy Jean" for Mom to being scared for my life while listening to "Thriller"— but loving every second of it—Michael and I were kindred spirits. He, also being raised with a J-Dub influence, *knew*.

And suddenly *I* knew.

I searched iTunes, found *the* song, purchased it, and listened to it interminably.

I listened to him sing about his need to be held, carried, loved, lifted up instead of trampled on, shown that someone would fucking be there, no questions. Unconditionally.

Michael—singing with the passion that only he can deliver, with a gospel chorus behind him—carried me that day.

I was in the zone when the General opened the bedroom door and said, "How many times are you gonna listen to the 'Free Willy' song in a row?"

I jerked my head to face him, then said, "But have you ever listened to the end? They don't play it all the way to the end on the radio."

"Can't say that I have."

"It's a poem of, of, of, I don't know what, but I think it's, like, an ode to the *Society*."

He bobbed his head and said, "Um, cool," then closed the door.

I came out of my Michael trance and stared at the script. I crossed out articles of English to focus more on word order, rearranging phrases; ASL's grammatical structure is vastly different from English word order.

I hung a white sheet on Stormy's Cody Simpson wall and propped my iPhone on her keyboard stand across the room. I wore a quarter-sleeved, black shirt—to cover my tattoos— and kept my hair tidy to minimize flipping.

I was ready.

After several takes, I sent the recording to Gregorio, he married my three-minute video clip to his documentary trailer, and that was that.

Only that wasn't that for me.

Over the next few weeks, I had panic attacks.

Having just taken part in legit apostate activity, I wondered if my family would find out. Or local elders. I—a grown-ass woman with two kids—was still afraid that they were going to summon me to the *second school* dungeon for another judicial hearing.

Interpreting for Gregorio's documentary meant quite a few things. It meant I was no longer standing behind the Mallory men, quietly, with Mom; I was finally front-and-center, the only shadow cast was my own. It meant my brothers weren't the only ones signing for video productions. It meant that I also had worthy contributions, and someone out there saw them, saw *me*, as invaluable and not the *weaker vessel,* not the

Mallory girl some folks didn't even know existed. And it meant I still had a lot of anger for those fuckers holding my family hostage.

Little did I know then, Gregorio and his trailer came into my life exactly when they were meant to. The experience allowed me to check my wound, inspect the source of my pain as I'd done many times before, and redress the abrasion again.

Christmas was on its way. I still disliked holidays and almost everything about them—forced mirth, going overboard with lavish gifts, the weird rules, all the lies.

I hadn't had too many opportunities, as an adult with no children in her life until that point, to fully understand and buy in to the many already-established holiday guidelines.

Our first Easter was a bit of a comical disaster, and before we'd moved to Austin, Cassie had the kids for most holidays. I'd been spared.

The most my family ever did during the holidays was enjoy long weekends with an Italian feast, watching old black and white movies together, huddled in Dad's office.

We watched *Gaslight* with Ingrid Bergman and Charles Boyer, *Arsenic and Old Lace* with Cary Grant, and *Abbott and Costello Meet Frankenstein* while eating lasagna and garlic bread. That was all I needed; that had always felt like enough.

But suddenly there was so much to do for this *one* day.

I'd been instructed that only some presents were wrapped, while the others were not.

"Why?" I asked, wrapping presents in the bedroom a few days before Christmas, wishing we could just watch old movies and that'd be enough.

"The wrapped ones are from us. The unwrapped, Santa."

"Oh. Why doesn't he have to wrap presents?"

"Because he doesn't have time to wrap shit between houses; he just drops them off."

"Did you come up with this?" I asked, still unsettled about lying to children.

"I think Cassie did and it just kind of stuck."

I shrugged my shoulders. "Okay."

I thought back to the previous year's Christmas in NH...

That year, 2010, I'd made homemade vegan lemon cakes with vegan lemon frosting and gave them away as gifts, and I'd vowed to do nothing more than that.

The kids had spent most of that Christmas vacation with Cassie, which was fine since holidays meant very little to me.

When the kids came back from Cassie's that year, at the start of 2011, we took them to Disney World. That had always been my idea of the perfect gift—travel and experience. I didn't think memories of Disney World would get thrown away like wrapping paper.

Yet there I was a year later, only wrapping certain presents.

I didn't begrudge the General traditions he and his once-upon-a-time-forever-family had created together; those were his to keep. I just struggled with my own recollections of non-traditional holidays and plastering an insincere smile on my face for the sake of fleeting Christmas joy and plastic crap from Walmart.

We placed our wrapped presents on the floor, underneath Christmas ornaments we'd nailed to the wall in the shape of a pine tree (it saved space), and strung lights across the "tree" in diagonal lines.

The kids gladly accepted not having a tree once they saw package after package, from Cassie and her side of the family in NH, flooding our living room.

On Christmas Eve, while putting "Santa's" unwrapped gifts under the "tree," I couldn't help but think, *that fat bastard is getting credit for shit I bought with money I earned on a campus I'm forced to share with religious nut-bags.*

That night I lay in bed and thought about how void some of my holiday memories were, yet how full and heartfelt random times of the year were. Missing calendar holidays wasn't too painful; to me they were always just days—nothing more. When you don't know what you're missing, you don't miss shit.

There were times my parents, and other parents in our hearing congregation growing up, found reasons to throw parties, so we wouldn't feel like isolated freaks among our *worldly* peers.

For the congregation's autumn costume party, my mother—being the talented seamstress she was—sewed a Supergirl costume, and I strolled in wearing a blue leotard, red 'S' in the center, red cape, and tacky tights. My intuitive superpower donned its own outfit, ready to save myself and others from mind control.

Every year my mother was gifted a frozen turkey from one of her housecleaning customers and we'd have a full-out Thanksgiving meal—but only on the Sunday following the sinful, harvest celebration, of course. It didn't matter to me which day we ate; watching old black and white movies together, full bellies, was what mattered.

As well as all the random gifts (dolls, stuffed *Muppet Show* characters, art supplies, other stuffed animals, pink Kangaroo sneakers) my father had brought home, just because.

I later realized the presents Dad gave me usually floated somewhere around my summer birthday. But never *on* my birthday.

It wasn't all shit.

It just didn't look like the holidays I now felt obligated to celebrate.

Ninth and Trinity

FOUR MONTHS LATER, Loretta flew to Austin for a two-week visit. We took her to all our favorite spots in the weirdest U.S. city and introduced her to our friends. In return she gifted the General and I with some well-earned alone time.

"Go spend a weekend alone together, and let me enjoy my grandkids," she said.

That was all the General needed to hear. He quickly planned a weekend getaway for us to Fredericksburg—a small city in central Texas popular for wineries, German heritage, and a thriving, quaint Main Street community.

The kids came barreling into the apartment after school in typical Friday afternoon fashion, thrilled to be spending the weekend with their mémére—who was sure to shower them with homemade treats once we were gone, and they knew it.

"Bekah, look at my book!" Max said while showing me a handcrafted piece of art made by his very own nine-year-old hands.

"Ooh, your very own published book!"

Thrilled, I opened his creation. With the turn of each page, my heartbeat echoed, my breath quickened; I felt like I was back in the quad being called *mentally diseased*—I wanted to puke.

"Do you like it?" Max asked.

"Yeah."

But what I wanted to say was, "Where's my stick figure?"

Max's book was about family. He had drawn stick figures next to short stories about his mother, her boyfriend, his new baby brother, their dog, Stormy, Squints, and the General.

He wrote about loving James Dean and Michael Jackson, placing those captions next to doodles of his mother. Things I had shared, taught, said, or done were stripped from me and pinned to Cassie. He'd drawn many doodles of me in the past, but in this book, nothing.

I was symbolically dead to my own family, and seemingly nonexistent to Max. I had given big pieces of my heart and soul to this tiny person. Without him knowing it, he tested me daily. I strived to be a better version of myself for both him and his sister, fighting my own inner demons day in and day out, and I felt like I constantly handed over pieces of myself for naught.

At that moment, I realized Cassie was holding up another mirror. Its reflection told me that she would forever hold a major piece of the General because she'd had his children. And I felt heated envy because they'd been together at a different time in his life, a time I'd never be able to experience with him.

All I had then were two casually dressed shitheads at my place of employment, sneering at me every day in the name of their Jehovah.

Max smiled up at me. His cheeks glowing, and his freckles danced in anticipation of praise.

"It's great, did you show it to Mémére?" My voice cracked. I handed the hardcovered book back to him. Tears welled up, and I hurried down the hall into the bedroom.

Squibbles chased me, bouncing off the walls of the hallway like a pinball on his way to see where his favorite human was headed. He pushed the door open with his snout and wobbled in.

Dogs get me; they may be the only creatures on this planet that do. I sat at the edge of the bed, tears trickling down, and pet Squibbs.

The General came in, closed the door behind him, and asked, "What was that?"

I sighed. "Did you see the book?"

"Yeah."

"I wasn't in it. Loving Michael Jackson, James Dean, that's me."

"Bekah, it's a book written by a third grader, a third grader who misses his mom. That's it. It has nothing to do with you."

"Exactly. My presence was disguised as someone else's. I'm overlooked. Ousted. Again. I'm, like, nothing to my own family and nothing to yours. I don't need to be his mom, I don't want to be his mom, but I want to feel like somebody to someone."

"Well, you're somebody to this someone," he said, kneeling beside the bed, looking up at me. "And I like your body."

"Oh, shut up," I said, sniffling.

"C'mon, let's get outta here."

The bed and breakfast was money well spent.

Fredericksburg's an adorable city teeming with shops and, for some odd reason, Volkswagens.

Walking down Historic Main Street on our way to dinner the first night, we saw Volkswagen Buses, Bugs, and Things. I had never seen a Thing before.

"Excuse me, why all the Volkswagens?" I asked someone, eyeballing the same Thing we were.

"This weekend is the annual Texas Volkswagen Classic. It happens every April. The big event is on Sunday and the buses camp at the Fairgrounds all weekend long."

"Thank you," we said and walked on.

"We should definitely check that out," the General said.

Well, we didn't just "check that out." We spent most of the weekend wandering the Fairgrounds, oohing and ahhing all the creative, crazy things people had done to their beloved Volkswagen buses, making them livable full-time.

I'd been a sucker for vintage automobiles, all things *I Love Lucy*, and the 1950s since I could remember, spending most of my life thinking I'd been born in the wrong era. I love the diners, the décor, the style, and elegance of that time. Though there was blatant misogyny and racism weaved into the fabric of American culture back then (that continues to merge into the now) the advertising was on point. And damn did that time in history ever sell the American Dream.

"I want to live a roving, Volkswagen bus life," I said, climbing into an open bus.

The bus was decorated with purple satin from top to bottom. The ceiling trim was lined with plastic, purple, beaded tassels. The walls were swathed in bohemian tapestries and sprinkled with yellow crescent moons and stars. Most of the buses were staged for a picnic, complete with a Yogi Bear basket. But the people occupying that bus were definitely living in the Age of Aquarius.

"Think we could live like this someday?" I asked, stepping out of the bus after the General snapped a photo of me, sitting in an antique armchair upholstered in purple, swirly fabric.

"Sure. Why not? I mean, after the kids move out, we can do whatever."

I sighed, knowing there would be more years of feeling like half a person ahead of me. There'd be more pieces of my own childhood to share that might all eventually be forgotten. I wanted to steal one of those buses and start my nomadic life right then and there.

It'd be so easy to just fall back on my tried-and-true talent for sabotaging relationships, so easy to just go. But not this time. This time I was in a relationship with a real-life trinity. And I knew it wasn't them; it was me.

The night before Loretta left, she, the General, and I sat on the balcony with some drinks while the kids stayed inside playing video games.

Loretta turned to the General, glassy-eyed; her Bud Light and neon pink straw began to speak.

"You know, son, you ain't gonna get any better than Bekah," she said, pointing at me. "She works hard. She cooks. She cleans. And most important, she takes care of my grandkids."

"I know, Mom," he said, attempting to hush her.

I sat quietly, watching the body language, eye gaze, and facial expressions bounce between the two. To them, and to most folks, those things mean very little. To me, they mean everything.

"If you don't marry her, I'll question how well I raised you," she said just before going inside to replace her empty can with a full one.

I looked at the General and thought back to a day—the year before—when I'd come home from work early and found him already there, playing hooky. He'd led me into our bedroom, pressed play on the CD player, and slow danced with me to a lineup of country songs. Just because. He teared up when Keith Urban sang "Thank You," and I knew then that he would marry me.

Knowing that the General was my person was all that mattered. He was the one, my 'til death. He knew it. I knew it. And my superpower knew it.

We didn't talk about it after that night or even after Loretta left. We both just knew it would happen when it was meant to happen.

My misfit family and I roamed the annual Wiener Dog Races in Buda, Texas one Saturday, and of course, I wanted every dachshund I saw. I still mourned the loss of Bartok and Moron, dreaming about them at least once a month, but there were fun, furry sausages everywhere.

The races not only had furry hot dogs running toward their owners in a race, but also food trucks, dog-clothing dealers, opportunities for dachshund rescue organizations to find homeless pups a home, and jewelry vendors.

Walking past a jewelry booth, I caught a glimpse of a sterling silver ring with one big, oval, maroon, and creamy white swirled stone, nestled inside a line of petite silver beads surrounding the rock.

"That is stunning," I said, pointing to the ring.

"Would you like to try it on?" the man at the booth asked.

"I would."

He handed me the ring and I immediately put it on my engagement finger. It was a bit big for my size four ring finger.

"I can size it for you," the man said.

I looked at the General and smiled.

"How much?" the General asked.

"That one is forty dollars. If you want it sized, I can have it ready next week and you can meet me on South Congress for First Thursdays."

"I love it. What kind of stone is it?" I asked, admiring the stone, studying its familiarity.

I almost fell over when the man said, "That one's a Mexican fire opal."

I slid inside the creamy mauve and deep maroon swirls I saw before me while remembering a photo and caption from my gemstone reference guide… "Mexican fire opals have the power to help those who've suffered abusive relationships, dissolving memories of rape and sexual abuse while fostering positive sexual health and increasing the libido. It symbolizes the most earnest form of love there is, replacing grief and sorrow with progress and hope."

Looking at the General, mentally going over all we'd shared together, it hit me. The times I'd visited the tracks after we began dating, I noticed that some of my painful memories mysteriously dissipated.

The General knew about my relationship with Dean, about some of the sordid experiences I'd had before and after Dean. He helped me feel better about them without even trying. His energy was the most calming and drama-free I'd been with in a long time. Nothing felt off with him.

He was my Mexican fire opal.

"This one. It has to be this one if we're ever gonna...you know," I said.

The General nodded. "I know."

He handed the man forty dollars and we made plans to find his booth the following week.

Engagements and weddings can sometimes be over-the-top extravagant, requiring months or even years (shoot me) of planning; bridezillas abound.

And sometimes they happen in a matter of two short weeks all because a Mexican fire opal comes along during a weekend Wiener Dog Race and reminds you that you're not *mentally diseased*; you're experiencing the most earnest form of love there is, the kind that allows each person to be none other than who they are. That was definitely us.

The General's proposal was casual.

Walking from the car toward Sixth Street for dinner one night, he stopped me on a random side street, faced me, and said, "The day you told me you shooed some guys away from my Puch (POOCH), I knew I was gonna marry you. And probably even before then."

His Puch was a vintage moped, circa 1977. A friend had given it to him, and some guys circled around it like vultures at our apartment complex one day. When I'd caught them, I told them to beat it.

"They didn't need to be snooping around it, lifting the tarp, asking if you'd sell it," I said.

He picked me up and lifted me above his head. Smiling that dimpled smile, he looked into my eyes and asked me to marry him.

I looked up, suspended above him, and noticed we were standing at the corner of Ninth and Trinity, in front of the First Baptist Church of Austin.

"Of course I will," I said.

He glanced up and said, "Ninth and Trinity. I won't forget that." Then he kissed me and placed the Mexican fire opal on my finger.

We called Loretta.

"You two should get married in front of Jo's Coffee," she said.

"Jo's Coffee? Why?" I asked.

"That's where the *I Love You So Much* mural is. I loved it there," she said.

"Yeah. It's cute but, I mean, we'd be getting married on a sidewalk."

"So? It'd be perfect for you two."

She was right. It was perfect for us.

We called ahead and made arrangements with Jo's Coffee to say "I Do" in front of Austin's *I Love You So Much* mural. The staff at Jo's were excited to host their first wedding as long as we didn't mind sharing the experience with people waiting in line for coffee, and we didn't.

"They'll make great witnesses," the General said.

"Yeah, and I don't want all the frills; just simple, you know?"

We'd both already experienced the anxiety and stress a showy wedding with too many guests and a mediocre buffet brings—we were having none of it.

205

I wore a short-sleeved, vintage circle dress with pink and white Albizia flowers I'd found in a costume shop; it matched my fire opal perfectly. The General wore jeans, a Red Sox cap, and a tan, polyester, vintage, disco shirt with a charcoal grey suit coat.

Standing casually in the heart of Austin, holding a wedding bouquet that I'd fashioned out of three melted 45-rpm vinyl records, we exchanged vows we'd written together the night before.

Our seven-minute ceremony was filmed by my friend, Blue, and officiated by her husband, Han, who was dressed in a pirate's costume. Holding a plastic sword, he sanctioned our rings while imploring the Flying Spaghetti Monster for its noodle-y blessing.

Stormy and Max signed our marriage license, and after the ceremony, Jo's Coffee gave us free t-shirts and coffee beans as a "thank you" for being the first wedding they'd ever hosted.

We drove around Austin for our wedding photo shoot. My favorite photos were taken at the graffiti park at Eleventh and Baylor (swanky condos now occupy the space). After photos, we went to Doc's Bar and Grill to celebrate with the kids and a few friends. No honeymoon, no trip, not even a night away. It was exactly what we wanted—just another day.

June swooped in, taking the kids away on a JetBlue flight once again, and thus began a summer-long honeymoon.

We spent a long weekend in Port Aransas, Texas jet-skiing with dolphins and drinking too many tequila sunrises while Jimmy Buffet songs played in every beachside bar.

A few weeks after our Port Aransas trip—for my thirty-fifth birthday—we flew into Denver to visit Kara and her SCUBA-diving-buddy-turned-husband.

We went to a Rockies game, climbed the steep steps of the Red Rock Amphitheater, went alpine sliding, and spent time picking up where we'd left off. It was like I had just seen her the day before, like no time passed.

Our remaining kid-free weekends were spent making one hundred bagged lunches to hand out to folks gathered in front of an Austin homeless shelter. One of the General's coworkers began the effort and we'd committed to supporting it each week.

Every summer, the kids returned with new school clothes, new electronic devices, birthday money they were itching to blow on just about anything, and a few questionable habits. The readjustment time was a long, drawn-out arduous task.

The General and I tried to keep each other in check. If I got too amped up while attempting to undo what time in NH had done (which usually equated to the kids lying about stupid shit and covering each other's tracks), he'd nudge me and vice versa. It worked sometimes, but unfortunately, no matter how hard I tried, I struggled.

Especially with the lying, it awakened my inner J-Dub Police Officer. I'm a horrible liar. A poker-face I do not have. My efforts to be a decent stepmom—who wasn't trying to take their mother's place or overstep boundaries while being ever-present and ready to deal with anything, including my own personal tumult—left me dead tired most days.

It took weeks to reorient them. While Cassie got to be the Disneyland parent every summer, we were the read-a-book-stop-playing-video-games-go-do-your-chores-and-go-to-bed ogres, tirelessly moving through the kids' confusion, angst, and turmoil upon their return.

Attempting to instill some good values, we enlisted the kids' help in making bagged lunches and brought them with us one Saturday to hand them out in front of the homeless shelter, exposing them to volunteering while expecting nothing in return.

I think parents forget that with each word and each deed—good or bad—they are teaching their children something, and I wanted to give mine something other than a damaged, lost ex J-Dub. Children are nothing more than mini mirrors, exhibiting a parent's best and worst behaviors. Having kids doesn't have to be rocket science. You lead others by leading yourself; kids are no different.

Halfway through the school year, we took a road trip to New Mexico for spring break. We didn't want to forever be seen as the read-a-book-do-your-homework-do-your-chores-and-go-to-bed parents, so we tried to find affordable things to do with them when we couldn't send them to NH.

Riding along west Texas highways, cruising at 80 mph, we headed to Roswell, New Mexico.

Roswell looked exactly as one might imagine. It was teeming with alien-themed street signs, murals, streetlights, vending machines, gift shops, and antique shops. Martians covered almost every building, and sidewalks were painted with green alien footprints, leading us into the UFO museum. There, we learned about the "Incident in 1947," ancient aliens, and every alien-centered conspiracy theory known to man.

After one night in a local Squibbles-friendly hotel, we drove on to Ruidoso and took the kids horseback riding through the desert.

The next day, we drove to Alamogordo and slid down white desert sandhills on plastic winter sleds. We did our absolute best to gift the kids with experiences, memories, rather than things; we were more than happy to spend time instead of money.

Back home in Austin we resumed our do-your-chores-and-homework roles, waiting ever-so-patiently for another kid-free summer. We appreciated that alone time just as much as the kids undoubtedly loved going to NH for the summer.

Little Bitches, Mighty Banyans

LYING IN BED, *I Love Lucy* reruns on TV in the background, the General and I finalized the itinerary for our long-awaited honeymoon.

"You've been there twice, what do you suggest?" the General asked.

"Anything, really. And the second time doesn't count since I was there for work in an underground, cemented bunker. But it's Oahu, you can't go wrong. I love how I feel there. I feel, I don't know, whole?" I looked back to my iPhone's tiny screen at the endless possibilities Oahu offered. "Luaus, snorkeling in Hanauma Bay, visiting Kualoa Ranch, the beaches, just sitting and watching the waves, whatever, really. Like I said, you can't go wrong."

"Would you, maybe, wanna marry me there?" he asked.

I turned my head and looked at him. "What? We've been married for over a year."

"So what? We could do it again. Like an elopement, a sexy elopement."

"Yeah?" I changed my Google search from "things to do in Hawaii" to "destination weddings/renewing vows."

We found a small, reputable company and put a deposit down on their short Magic Island ceremony package; it came with a professional photo session, two leis, and a renewed marriage license.

"We need to get in shape for this," the General said.

"Huh?"

"My dad sent a gift card and I've been wanting to try this at-home workout—"

"There's a gym here."

"I don't like going down there. I'm buying it," he said, putting the DVDs into the Amazon cart from his phone.

A week later a DVD set, how-to book, and meal plan booklet arrived in the mail.

"HB3?" I asked, scowling at the contents of the box.

"Yeah! Hard Bottoms in three months," he said, inspecting the DVDs.

I flipped through the how-to booklet. Pull-ups, push-ups, weights, resistance bands?

"This is a dude's workout. I'll stick to my kickboxing classes at the gym, thanks," I said, tossing the booklet onto the coffee table.

"C'mon. Do it with me. We've got about four months before we go to Hawaii."

It wasn't easy for me to turn down all three dimples with a hard no. He'd already spent the money, had secretly wanted to do it for a while, and there it was on the coffee table, staring at me. I took a closer look at the booklet. Three months. A workout every day. There were no workouts less than an hour long.

I sighed. "Okay. I'll try it."

The General came home one day after work with heartrate monitors and a set of weights, then made me pose in a sports bra for "before" photos. I almost lost my shit.

"I don't wanna do this. I changed my mind," I said, flexing my non-existent muscles.

"Too late. We get to do the fit test after this. Turn," he said, snapping pictures with his phone.

"Oh, do we?" I said, unenthused, turning to the side.

I survived the fit test. Day one fell on a Tuesday. Sometimes we worked out together, sometimes separately, depending on our schedules. The day we did one hour of plyometric training together, I thought I was going to die.

I huffed and puffed while leaned over, grabbing my knees.

"Is this guy high?" I said, panting. "Did he like… Do a line…of coke…or something before filming?"

I wheezed then opened the balcony door for some fresh air only to be hit with Austin's wicked humidity.

The General was just as winded. "Jimmy," he said letting out a gust of air.

"Huh?" I looked at him, brows knit.

"The trainer…" He huffed. "Jimmy Heston." He leaned over panting, hands on his knees.

"Oh. Well, fuck Jimmy."

The videos were such a fixed part of our daily routine that even the kids knew the trainer's corny jokes.

"Hey, Bekah?" Max asked.

"Yeah?" I answered, short of breath.

"How's your heart rate?" he asked, mimicking Jimmy.

"What's your zone?" Stormy added.

I rolled my eyes mid-jumping jack.

We kept at this diabolical workout regime for three months. On the last day, we took "after" photos and barely recognized ourselves.

"Is that me?" I asked, eyes wide open.

"Sure is. Look at your cute, little booty," the General said, getting excited. I grabbed my ass and felt the junk in my trunk; it was tight.

A month before sending the kids to NH for the summer, Loretta tagged me in a post on Facebook and I immediately felt every inch of my body come to life.

"Go get her, Bekah. She needs a home," Loretta's comment read under the photo of a ready-to-adopt-right-now, short-haired, tan and red dachshund.

It had been three years since I'd been around a furry wiener of my own, and I kept telling myself I wasn't ready to fall in love with another one just yet. I'd never picked out a dog from a rescue or breeder going by an online picture before (I prefer to rescue), and I'd never owned a bitch.

But there was something in this little girl's face; I felt like I already knew her. I called a shelter in San Antonio and spoke to a woman named Penny.

"That little girl is about ten-months-old and scheduled to be euthanized tomorrow," Penny said, distracted; I could hear her flipping through papers.

"What? Why? She's just a baby."

"We don't have enough space. Unfortunately, we're not a no-kill shelter."

"Don't, don't do anything. I want her. I'll take her."

"Okay. Send over the adoption application, eighty dollars, and she's all yours, microchipped and fixed."

I rushed through the paperwork, scanned, and emailed it. The General paid the fees, and we saved her just in time. I called the foster family to arrange a time and meeting place to get my bitch.

"She's a very happy girl. She seems a bit anxious, but her tail is always wagging."

"Does she have pudgy paws?" I asked.

Moron had paws that looked like furry, little boxing gloves; I'm a sucker for pudgy mitts.

"Um, I hadn't noticed," the foster mom said.

Hadn't noticed? I had to get my little bitch from that blind-to-pudgy-paws woman as soon as possible. Hadn't noticed, psshh.

I picked our girl up the next day from a Buc-ees parking lot in New Braunfels. She was wrapped in a bath towel with a clear, plastic cone on her head; she had a small green tattoo on her belly and the pudgiest little boxing gloves. She was shaking, visibly nervous, but her tail was going at warp speed.

On the ride home Little Miss No Name attempted to cuddle with Squibbs, and he was having none of it. He wobbled his unstable ass to the front of the car and put himself in the passenger's seat while I drove, leaving my little bitch alone, shivering in the back. That was the only time he rejected her. Once we were home, he loved her as much as we all did.

The first night the General and I spent in bed with her and Squibbs, we picked a name—Liesel Hauser Von Patten Pants. Though she has many aliases: Babyface, Sweetpea, Little Miss Mouth, Little Girl, Brat, Stinky, Gross-y, Truffle Pig, and Little Bitch.

She fit right in without trying, introducing us to new things.

"What's that sound?" Stormy asked.

The General paused the movie we were watching and the four of us looked around the living room, trying to locate the *thud, thud, thud* we heard. We found Liesel, under the coffee table, wagging her tail at nothing.

"It sounds like a helicopter is landing in here," I said.

Another noise we detected was when a familiar buzzing sound could be heard throughout the apartment. The four of us searched each room and finally found Little Miss Mouth in our room, chewing on something.

The General crawled under the bed to find our little bitch— mouth and paws wrapped around a vibrator that she'd turned on all by herself.

I saw the sex toy and covered my face with both hands. "Oh, my god."

"What is that thing?" Max asked, trying to get a closer look at a relic from the tin-of-toys.

"Nothing. Don't worry about it," the General said from under the bed.

"C'mon, kid. Out," I said, shooing Max out of our room.

The last day of school came, the kids had flown to NH, the fur brats were getting the royal treatment while boarding at Bluebonnet Animal Hospital, (I trusted them explicitly) and we were Oahu bound with new-to-us hard bottoms.

Stepping off the plane in Honolulu, the smell of sweet island air encircled us, and we fell right into a Waikiki groove.

We crashed Hilton beach parties; day drank; partied with drag queens; renewed our vows on Magic Island by the shore with a local ukulele player; rode all around the island on a motorcycle; walked from our equestrian-themed hotel to Diamondhead; hiked Manoa Falls; followed the trail to Makapu'u Point to ooh and ahh at the lighthouse on its edge; and against our better judgment, we climbed the steep stairs of KoKo Head Trail where the city below is so beautiful it almost looks fake.

While roaming Waikiki beach after a private yoga session— with a very eccentric instructor who had us doing handstands on rickety picnic tables—I saw the Banyan trees.

I swore I was standing in front of the exact same one I'd seen six years before. It was stronger, and it had re-root itself once again, growing into this massive, beautiful beast of earth. It stood tall, shameless, unrepentant. It just was. Although this incredible tree had roots keeping it ashore, it was still alone. It still faced rough island winds and high tides, alone.

Like the tree, I knew that even if I had people keeping me grounded, I was still one hundred percent alone in this world. I was a mighty Banyan—messy roots, shameless, unmoving, tough, veritable.

Factor in my superpower that no one fully understood— hell, I was only halfway to understanding it myself—and it was clear why my sixth sense and the General's paranoid hunches clashed during our last night on the island.

The General wanted to find someone on the island with some green. I hadn't been much of a toker since my Dean days but was confident I could help him find someone local; I had a knack for finding what I, or anyone with me, was looking for.

I spotted a muscley, tattooed Samoan and made a beeline for him on the Waikiki beach strip. His name was Moses, and like I'd suspected, he was safe, down-to-earth, and had some green.

He, two of his buddies, and the General disappeared down a dark alley. They smoked a joint and came back about fifteen minutes later, laughing, patting each other on the back as if they'd each just got a hole-in-one—though none of them looked like golfers.

"Feel better?" I asked my glassy-eyed General.

"Yeah, after the panic wore off," he said, sitting beside me on the sidewalk in front of a bar.

"Panic?"

"I got a creepy feeling walking down all those alleys and side streets with them, like, maybe Moses and his buddies would mug the unsuspecting tourist out of the blue."

"Moses? Really?"

"Yeah, I read an article before coming about how some locals lure tourists then mug 'em. So, I kept my fist clenched in my pocket, keys between my knuckles, just in case."

I thought back to the creepy tour guide from my first Oahu trip, offering me a private look-see around the island. Moses' energy didn't feel anything like that guy's. My face scrunched. I couldn't help but scoff at my new-again husband.

"No. No way." I shook my head.

"How do you know?"

"Because I didn't get that feeling from him at all. I can't speak for his friends but if I didn't get that feeling from Moses, I doubt anyone he hangs with would've burgled you, haole or not."

215

"Are you chalking this up to your superpower?" the General asked using air quotes.

"Abso-fuckin-lutely." I smiled at him.

The General shoulder-checked me and grinned. We had a way of complementing each other's existence, fusing together naturally, like peanut butter and jelly.

We both teared up at the airport when it was time to leave. Saying aloha to that sweet island air and the indescribable magic of Hawaii was harder than expected.

In Austin, we made every attempt to mimic the enchantment we felt on Oahu but failed miserably. Trying to hold on to all the aloha we'd left behind, I found a tattoo artist I loved and had him draw up a huge back piece to cover up my Paul Booth, Alice in Wonderland tat. We spent weeks going back and forth with a design to honor the magical week spent on Oahu.

Some folks come into your life and though you barely know them at all, they get you immediately. That was Paul at Bijou Studio. There was something in his face that comforted me, something in his eyes. He was kind, full of creative ideas, and quite discerning because he drew up something powerful and elegant that was meant for my body and my body alone. Everything we collaborated on, tat-wise, from that point on was a custom design because he got me without much effort. I loved that. It felt good to be seen.

The day came to start the tat, and while Paul and I talked about how and where to situate the design, the owner of the studio chimed in.

"You're going to cover your back piece?" she asked.

I smiled and nodded. "I'm so excited." I held the drawing in my hands, eager to have it etched on for life.

"But, honey, the piece you're covering is a part of you, of who you are," she said.

I looked at her, tilted my head, smiled, and thought, *yes, a part of who I was that I'd like to forget.*

"Well, she'll always be there," I said, smiling as Paul pressed the transfer paper onto my back. Then I wondered, *what if tats could talk? Would Alice be upset? Angry? Sad? Slighted? Will she miss me? Will I miss her?*

"That look right?" Paul asked.

I turned and looked in the full-length mirror. A tear pooled in the bottom of my eyelid as I looked at the design, then to my face. There was no abused teenager staring back at me wondering why we were staying in Franklin; no adulteress glaring at me shamefully; no desperate woman clinging to a meaningless engagement. There was just me, becoming who I felt I was always meant to be.

"Ready?" he asked, patting the cushioned table.

"Yep."

Laying on my stomach, naked back to the ceiling, I relaxed to the sound of bees buzzing and the sensation of needles scraping. For me, every tat was a therapy session. Sometimes I even fell asleep.

That piece took Paul a few weeks to finish. Once complete, it was perfect. Alice could still somewhat be seen behind a grey and red koi fish that was swimming upstream, splashing water, surrounded by Plumerias and one giant, purple Water Lily. Through many conversations, Paul told me he drew that piece up for me because koi fish swimming upstream depicted the strength of a person fighting their own demons.

That was me, all right. I'd never shied away from challenge. I loved the tat; it was one hundred percent me. The magic of Oahu was set to linger on my skin 'til death.

When the kids came home, however, the magic was definitely gone. Of course, we were happy to see them, and we began our annual end-of-summer kid-activities—a day trip to Six Flags and our customary day-turned-into-night at Zilker Park for that year's theater production, Little Shop of Horrors—but once again, we were faced with reconditioning NH habits.

It got harder every year.

The start of Stormy's freshman year in high school brought many unforeseen challenges (not unlike some of mine). Since she wasn't my child, discipline was better left to her father. But he had almost no clue what to do with such a mercurial teenage girl. We were often trapped in these never-ending battles with Stormy.

When these exhausting clashes repeatedly ended in a stalemate, Stormy would bring up living in NH with Cassie, and the idea was brutally rebuffed year after year.

"Your mother doesn't have health insurance for you."

"Your mother just had a baby."

"Your mother isn't working."

The General finally conceded to the idea of Stormy in NH when he said, "Okay, but your mother needs to start and file the custodial paperwork."

As soon as the General and Cassie fleshed out child support concerns, she very quickly filled out and sent the paperwork. Stormy wasn't even halfway through her freshman year at Austin High when she boarded a plane back to NH.

Stormy's leaving awakened my fear of abandonment; it felt like betrayal. No matter how close I got to people, allowing them a space inside my heart, I felt cast aside. I remembered why slamming the door was easier than leaving it open. Leaving it open meant I left myself vulnerable to rejection.

Memories and aftereffects of being ousted from my own family shot up to the surface, and those uninvited esteem-squashers were something I struggled with more often than not, and I'd have to remind myself: *I am a Banyan tree. I'm motherfucking solid.*

As for Max, he was angry with us for "sending Stormy away." We could do nothing but accept the blame.

"We should move. Maybe a fresh start is what we need," I suggested to the General one night.

"Maybe," he said.

I had been in the habit of moving and making fresh starts long before the General and I crossed paths. I always believed up around the corner there was something better waiting for me; something else, some hurdle to leap over, running toward some foreign version of myself I was destined to be.

The General was willing to move since we were paying for a three-bedroom, only using two, and the third was nothing but a reminder of who had left.

So, we moved across town when we happened to find a two-bedroom house with a fenced in yard and doggy door—not that Squibbles was able to pinball-bounce his way through it, but the door was perfect for Little Miss Liesel. After securing a deposit and moving in, we settled into Austin's North Loop neighborhood.

We loved it.

We lived a three-minute walk away from Epoch (an all-night hipster coffee shop), The Tigress (our go-to for fancy cocktails and *Walking Dead* viewing parties), several vintage shops, a record store, one of the last video rental stores in existence—Vulcan Video—and an authentic Mediterranean restaurant hosting Saturday night belly dancing and hookah parties.

Max quickly made neighborhood friends that he spent time skateboarding side streets with, and the General and I learned we had a knack for gardening.

In a raised garden bed, in our mini yard, we grew spinach, carrots, potatoes, herbs, radishes, and tomatoes. We ate from our own garden, and only shopped for essentials. We made a few friends, hosted barbecues, bocce ball parties, and found a rhythm that worked.

219

Things seamlessly fell into place, but it wasn't long before my superpower woke, rubbed her eyes gently, and whispered, *Something's off again.*

I'd started working with another college part-time—one *without* a quad full of booths—and was paired with different interpreters, for a variety of classes. Most were great and likeable. But there was this one interpreter who looked at me oddly while we teamed, and I couldn't put my finger on why.

"Could it be the 'terp recognized you?" the General asked, stir frying chopped Roma tomatoes from our garden.

I scraped minced chili pepper from the cutting board into the cast-iron. I watched the General while he mixed peppers and tomatoes with a wooden spoon and lost a tiny version of myself on the pan, surfing on the waves of hot virgin olive oil.

I'd forgotten that my last name and eyebrows were still a dead giveaway. I am my father's daughter. Some interpreters, and J-Dub interpreters especially, knew exactly whose loins I'd sprung from.

"Maybe," I said.

It was becoming more and more obvious that I couldn't escape the Mallory-Girl-J-Dub-CODA label unless I stopped interpreting. God, that thought was appealing—retiring from interpreting. I consistently fantasized about myriad careers that wouldn't jab at the despondency I felt over being cast out of the renowned Mallory nucleus. But with no degree, and every year ushering me toward middle-age-dom, interpreting was my it, my career. What else could I do?

I didn't (and don't) take issue with the language, culture, art, stories, Deaf norms, or the community that raised me, but I'd become so exhausted communicating through eyebrows that were hard to miss in the small J-Dub Deaf community. For me, the Deaf community and the J-Dub Deaf community were synonymous. And to this day, the only

220

people I see in front of me while working are my parents, sitting in our very own Deaf section at the Franklin Kingdom Hall.

The General sautéed, and I thought back to when Carter and I had gone to see an ASL show with some friends in Boston.

The act starred a well-known CODA and his interpretation of the song, "Tears in Heaven." He didn't interpret the song lyrics, per se. What he did was sign a letter he'd written to his parents after they passed away as the song played in the background.

And when he signed, "Now that you're gone, who are these hands for?" I cried because I knew exactly what he meant, and I realized I'd been interpreting all this time so somewhere in my mind I could be satisfied with the idea that my parents were proud of me, even if I wasn't in the Truth.

And they *were* proud, especially my dad. Over the years, whenever we *did* talk, he'd ask how things were going in D.C., curious if I'd interpreted for anyone famous.

Then it hit me.

Kyrie eleison! All I want is my parents' approval!

How had I so easily forgotten that my disenchantment with interpreting was because my hands were whored out to people I didn't care about nearly as much as I cared for my parents? How had that slipped past me?

I supposed my years in D.C.—working forty-to-fifty-hour weeks at SLA, being distracted by Kelly, therapy sessions with Joel, happy hours with colleagues, salsa nights with Kara, *I Love Lucy* and *Sex and the City* marathons with Bartok, Moron, and Spork, Asshat's lame bullshit…all of it—had diverted me enough to not think about my parents.

Though somehow, Mom and Dad found me on an Austin college campus then followed me home to slide around a red-hot pan of tomatoes and peppers.

Extraterrestrial Fantasies

KID-FREE SUMMER didn't feel the same that year. It didn't feel earned, deserved. Stormy had just vanished. The Winged Devourers from *Beastmaster* had taken her into their slimy, webbed arms and consumed her whole. Every day I had to tell myself, *it has nothing to do with you, Bek.*

Deserved or not, the General and I planned to spend two weeks on the Big Island, at an eco-hostel in Pahoa, occupying a tent in the jungle, surrounded by Guava trees.

Aside from working on the property—painting, cleaning, gardening, planting, raking, and weeding—the most notable part of our trip was being chased by wild donkeys the size of Clydesdales. They were massive, and those beasts were not happy when they saw us picking limes from *their* trees for *our* Coronas.

Being chased by enormous, wild donkeys made me feel amazingly alive. It wasn't the running. It was remembering that in one fleeting second anything can change. I saw how small I was. Everything else—the worries, the discomforts, the bullshit of the everyday, the lingering J-Dub trauma, the reservations about my career—all seemed inconsequential. I could feel a bigger picture shifting inside me.

New life perspective aside, even though I'd tried to find my place with the General and his family, no spot I wedged myself into felt right. The only place I ever felt just right was inside my own head. Things made sense there.

During our Big Island trip, I started writing again. And when I couldn't handle my own thoughts, I drank—bookending all the time I spent pulling weeds from the lily pond with alcohol.

Laid over at the Portland, Oregon airport on our way back to Austin, I had a drink at the bar.

"Hittin' the bottle lately, huh?" the General said, sitting next to me with our luggage.

I shrugged, sipping my to-the-brim Cosmopolitan. "Write drunk, edit sober," I said.

I pulled out my journal and started scribbling. The more I drank, the more uninhibited I was with my own words; the angst was easier to handle drowning under the influence of alcohol.

An announcement at our gate blared through the speakers. "Passengers boarding flight five-one-two to Austin, Texas—your flight has been delayed."

I looked up from my journal. "That's us."

"Lemme go see what's going on," the General said, leaving his Coke at the bar.

Once my empty martini glass bared the symbol of a budding alcoholic, he came back.

"There's an issue with the engine." He sighed, wearing his dimpled think-y face. "I don't want to wait at the airport all night. We have the option to bump ourselves to tomorrow, no extra cost. Let's pay this tab and find a hotel." He motioned to the bartender, pointing to our drinks. The bartender nodded.

In the cab, the General called around looking for a room and found one at The Westin.

"From a jungle tent in Pahoa to The Westin. I'll take it. I'm dying for an indoor bathroom, maybe even a soak in the tub after our outdoor shower and shared bidet experience," I said, enjoying the start of a good buzz.

We checked into the hotel and called my brother-in-law, who'd been house and dog-sitting, to let him know we'd be at least another day, depending on when we could get back.

By the time we settled into our room it had started to rain. In our luxurious suite, with a king-sized bed, we had a view of Portland. Pastel-grey clouds hung over the city, and a light rain dragged itself down the windows in long, sad streaks. The weather outside, coupled with the unrest inside of me, created the perfect storm—perfect for more drunk journaling.

"Hey, let's get room service," I said, excited by the thought of someone delivering drinks to our room. I'd already made plans to drink, soak in a tub, dry off, then journal wearing a plush, white robe.

As I watched the infamous Oregon drizzle move through the city, I sipped my DIY Cosmo via room service. Snug in a fluffy hotel bathrobe, I wrote more and wrote hard. With every sip and with every scribble, I found more hidden harm buried in deep, dark corners. Only the pain didn't occupy my mind—I found it lingering in a hollow cave inside my chest.

I crawled inside, moving heavy cobwebs, teeming with memories that stuck to my hands. Pulling apart long strands of viscous netting, Trauma revealed herself to me and she was ugly. She slithered toward me, reached out, and squeezed both my wrists, affixing herself to me.

Scowling, I managed to free one of my arms back in haste. She threw her head back and laughed, yanking me in further. I clawed at her gelatinous tentacle with my free hand, trying to wiggle loose, but her grip was too firm. She grasped tighter and pulled at me again, unwavering.

I tried to tell her that I'd seen more than enough, I couldn't take any more, but Trauma forced me to stay. She showed me more humiliating things I'd done and said, things other people had done, lies, more fear, more loneliness.

She latched onto my budding self-acceptance and dignity, twisting their limbs around her fist until they almost snapped away from me, becoming hers forever. I pulled them back while screaming, crying, pushing, and kicking. When I finally escaped, she slid after me, laughing freakishly. I bolted.

Free from her disgusting cruelty, I caught my breath, wiped away the remaining slime, and stood erect. Ensuring I had not lost self-acceptance and dignity, I cautiously walked down a cavernous hallway, relieved to be free from Trauma's lair.

I ran my fingertips along my ribcage, feeling them strum over my distal bone, *thhrmm, thhrmm, thhrmm.*

I came to where my heart dwelled and saw it pumping life over and over—beating, contracting, swelling. I stood in awe watching it, noticing that nothing destructive dared getting close. It was pure. Untouched. Content. *Thump, thump, thump;* it beat happily.

If my heart can keep going with Trauma skulking nearby, I have nothing to worry about.

I backtracked, running my open palms over my ribcage—*thhrmm, thhrmm, thhrmm*—walked down the hallway, and back inside the cave.

I snuck past a now-sleeping Trauma, slovenly lying in her own mucus and filth and made my way out of her webbed mess to find solace back in our suite.

Settling into a Cosmopolitan-drenched fog, while sitcom reruns played on the TV well past midnight, I lay safe in the General's arms.

Over room service breakfast the next morning, I sat by the window and looked out to see Portland post-rain. Beautiful.

"What time is our flight today?" I asked, sipping coffee.

"It's not."

I scrunched my face. "What?"

"I moved it to tomorrow, no fees. I booked another night and rented a car. Since we're here, and Portland is Austin's *sister city*," he said, quoting the air, "why not check it out?"

"When the hell did you do all that?" I asked.

"While you were sleeping off your DIY drinks."

I looked at him through squinted eyes. He winked.

The first place we went to was Powell's Books. Bringing me to a bookstore that required a map upon entry was a sure sign that the General was buttering me up for something, and my answer would most assuredly be *yes* to a question he hadn't asked yet. I ignored the map, allowing myself to get lost in the stacks for as long as the General could stand it. I got as many books as my carry-on bag could handle.

From Powell's we moved on, briefly taking in the cityscape then venturing out of Portland, going deep into Oregon's wine country. We walked along Third Street in McMinnville, and I fell for its quaint charm immediately.

"What're we doing? Touring random cities on an extended layover?"

He ignored my question, said "Let's go to a wine tasting," and dragged me into a local winery.

"I don't drink wine that often, you know I'm allergic. The sulfite—"

"C'mon, who ever heard of an Italian allergic to wine?"

I don't know what it was about local Oregon wine, but I had no allergic reactions to it. In fact, I had a decent buzz going. Walking down Third Street toward another tasting room he finally admitted that he was buttering me up for something.

"I thought so. Books, wine, walking around cute, little cities. *Antiquing!*"

"Remember the guy I worked with when we first moved to Austin?"

I nodded.

"He's vice president of a shop just outside of Portland. They do some kickass welding there and he offered—"

My eyes bugged. "Offered what?"

"Offered me a job."

How had I not seen this coming? I typically felt something on the horizon long before it arrived. My super-gut's silence unnerved me.

"We don't have to move if you don't want to, it was just an idea."

It wasn't the idea of moving that ticked me off. I didn't mind uprooting myself. I'd done it so many times I was a pro at knowing what to pack first, what to pack last, the best routes to take, and which rest stops had the best food. What got to me was the sudden absence of my instincts.

"It's not the moving, even though we have a wicked, badass place in a sweet neighborhood. What about Max? Stormy just moved away; I mean…" I sighed and looked away, fighting off the tears of Stormy's absence. "We have a fenced-in yard, a doggy door for Liesel, a garden, friends, Max loves his new school—he's in a magnet school for Christ's sake," I said.

"Being in Austin's been great. But it's jam-packed; I can't go ten miles without being in my truck for an hour. And all the things we've talked about—getting a Volkswagen bus, living off the land…Oregon would be the perfect place for that. And this welding opportunity…" He looked into the distance, no doubt seeing sparks fly at the mere thought of working on whatever kickass welding projects this Portland company had.

I looked at my General with pure envy.

What would it feel like to harbor no resentment for your job? What's it like to create something from nothing without childhood memories getting in the way? This dimpled jerk puts his gloved hands up and builds something with passion and zeal, every day. And most days I just—

"We don't have to decide here and now. C'mon, let's go get some dinner."

We walked down Third Street and stopped at McMenamin's.

"McMenamin's in McMinnville," the General said.

"Say that five times fast."

I could feel a shift in energy when the door opened. As soon as we walked in and were seated, I felt ancient spirits circling above me. The dimly lit pub emitted a comforting mourn. Contented sadness wrapped itself around me, like a light, warm blanket, and said, "Come in; we've been waiting for you."

That was the moment I decided that my dark insides had met their match. *Oregon might be just what I need to calm this pent-up J-Dub, CODA bullshit.*

I silently consented to moving to the Pacific Northwest while eating hot-sauce-drenched tater tots and drinking an Old Fashioned.

By the end of Max's sixth grade year, I was asking my part-time VRS boss for a transfer.

"A transfer? To Salem, Oregon?" Sitting across from me was Jack with the saddest look I'd seen him wear in a long time. "But Kebah, we're like family."

Kebah was a nickname most people at the VRS center called me. One of the Deaf managers could *not* grasp the spelling of my name. The K, B, and H moved about aimlessly in her brain; "Kebah" was the name that stuck, it was better than "Rehak." Everyone thought Kebah was cute.

Except me. Not because I hated it but because I'd given up on correcting people when they misspelled my name, and I grew tired reminding them what I preferred to be called. The sad truth was, I didn't know who I was, so what would I have had them call me?

"I'll start the transfer and introduce you to the manager in Salem via chat but let me leave you with one thought-slash-question. Are you running toward something or away from something?"

I opened my mouth to answer, but he interrupted with the palm of his hand.

"Don't answer. Just think about it," he said.

I did think about it. All the way to Oregon I thought about it. The only time I didn't think about it was when Stormy (she'd flown to Austin to help us move) and I stopped at the Area 51 Alien Travel Center in Nevada, just to be sure civilization still existed.

Relieved to find life, we got gas and food. We saw people, antique alien exhibits, cardboard stand-up aliens for photo keepsakes, and a brothel. Yup, that's right. Behind the Area 51 combination gift shop, restaurant, and gas station was a hidden alien cathouse for all the extraterrestrial fantasies you can handle.

Thinking back to my Big Island Wild Donkey Chase and the lush canyons surrounding Hedonisia in Pahoa, I remembered how small I felt then, and it mirrored that moment.

Nothing throws you into existential wonder quite like isolated desert canyons, wide open highways, alien-themed whorehouses, and the recent memory of running away from monstrous donkeys with a fistful of limes.

"I wonder if anal probing is part of the package or if that's extra?" I said, putting my sunglasses on.

Stormy rolled her eyes and plopped into the driver's seat.

In northern California, I feared for my life. Stormy drove on a very narrow road that curved around the edge of a cliff; there was no guardrail to block the fall I was certain would happen. My anxiety sprang to life, and I was sure we'd die right there.

"Do you remember that movie with Lucy and Desi, *The Long, Long Trailer*?" I asked, gripping the door handle, closing one eye.

"I think so. The one where they buy a trailer and drive all over the country?" she asked.

"Mm-hmm," I said.

"Why?"

"No reason."

I reimagined Lucy and Desi, towing their forty-foot trailer, rounding the edge of a cliff as I heard my heart thump in my ears, readying myself for the imminent fall.

Multi-Level Culting

THE GREY RANCH set on a small plot of land halfway down a dead-end street in McMinnville, Oregon. Not unlike the road I grew up on in Northfield, NH. Only this house was surrounded by thriving, green grass, a beautiful garden, apple trees, and a grape vine.

The three cement steps leading to the front door felt a bit unwelcoming. I unlocked the door and felt *something* hit me as soon as I stepped in.

The front entrance spilled into the living room. Directly across from where I stood, a wall of small, square mirrors was grouped into one large body.

And that was the first time I felt *her*.

"Whoa. Have some mirrors," Stormy said, putting Squints down on the carpet—his condition had worsened; we carried him everywhere like a sack of potatoes.

Liesel ran in and rubbed herself all over the thick, sandy-brown carpet. Squints, already on the floor, joined her.

I stepped in further.

Standing in the living room, I looked to my left and saw a long hallway. Pulled in, as if by force, I walked left. Stepping cautiously, the first room I saw was on my left. *Max's room,* I thought.

I looked ahead and saw a full-length mirror at the end of the hallway on the back wall. I walked toward my own reflection. Standing in front of myself, there were two rooms. The one on the left was spacious and carpeted—

"My room," Stormy said, walking into the empty space.

This left the room on the right. I turned my head and saw the master bedroom with light grey, industrial-type linoleum covering the floor. The windows overlooked the backyard.

I turned around and walked back toward the living room, the wall-of-mirrors now on my left. Next to the mirrors was an entrance, leading into the kitchen. I walked through and to my right saw just where my Formica table would go—next to the windows on the side of the house, facing the driveway.

An old rotary phone hung on the wall by the windows, and I chuckled. *At least this one doesn't have a strobe light above it.*

To my left were vintage, Formica countertops, a stove, and a pantry. It all seemed normal. Except for the hollow window frame, no glass, above the kitchen sink. The window frame looked over another room.

I walked straight and down one step. It seemed the further and further I stepped into the alternate reality that *was* this house, the stranger it became.

In the left-hand corner was a fireplace. Next to that were sliding glass doors leading to the backyard. The backyard was gorgeous and inviting. But there was a curious door to my immediate right.

I opened it and found the garage I knew the General would be spending most of his time in, tinkering with tools and metal scraps. Bored by the thought, I turned and walked back into the mystery room.

Across from where I stood, there was another door between the fireplace and washer/dryer leading to the back corner of the house.

Why so many escape routes?

I spun around and walked back into the kitchen. I turned right and found the bathroom behind a closed door, next to the pantry on my left. I walked in.

To my right—a sink and a tub with no shower head or curtain rod. Straight ahead and to the left was the toilet, behind a half-partitioned wall. Across from the toilet was another sink and medicine cabinet.

Not only did the bathroom have two sinks but two doors—one behind me leading back into the kitchen, and the other, to my left, leading into the long hallway across from Max's room. I stepped through the door connected to the hallway, and to my immediate left was another door that was already ajar.

"Bekah, come upstairs!" Stormy said from afar.

I pulled on the antique door handle and looked up to see a set of old, wooden stairs.

"It's like an attic, only—" Stormy said.

"Only what?" I asked, a bit guarded, walking up the stairs.

"Well, it's weird up here."

At the top of the stairs, I turned to my right. Around the corner—a big empty room was nestled under a pitched roof. A wooden, raised platform was built into the rickety floor, butted up against the wall, near the only window the attic had.

I envisioned someone strapped to it as cruel experiments took place. I could clearly see the victim wiggling in a panic, releasing muffled screams from behind a cloth gag.

"Find anything else besides that?" I asked, pointing to the platform.

"No."

We both scanned the room, searching for a secret trapdoor inside the eaves, hiding a pile of dead bodies.

"No dead bodies?" I asked.

"Nope."

We heard the General's truck pull into the driveway, and we did our best to settle in. I did my best to make peace with the floating vibe I'd felt as soon as we arrived.

On my thirty-eighth birthday, I woke to the smell of warm apples coming from the kitchen.

"Is that how it's supposed to look?" I heard a now-twelve-year-old Max ask from the kitchen.

"Yeah, it looks good, buddy," the General said.

I walked past the wall-of-mirrors into the kitchen. "Hi."

"You're not supposed to be in here," Max said, nudging me.

"Whoops, sorry," I said, walking back into the living room, unsure what to do with myself.

"Oh, and happy birthday," Max said.

"Happy birthday," Stormy said, elbows deep in her own cooking project.

The General handed me a cup of coffee, kissed me, wished me a happy birthday, and put a DVD into the player. "Just relax. We're making you breakfast."

I looked at the TV perched atop my old bookshelf, where books were already arranged on shelves according to size, and *The Long, Long Trailer* had begun.

I thought about how weird it felt for our misfit family to be celebrating my birthday. The four of us hadn't been together on this day since the Mount Washington cruise five years before. The kids had always been in NH with their mother.

The apple trees in our backyard allowed them to make homemade apple crisp for breakfast using a recipe from Jodi's cookbook, *Homemade and Wholesome*. Afterward, we went to Powell's Bookstore, followed by a late lunch in an old Italian restaurant where I drank cilantro martinis.

That summer, we took gorgeous hikes, ate in restaurants, drank hard cider and more cilantro martinis, attended two of McMinnville's Annual Third Street Festivals (Turkey-Rama and Dragging-the-Gut), strolled the McMinnville Farmer's Market, and spent hours at Powell's.

One Saturday, the General, kids, and I went to Portland for a live workout with the Hard Bottoms trainer that nearly killed us two years before. We heard Jimmy Heston was visiting the area, and we wanted to see if we could survive an hour with him.

During the presentation segment, my inner compass spun in several directions when I heard the CEO say, "It's not multi-level marketing, it's multi-level *helping*."

I looked at the General and whispered, "What's multi-level marketing? I thought we were just working out with Jimmy?"

He shrugged.

I looked around and saw some fit, muscular people, some not so fit people, and all body types in between wearing yoga pants, clutching chocolate shakes, and neon yellow-colored drinks. Everyone was seated quietly, hanging on every word tearfully while diligently taking notes.

The veins in my body switched on full force. I realized the only thing missing from this event was a Bible, accompanied by a *Watchtower* magazine, in every lap.

After the kids flew to NH, and after this multi-level *helping* workout event, an old friend I'd reunited with via social media talked me into becoming a fitness coach with Hard Bottoms.

She added me to Facebook groups full of women I knew I wouldn't be friends with if I'd met them on my own; I had nothing in common with them. Most of them were religious, athletic types, tying their fitness coaching in with their own belief systems.

"God wants you to be healthy!"

"I work out to glorify Him!"

"God gifted me with this body and I'm taking care of it!"

I forced the chunks rising to slide back down my throat while mentally going through my closet-of-chameleon suits, looking for an appropriate one to wear.

The friend I'd reunited with gave me marketing advice.

"You're already doing the hard part—the workouts—now you just need to share what you're doing on social media, take selfies while holding the shake, and oh! You need to buy the shake every month to remain active; getting the pre-workout, wouldn't hurt, either. And pop into people's inboxes, inviting them to your online challenge club," she said.

That's when the gut-jab was too intense to ignore.

"Invite them?" I asked, roaming our backyard, one eye on Liesel and the other on Squibbs.

"Yeah. When you post a sweaty selfie—"

"Which is lame, by the way," I said.

"Get used to it. When you post, make a list of who likes or comments on it and send them a message like, 'Hey, girl! I saw you liked my post! I have a little group online you might—"

"Hey, girl? I wouldn't say that." It all sounded so fake. Not me. And "popping into someone's inbox" with an "invite" felt a lot like going door-to-door did as a kid.

"And make sure you're reading."

"I am. I'm Reading *Darkly Dreaming Dexter*—the books the show *Dexter* is based on."

She laughed. "Um, try something a bit more uplifting. Like, *Miracle Morning*."

Miracle Morning?

The most I'd done up until that point was try a different workout with a new trainer, drink the company's protein shake a few times, and workout at home. I had no interest in "building my business" or trading in my *Dexter* paperbacks for inspirational boo hockey.

But once the General adorned himself with coach status after our live workout experience—placing himself beneath me in the coach pyramid for moral support—things changed. I moved up in a company that I had no intentions of staying with.

I suddenly had a small, private, online community and was publicly posting sweaty selfies, workout tips, recipes, fitness memes, and even some of my own very personal experiences.

"It's all about relationships; engagement. Talk about your struggles—not only your fitness-related struggles, but real-life battles. You want your followers to relate to you, feel close to you, confide in you about their own struggles, and then, when you've built a relationship, ask them to join your next workout group," a top-earning coach advised in a live, online training.

My intimate social media posts got lots of traction. They were one hundred percent true, but I was using them for attention and the potential sales that followed. I hated how that felt, but I started ignoring my moral compass like a pro. Hell, I'd done it so many times before—in the Truth, with Dean, with Asshat—what would one more time hurt?

Then, things I'd learned on my journey down the ex J-Dub rabbit hole appeared in my mind, arranging themselves into sentences, and it all started to make sense.

I thought about the little butterball that had witnessed to my parents all those years ago. Knocking on their door, she had found them in a vulnerable state. My parents relayed their woes at the kitchen table with her, confided in her, and no doubt felt close to her. Then they began home bible studies, went to meetings at the Kingdom Hall, and the rest is history.

Though I knew the "Hey, girl!" shit wasn't me—whether for the false promise of life everlasting, or for a quick sale to move up the rungs of a multi-level marketing company—I did it anyway. I had already done it for most of my formative years; it didn't take much to fall back into old cult-like habits.

An unknown autopilot surfaced and began flying a plane I thought I'd retired and sold for parts years ago. I didn't have to think twice about sending "Hey, girl!" messages once I was in flight at thirty thousand feet.

And boy, did I love the shit that sent me flying.

Waking sometime between 4:30 and 5 a.m., I'd stumble into

the kitchen. Retrieving a small, plastic tub from the cupboard, I'd unscrew its lid, and the whiff of lemon-scented powder would wake me instantly.

Shaking the contents, a clear, plastic ladle came into view. I'd dump one heaping scoop of yellow powder into a glass, fill it with eight ounces of water, and stir with a hard, reusable straw.

The first sip hit me the same way cocaine had years prior: it stung my nose as it dripped down the back of my throat. The label said, "all natural," but all I could taste was thick lemon, saturated with unpronounceable chemicals.

I'd sit on the couch, scrolling through my social media feeds, then take another sip. Then another. Before I knew it the glass was empty, and my entire body was on fire. My veins were highway lanes, permitting 80 mph.

My skin itched and buzzed. The container said (in very small print) "Some people may feel a mild tingling from the Beta-alanine."

Mild tingling?

I felt like I could lift any weight, climb any mountain, give a powerful speech ending in thunderous applause... *I am the Lizard King! I can do anything!*

I'd send messages to "at least five people a day," inviting them to my next challenge club, which I didn't even have plans for until suddenly, I did. I'd lose count of how many messages I'd sent and to whom. My focus was intense, but names rushed past me in streaks.

When I tired of that, I'd grab my latest personal growth book, amazed by every word I read. (Later, I'd look at this same book and ask, "Who edited this garbage?").

By that time, a groggy version of the General would saunter into the kitchen and for a good fifteen minutes, I'd ramble on about some epiphany I'd had within the last *three* minutes.

Then I'd leave him, bewildered at the kitchen table, and workout.

I'd do plyometric jumps with dumbbells, knee-tuck jumps, jump lunges with weights, squat jumping jacks while pressing weights overhead, and more, for thirty minutes. By the end, I was soaked, out of breath, and dizzy with blurred vision. It would take another thirty to forty minutes after my cooldown to get centered.

I'd subsequently go about my day at work, sharing relatable snippets on social media, remembering that my team lead had shared social media post suggestions. Mondays, motivation. Tuesdays, transformation. Wednesdays, recipes. Thursdays, vulnerable throwbacks, "I used to be so miserable but look at me now!" Fridays and Saturdays, our choice but usually an opportunity to share some deep passage, gleaned from a self-help book. And for Sundays, an eye-catching 7 p.m. post inviting everyone to join you on your wellness journey.

I made videos, posting them on social media openly talking about incredibly personal things. I shared before-and-after photos, then friended and invited strangers to my "challenge clubs." I "put myself out there" every day, became someone I wasn't. Even though I saw it coming, I didn't feel it happen; I'd been swept away by pre-workout and chocolate shakes.

If I found someone who was interested—which still felt too much like going door-to-door, pre-workout or not—I slowly introduced them to the idea of working out, meal-plans, and self-discovery. After sharing personal things about myself to be more relatable, I followed up, practically badgering folks.

Why was I so hellbent on selling when I instinctively knew multi-level culting was not my jam?

Simply put, I'd fallen for their low-hanging lemon-y fruit and when I looked up, I saw the pie in the sky. The more people one *helped*, the higher in the company they got. The higher they got, the bigger the paycheck. The bigger the paycheck, the bigger the heart.

Some coaches were master helpers with big hearts (and McMansions). But those top-earners were a mere handful in a sea of rank-and-file coaches, barely keeping their bills paid.

Hard Bottoms and their own prescribed cult-code of sleep deprivation via fucked up cortisol levels; intense workouts; strict calorie-counting meal plans; products auto-delivered monthly; and tiny slivers of hope buried in self-help books and an online community was more than enough to keep me one click away, wide open to anyone, ignoring gut-pokes and my own depleted inner battery.

Until *she* appeared again.

I loved her. I don't know why, but I loved her. She showed up exactly when I needed her. She knew it. I didn't. And she used it against me.

Her presence was benign at first. A light breeze would whoosh through the living room, then the faint smell of a lingering perfume would drift down the hallway. I wanted her intriguing presence to wrap itself around me and carry me through the vertiginous days that lay ahead.

Oftentimes, Liesel would rest in our bedroom snuggling Squibbs. Then, almost as if she heard a gunshot, she'd rush out of the room and race down the hallway into the living room. Stunned to find just me sitting on the couch, she'd look around like she missed something. Then, she'd meander back down the hallway confused.

The disturbed air I felt in the house on move-in day became much more prevalent once the kids had gone to NH for the remainder of the summer. I was left to face all those mirrors alone. The light breezes and lingering floral-scented perfume soon became shadowy whispers, impossible to ignore.

"Do you hear or feel anything, like, weird in this house?" I asked one night over dinner and local Oregon wine.

"Like what?" the General asked.

"I dunno, like, gentle breezes. Whispers?" I was slow to ask. I wasn't convinced I'd felt anything myself.

"Are the windows open?" he asked.

"No. Not like that, but I think even Liesel senses something. She'll bolt from the bedroom into the living room, look around all anxious, then walk back into the bedroom. And I hear, like, murmurs."

"No, I can't say I've sensed anything."

"Ugh. That's because you're the Tin Man."

Was it me and possibly the stranger I had become to myself? Or was there really something lurking, living between all the mirrors strategically placed around the house?

I was confident we were living with *something* the day I got home from work and noticed a black SUV parked in front of our house. I saw an older couple sitting in it, talking, pointing at our house. I walked toward the SUV.

"Hi, can I help you?" I asked, assuming maybe they were lost.

The gentleman from the driver's seat spoke. "Oh, no. Thank you. I was just showing her the house I was raised in."

"Oh, yeah?" I smiled, hoping he'd continue.

"Yeah, my brother and I shared the attic room. The two additions—"

"I wondered about the attic. You know, there's this wooden platform up there?" I said.

"That's where we slept. The additions, the large, tiled back bedroom and family room off the kitchen, weren't added until years later," he said.

"We thought so since the kitchen window above the sink is now just an open window frame-slash-shelf, overlooking the family room."

"Lots of memories there," he said, smiling.

241

"Did you want to come in? You're more than welcome to—"

"No, thank you!"

With that, he sped down the street, barely braking at the stop sign. I slowly turned to stare at the grey ranch. *Something is in that house.*

Thinking back to when my friend Diane and I had drinks at an outdoor Austin bar, I remembered her telling me that she and both her pit bulls had had several experiences with the other side in Hawaii. Experiences that gave her "chicken skin," as she put it. Her pit bull, Malia, often paced their apartment, checking doors, whenever *he* showed up. Those stories stuck with me.

I texted her.

"Hey, remember those spirit conversations we've had?"

"Yep. Why?"

Diane was a mirror I liked looking into; she housed hidden, positive pieces of me that just hadn't surfaced yet.

I explained all I had been feeling and experiencing. I told her about the previous resident's recent visit and how he hit the gas when I invited him and his lady-friend inside.

"There's something there. Does it feel harmful? Malicious?"

"I'm not sure? She feels heavy, mournful almost, and I think she wants something, but I don't know what."

"So, talk to her."

"Talk to her?"

"Yeah."

After my shower the next day, I walked into the bedroom. Dripping wet, wrapped in a towel, I stood before the mirrored closet doors.

A cold air passed through me, and I froze. I looked at my reflection and, directly behind me, saw Liesel on the bed with Squibbs, shielding him. Her head shot up and she looked around the room at warp speed. I backed myself toward the bed and sat down. The dogs didn't budge.

"Um, I know I'm not alone right now and I'm okay with that. I know you're here. I can feel you. I'm also okay with that. I won't get in your way. I'll take care of the house while I'm here then you can have it back. Stay as long as you like, do what you need to do. I'm okay with that."

I felt stupid talking to an entity I couldn't see, but I knew she was there. I held my breath and waited. The air around me lifted. Both dogs unclenched. But it wasn't enough.

I should never have told her I was okay with anything.

Charlotte's Place

I TOLD THE General about my encounter with the couple in the SUV and Charlotte.

"You named it?" he asked.

"No. The name surfaced on its own. I didn't name shit."

He looked at me like I had seven heads. He sighed, lightly shook his head, and said, "Well, this is all very...you."

"Meaning?"

"Doesn't your super spider-sense start its motor every so often?"

I nodded.

The General had quieted my inner force since we'd been together, the second-guessing had decreased significantly, but my superpower still kicked itself into high gear from time to time.

This wasn't that, though.

"Maybe since you're so in tune with it, you feel things that can't be explained."

"But why here? Why now? Why Oregon?"

He shrugged.

"Know what else is weird?" I asked.

"What?"

"My being able to spot a cult almost right away."

"What do you mean?" he asked.

I told him about the weird vibes I was picking up from Hard Bottoms.

"I don't feel any of that."

"Need I remind you that you're the Tin Man?"

The General didn't pick up on vibes very often or have sudden hunches. Sometimes he did, but it was pretty rare.

"Very funny. I'm only in it to support you. I don't mind the shake sometimes, and I do like the workouts. But you're in those groups way more than I am, and I don't post shit online."

"Yeah, there's that. I see all kinds of shit online that makes me feel..." I knit my brows and dipped my head to the side.

He shrugged and said, "Well, trust it, then."

Those kinds of conversations transported me to the tracks in my old backyard. Even though it had been years since I'd visited, whenever I felt confident enough to trust myself, I was instantly brought home to NH. Sometimes I could feel myself balancing on the rail, arms outstretched to avoid falling.

The truth was I didn't need my husband to tell me what I already knew, but he'd become a gut-check I relied on, a sounding board, a mirror, my own personal Joel.

I didn't mention Charlotte again, but I still felt tiny zephyrs and heard indistinct secrets floating around the house. She wasn't doing much more than that, so I figured we could cohabitate.

Max flew back to Portland as one somber twelve-year-old. No doubt he missed his NH family, felt left out, and fretted about fitting into a new school; his little life had been shaken by Stormy's absence.

I was consumed by my day job at the VRS company, sweaty smiles for my wanna-be fitness business, and entertaining the apparition I seemed to be on good terms with. I couldn't be bothered with a pre-teen.

I didn't love Max any less or stop doing what any parent is expected to do. I showed up to his school events in body, but my mind was usually preoccupied with how any event could be Facebook post-worthy, bringing in the most likes and comments to find potential workout buddies, and get them hooked on protein shakes and pre-workout.

And Charlotte—the starving, displeased specter that she was—found ways to thrust herself into everything I did or tried to do. And sometimes, she was a demanding bitch.

I thought I was the only one who felt her but when Max said, "I see a shadow sometimes. She's angry," my ears perked.

I asked him what it felt like.

"Like she's mad about something. It feels like she's following me, like she wants to hurt me."

The General listened, then said, again, that he felt nothing and didn't know what Max and I were talking about; he wasn't experiencing what we felt.

It'd be easy to say the energy in that house had spawned from our own personal suffering—ricocheting off the oddly-placed mirrors in that house—but Max felt it too and called it a "she" without prompting.

Soon enough, Charlotte began attacking Max through me; I chewed that poor kid a new asshole every chance I got. *I* was the sinister wraith—prowling, searching for anything—and when I thought I'd found something to browbeat him with, I'd pounce.

"Max, did you eat all the pepperoncini?" I shouted from the kitchen.

No answer.

"Max!"

He walked into the kitchen, visibly frightened, and said, "No. I saved some."

I screamed in his little freckled face.

"I was saving these for a salad! I need a specific amount to fill the Hard Bottom containers!"

He backed up.

I stepped closer. My face reddened. I shook, roaring that he was selfish, leaving barely enough in the jar for someone else.

246

The General came into the kitchen from the next room. I could feel him glaring at me from the corner of my eye. I knew better than to argue with a man holding two thirty-pound dumbbells.

"Lay off, we can buy more," the General said.

"That isn't the point! These were for me!" I said, eyes still on Max.

"Stop yelling at him."

Max started crying and flew into his room. The General went back into the all-purpose room to work out, leaving me in the kitchen to wonder why I was holding an almost-empty jar of pepperoncini.

I opened the fridge and put the pepper jar back, like it was possessed instead of me.

Get out, I told myself.

I grabbed my purse and left.

I drove down the street and took a sharp right, heading down Second Street. My car knew where to take me because before I knew it, I was parked by an old train station behind Remy's Winery.

Way too embarrassed to get out of the car, I sat, blubbering aloud, wondering why I cared so much about a jar of sour peppers.

Once calm, I went in to drink my misery and self-reproach away. I stayed until Remy closed, then sat at one of the outside tables, staring at the train tracks, curious if they'd lead all the way back to my beloved rails in NH.

Somewhat sober, I drove home, rushed inside, and went straight to the bedroom. I stayed there for the rest of the night, punishing myself with a time-out.

The air in the house was stale and unwelcoming. The three of us didn't speak to each other and Charlotte's presence was quiet. Almost as if she got what she wanted: friction.

The next morning, after Max left for school I went into his room. Unsure what I was looking for and unprepared for what I'd found.

His black, tubular, metal bunkbed was a twelve-year-old's dream. His bed was up top, and the bottom half was a desk where he read, did his homework, and played handheld video games. Nothing new there.

There were framed pictures on his desk—photos of him with his mother, him with Stormy, and other family members. I had given Max a framed photo of me and him, taken the day the General and I got married; we were locked in an embrace, smiling in Austin's graffiti park. That photo had taken up space on his desk before the Pepperoncini Incident. It was now face down, behind pictures of Cassie.

And could I blame him?

The house quickly became a dark den of shame. The air was thick and suffocating. Liesel was back to darting down the hall at odd hours of the day and night and poor Squibbs could only sit and wobble his way through any discomfort Charlotte cast upon the spaces we all shared.

"I'm sending Max to his mother's for Christmas," the General said.

"I think that's a good idea," I said. "I think we should take off for the holidays, too."

I didn't feel welcome at Charlotte's Place and was surprised the General had agreed on a weekend away, especially since he hadn't felt her presence at all.

Christmas Day, the General, the pups, and I drove to Depoe Bay, Oregon—a small oceanside town deserted during the winter months.

We'd made reservations for The Inn at Arch Rock and were met with a comfy room, overlooking a private cove. There was a welcome note on the kitchen table next to a decanter of sherry, with two crystal glasses just eager to be filled with liquor.

Our first night there, inside the Arch Rock's quaint kitchen, I'd made a tofu and broccoli teriyaki dish and we played cribbage game after cribbage game while drinking a bottle of Remy's Old-World Wine.

I savored that dinner because visiting an oceanside town for the weekend would mean I'd have seafood on my plate, which I hate. I imagined with each bite of over-greased Surf n' Turf, I'd need to take a big gulp of something alcoholic just to wash it down. The thought of fried scales rolling around in my mouth was despicable.

During our lunch date the next day—as scales were being broken down by my obstinate mouth enzymes—Charlotte had either made an appearance or summoned her Depoe Bay posse because I started to drill the General about the kids, Cassie, everything about being a stepparent that ailed me, and his e-cigarette: his precious binky.

I had gotten so loud, so drunk, and so obnoxious, people stared. The General stood up—tired of my bellyaching—and left me sitting in a booth in a dark corner of Gracie's Sea Hag Lounge. I paid the bill, stumbled to the downstairs bar, and joined the other sorry suckers alone for Christmas.

There was a time Christmas meant nothing to me, a time I didn't care about gifts, holiday lights, music, or movies—I was okay with that. When you don't know what you're missing, you don't miss shit.

But the General and his kids had made me care. They made me want to wrap presents, decorate, watch Christmas movies, go to a stupid Christmas parade, and gawk at Austin's Holiday Tree. They made me miss something I'd never missed before, and I was pissed. They'd made me part of the family, made me care too much, then suddenly they weren't there. And I felt orphaned again.

"What'll ya have, honey?" the bartender asked.

I really shouldn't drink anymore.

"A Cosmopolitan with an extra drop of lime juice. I like them sour and a bit unwelcoming, like me. And don't be shy with the vodka."

Cosmo after Cosmo I sank deeper into my own loneliness and angst. In a drunken haze, I grabbed the journal out of my bag and started to write about how much I hated Christmas, the General, marriage, being a stepparent, and the stupid dive bar I was drunkenly scribbling illegible words from in a sad, desolate, oceanside town. I calmed myself long enough to wax drunk and stupid with a few strangers at Gracie's bar, then collected the shattered remains of my dignity and left her Sea Hag Lounge.

Then I remembered I was without transportation.

Cursing the General for ditching me in a local watering hole, I zig-zagged down the street, passing all the novelty shops that would've been open had it been July.

Mannequins, dressed in neon-colored muscle tank tops that flaunted "Surf's up!" "Beach Bum," and "Tons of fun on 101!" caught the corner of my eye while stumbling down the hill.

I wasn't planning on calling him. I was sure I could find my way back to the inn. It was just a straight shot toward the bay; one blurry, far-off-in-the-distance bay.

After vaguely making out the ass end of my car at the inn's parking lot, I found the door to our room. Stumbling in the dark, trying to locate the room key didn't come easy and, in the process, I had broken my glasses.

I opened the door to find a sleeping General. If anything upset him, that's what he'd do—sleep. He'd been sleeping a lot.

I greeted Liesel and Squibbs, got into bed, closed my eyes, and tried to focus on the spinning black circles behind my eyelids.

In the morning not a word was spoken.

But as was custom, any argument could be remedied with sex. There were times we wouldn't speak for days due to some fight gone bad, but we could usually soften the tension with angry sex, complete with mild choking and hard slaps across the face.

And sometimes, he'd just find a rug to sweep the discomfort under. We often resolved our differences via violent sex or vigorous sweeping.

Back in Mac (McMinnville's nickname), on New Year's Eve, we stayed home with wine and pizza. I fell asleep long before midnight with a vegetarian magazine in my lap while the General watched *Making a Murderer.*

Max was scheduled to fly back to Portland just after the New Year. Things between us had been off since the Pepperoncini Incident. The framed photo of us at the graffiti park was still face down on his desk.

Standing at the gate, waiting for our unaccompanied minor, I stood with my arms outstretched, ready for him to bounce into my embrace the way he had in Austin years ago.

He sauntered down the jetway, an embarrassed half-smile escaped his lips, and he stood limp as I hugged him. I could remember being embarrassed by my parents' very existence and how dreadful my pre-teen and teenage years were. I tried to hang my disappointment there, but I couldn't help taking it personally.

The General had no problem chalking Max's sullenness up to pre-teen angst and his attempt to hold onto the jagged pieces of a broken family. Stormy was in NH—now sixteen, with a driver's license, looking into colleges. Max was with us, lonely without Stormy and Cassie's huge side of the family around.

Max went to his room, unpacked, then came out while I was making dinner to say he no longer wanted to live with us in Oregon. He wanted to go back to NH.

Logically, and because the General had repeatedly said so, I knew Max's desire to be with his mother had little to do with me and more to do with the family unit that had been broken long before I came along.

Just the same, abandonment, shame, worthlessness, and betrayal came back with a vengeance. My family obeying a group of religious, old men; Kelly going to Memphis; Asshat jilting me; Stormy leaving us in Austin; and Max wanting to leave all surfaced simultaneously.

I couldn't figure out why almost everyone I'd let into my life left. Was it me? I am not, after all, a soft, airbrushed Olan Mills picture. I'm a gritty Old Western photograph.

Without invitation, I told Max no; it wasn't going to happen. Being twelve, the decision wasn't his to make. It wasn't my place at all, but my train-track self had spoken and wasn't about to let someone else leave.

Max looked at me with tears in his eyes.

"Let's talk in your room," the General said as they left me in the kitchen, holding a wooden spoon.

They were in there for hours. I knocked once and was met with a gruff, "What do you want?" from the General.

"Um, supper."

"Not now," he said.

A little while later, the three of us ate a lukewarm dinner in silence. As the days went by, Max distanced himself more and more.

Again, could I blame the kid?

Charlotte's Inedible Truths

THE GREYNESS OF an Oregon winter had gotten to me. I could almost understand Bundy, Kemper, and Dahmer. Leave it to someone like me to get guys like them, but from what I'd read about their abandonment issues—along with the sadness that complements the soggy Pacific Northwest—I was convinced I shared something dark with these men.

"I stopped at the store on my way home," the General said, holding a small, brown paper bag. He dumped the contents onto the kitchen table.

"Ooh, brownies," Max said, eyeballing all the prepackaged treats on the table.

"Those brownies aren't for you. You can have this one," the General said, handing Max one particular brownie, "but not those."

"Why not those?" I asked, pointing to the table.

"Those are special brownies. For us. It's legal here, and I think we could use it."

"Okay. I've never had an edible before." I opened a package and took a bite of the brownie, eager to leave behind the serial killers I was beginning to understand.

"Whoa. Take it easy. Eat a quarter not the whole thing. Trust me," he said, breaking the brownie into quarter pieces.

We each ate our piece.

"Ooh, those are yummy, just one more bite," I said, taking another piece.

The General gave me a look of caution.

After supper and kitchen cleanup, we sat on the couch and played cribbage. Halfway through one game I looked at the General.

"Is it my turn?" I asked.

"I think so. I don't know… Did I just count?" he asked.

"I don't know?" I studied the eight and seven cards intently. "Am I holding fifteen?"

"I'm not sure," he said, inspecting the Seven of Spades.

"I don't think I can play anymore. I can't count." I started to giggle.

"Maximus!" the General bellowed.

Max peeked his head out of his room, which was right off the living room. "Yeah?"

"What're you doing? Come here and sit with us," the General said.

"Playing a game. Why're you yelling?" he asked, coming into the living room.

"Am I? Sorry. Wanna watch *Inside Out*?" The General clicked on Amazon and searched our video library.

Max sat at one end of the couch, looking at us. "Did you guys eat those brownies?"

I ignored his question.

"It's kind of cold in here. Are you cold? I think it's cold. I need a blanket."

I grabbed the thick, king-sized, t-shirt quilt I'd sewn three Christmases ago—with my, the General, Max, and Stormy's t-shirts stitched together, bound to fleece backing. I wrapped myself into a burrito, attempting to ground myself.

The room inhaled, exhaled, swelled, receded. The mirrors on the living room wall, leading into the hallway, beckoned me. The room felt smoky, unreal; like a low-budget MTV heavy metal video.

I waited for a sleazy lead singer, wearing leather pants and a shredded crop-top, to peek his teased head out from behind the bathroom door, mid scream. It didn't happen, of course, but it might've been enough to distract me from the dizzying thoughts that followed.

I trembled, fixing my eyes to the TV.

Once *Inside Out's* main character, Riley, and her parents moved across country, her budding emotions drove her into a frenzy. Pixar's rendition of her animated feelings was vibrant and loud, demanding attention.

I looked at Max—innocently engrossed in the movie—and felt a wave of guilt come over me, driving me further into the confines of a poorly-sewn, quilted-patchwork of our family's recent past.

He looked at me while I stared at him.

"What?" he asked.

I reached over, wrapped him inside the safety of our family quilt, and hugged him. "Oh, god, do you feel like Riley? Do you hate us for moving so many times? Did we fuck up?" I swayed back and forth with an irritated pre-teen in my arms.

"I'm fine, Bekah." He reassuringly tapped my forearm.

"We're horrible parents. You must hate us."

I couldn't stop the guilt, shame, or irrepressible quiver from seizing my body and mind into total dishevelment. Then, paranoia set in. I released Max from my embrace, coddled myself inside the quilt, and stared at the TV screen.

I hadn't been myself since we moved to Oregon. It wasn't Oregon's fault; it was a beautifully sad and soggy place, full of wonder, homeless spirits abound. It was more the stress of not feeling like I belonged with anyone, anywhere.

And it was also her.

Charlotte had made it clear: we were on her turf, and she did *not* like children. I had given up on explaining her ominous presence to the General; he didn't feel a spirit whatsoever. But Max and I knew better. Charlotte shat all over the relationship we once had, transforming it into uncomfortable tension.

I could remember carrying Max around when he was just six years old...

"Bekah, can I play Brick Breaker on your Blackberry?" Max's tiny voice asks from below my waist. I look into his green eyes, surrounded by freckles and gorgeous blond hair, knowing it'd be hard to ever tell him "No."

"Yeah." I smile, handing him my Blackberry.

"Pick me up. Watch me play, I'm good," he says.

I pick him up, setting his boney six-year-old butt on my hip and watch him break bricks on my smartphone.

Six years later, framed photos of us hugging sat face down on his desk. Hugs turned into reassuring taps on my forearm, and he no longer wanted to live with us.

I didn't know whether Charlotte was some separate entity wreaking havoc on our lives, or if she was a suppressed part of me, come to life. All I knew was I had to get out of Oregon, I had to get out of that house. It was clear Charlotte had not shown herself so she and I could become friends.

My people, my dogs, and my possessions had all surrounded me. The house should have felt like home, but it didn't. It was Charlotte's Place through and through. Each time the living room breathed, it cried. The inhalation and exhalation I'd just felt became desperate and panicked.

The mirrors didn't help. They were everywhere, making it impossible for me to avoid myself. Even a medicated brownie wasn't an escape, it was just another mirror. All my doubts, insecurities, mistakes, and sadness morphed into a hand (*was it Charlotte's?),* grabbed the back of my head, and forcefully shoved it into the mirrors within me, screaming, "Don't turn away! Look!"

"I can't watch this movie anymore," I said.

Dressed in heavy homemade armor, I got up, staggered down the hall—passing mirrors along the way—and went into our bedroom. Liesel followed.

I lay on the bed, in the dark, staring at the ceiling. Moments later I heard the General shuffle down the hall and come into the bedroom, giggling.

"Hey, whaddya doin' in here?" his thick New England accent asked.

I waved him away with the flitter of my hand from my limp wrist, and said, "I think I'm freakin' out."

"Why?" He sat down on the bed and looked at me—the dark outline of his face was utterly adorable.

"Oh, no. You can't be in here. I told you, I'm freakin' out. Go away."

I turned my head away from him and closed my eyes, attempting to find solace behind my eyelids. I inhaled and exhaled, like the rooms in that house.

He rubbed my limp wrist, still midair, propped on the bed via my elbow. He wouldn't leave.

I calmed my breathing, collected my thoughts, and went deep into Charlotte's existence. I thought if I could fully describe it, he'd believe me.

Again, I told him about the whispers; the faint smells coming from nowhere; quick gusts of wind inside the house while windows were closed; the fact that Max also felt her and saw shadows; Liesel running up and down the hall searching; and poor Squibbs bobbing his head at random moments, looking for something.

I expressed a deep, uncertain need to leave Oregon. I didn't understand it myself, but we had to get out. I said I was afraid of what might happen if we stayed. I didn't trust my feelings. I didn't want to do or say anything more I would regret. I had already said and done enough.

I shook inside my quilted burrito, anxious for his response.

"Well, I guess we make plans to go home then," he said.

"Which home?"

There was our childhood home—riddled with trauma we didn't want to revisit—and there was our adult home.

"Austin. I'm not ready for New Hampshire now, maybe not ever."

If I could have loved this man more, I surely would have. The General still wasn't convinced about Charlotte's existence, but he said he'd been battling his own demons and Austin was the best place for us. My lifeblood was returning to normal with the mere thought of going back.

To say Max was ecstatic would be an understatement. He'd made friends in Oregon and seemed to enjoy our sporadic day trips—taking in lush scenery while searching for Bigfoot—but his friend base, along with memories of Stormy when she'd lived with us, were still roaming the streets of Austin. Going back was sure to make us all feel better.

We secured an apartment online; finding a rental in Austin from afar was stupidly easy. Come April we'd be basking in the sunshine of an Austin spring and be back just in time to attend a Blue October concert at Stubbs BBQ. I filled days with my own personal Blue October soundtrack to hush Charlotte's incessant protesting.

We resolved to make the most of our time by seeing all we could before we left. We spent many an afternoon at Remy's with our wine crew, we strolled along Third Street in Mac while window shopping and drank in the back bar at Nick's Italian Café.

From Third Street, Nick's was an upscale Italian restaurant drawing in tourists. Passing a small dumpster on a narrow side street/alley was how we locals—we'd been in Mac long enough to call ourselves that—entered Nick's.

The back room had a pool table, timeworn brick decorated with old Italian photos, and a wooden shelf, wrapping around the entire room, lined with dusty wine bottles. I sat at the bar and waited for Johnna, the bartender, to come around.

She looked at me and smiled, "Cosmo, sweetie?"

I nodded, fishing the most recent library book from my bag—*A Clockwork Orange*. I'd seen the movie with Carter once and hoped the book would be enough to distract me until we left.

With a fresh Cosmo in front of me, I shielded myself from hollow bar conversation with the book. I sank deeper into my stool, leaned back, and for a moment felt peace.

People intrigue me. I love their energy, stories, and genuine goodwill. I don't think most people are ill-intentioned and if they are, it only makes me want to talk to them more.

What I don't like is idle, meaningless chit-chat. I could feel the gentleman sitting next to me dying to do just that—talk small. He peered at me from the corner of his eye. I felt his stare.

I looked over and smiled.

"*Clockwork Orange*, huh?" he asked.

"Yeah." I looked at the front of the book as if I had no idea what I'd been reading. "I was hoping to expel some demons."

"I dunno how to tell ya this, honey, but readin' that will only wake 'em up." He released a gruff laugh; the backed-up smoke in his lungs rumbled.

I laughed and said he might be right about that.

After I'd decided to chat with the guy who seemed to know *A Clockwork Orange* was risky reading, the General came up behind me.

"Hey sweet-haaht," he said.

I love his stupid accent.

"Hi. Where's Max?" I asked; it was a random weekday, just after school had let out.

"He's with Carlos. They're gonna get some pizza on Third Street and play video games."

The General ordered a Moscow mule, then summoned me to the pool table. He suggested we make a list of pros and cons, for both Austin and Oregon.

I leaned against the exposed brick, furrowed my brow, and folded my arms in protest.

He said he wanted to be sure. He loved his new job, the people, the food, the environment, and all the beauty that *is* Oregon.

"We have no ties here," I lamented.

"Remy's?" he asked, smiling.

"Don't you dare use Remy's winery against me."

I loved Remy's wine. Sometimes I'd go to her place to watch her dad drive the forklift, moving squished grapes into a barrel to ferment while I sipped the fruits of their labor.

"What about Sarie?" he asked, sipping his Moscow mule.

I had one coworker-turned-friend from Maine, Sarie; we shared past lives in New England, but we didn't see much of each other outside of working at Western Oregon University.

"I love Sarie, but she's leaving Portland soon, too."

"Didn't you just make a friend at your Hard Bottoms live training?" he asked, arranging balls on the pool table.

The little voices telling me Hard Bottoms was a cult were hushed because my social life was almost nonexistent. I was lonely and bored, looking for a purpose, a distraction. I instinctively knew religious, stay-at-home #BossBabe moms building an online empire while obsessing over their social media following, team volume, rank points, bonuses, and six-figure incomes weren't my people.

I shook my head, sipped my Cosmo, and thought, *the only other friend I have is Charlotte and I wouldn't necessarily call her a friend.*

I set my martini glass down, readied myself for a break shot, and said, "You're forgetting one major reason Austin wins."

I hit the cue ball. A few stripes and solids scattered. None found a pocket.

"What's that?" he asked, lining up his shot.

"Max. He was happier in Austin, maybe he wouldn't want to leave us if he's closer to Hawk and Felix." Hawk and Felix were Max's best friends, they'd sort of become our buds, too.

He nodded, calling the striped eleven into the corner pocket.

The General made the lists anyway. One pro for Oregon was Bigfoot; he knew how to tug at my morbid curiosity and use it against me. Even though I hadn't seen the evasive sasquatch— and might've stayed in Oregon longer for that reason alone— by the end of our game, the Austin pro list was much longer.

We had close friends, Austin had a huge CODA presence, our previous jobs were ours if we wanted, and let's not forget— Texas owns the sun for more than three hundred days a year. The rain in Oregon had left me incredibly droopy.

And then there was Max. He'd become my reason.

"Okay, we go back. I just wanted to be sure. I do miss Opa," he said.

What I had felt all along finally paired up with the General's need for logic. He filtered information via mental lists until he could extract lucidity, whereas I experienced tidal waves of overwhelming feelings. Understanding my own emotions was often a challenge, but I couldn't rely on much else.

A few weeks before leaving, we took a day trip to Newport, Oregon; a charming oceanside town. With the clouds at bay, I was able to appreciate the same Pacific Northwestern beauty I knew the General had fallen in love with.

Wandering inside Newport's empty *Ripley's Believe It or Not!* museum, I felt her again. Only, this time, she didn't seem angry. She was melancholy, dejected. She came to me as I stood in front of an unsettling Bigfoot exhibit, and I couldn't turn her loose.

She lurked around the exhibit, slowly weaving her way in and around massive pines and Douglas firs. Behind the fake trees stood Bigfoot. There was nothing inviting about this yeti's presence. He was formidable. His eyes glowed between the trees. His mouth was slightly open, he gritted his sharp, crooked teeth in anger.

I moved on from the display with haste.

At an outdoor table, sitting at Ocean Bleu Gino's for lunch, we perused the bustling main street of Newport's tourist shopping district. Being among living people, as they strolled the sidewalks with their bags of designer chocolate from upscale candy shops, felt much safer than staring down a yeti from inside an empty museum.

Max, using his keen eye for photography, took pictures of neon boat fenders hanging from the slat-wood ceiling just above our heads. As he went on about how much he loved the detail, texture, dips, and crevices running along their surfaces, a tear fell down my cheek.

For the first time since we'd made the decision to go back to Austin, I felt an indescribable pull to stay. I felt a sudden shift; personal growth was just beginning to stir. To leave my own fated evolution felt blasphemous. I let the tears fall and barely made it through another scaly, greasy, Surf n' Turf lunch.

Walking along Bay Boulevard, ogling sea lions lounging on the docks, I found a wine tasting room. I tasted every red they had. I bought three bottles and three pieces of framed art before leaving Newport.

I drank every day until the house was packed. Notice to the property management company was given, and Stormy had flown to Oregon to help us drive our lives back to Austin.

The night before we left, we camped out on the living room floor; beds and mattresses were already in the moving truck. The last time we'd had a camp out with the kids was six years prior. After I had just moved into the Cold Empty, we'd made forts out of sheets, had a *Shrek* marathon, and the kids fought over who got to sleep (and snore) next to me.

Times had changed.

I looked over at Max, recalling a time when photos of me weren't face down, a time he competed with the General for my affection. I looked at Stormy, scrolling through her phone, and remembered reading *American Girl* stories to her at bedtime.

Wrestling free from memories of days gone by, I grabbed the remote and snuggled on the floor with Squibbs and Liesel. I watched a Bigfoot documentary and lost myself among the film crew, pushing past Douglas firs, in hot pursuit of the King of hide-and-seek.

Hours later I awoke. The TV was still on. Everyone around me was snoring. Max slept on a pile of blankets in the corner of the room, Stormy was on the couch, and the General and I lay on Jesse's old air mattress. Squibbs and Liesel snuggled next to me.

That's when I heard the whispers louder than I'd ever heard them before. Hisses and sinister moans floated past my ears, refusing to be ignored. I lay awake, eyes and ears wide open, afraid to move. It felt like I was being held down with someone sitting on my chest.

With a pounding heart and a hushed whisper, I asked, "What do you want, Charlotte?"

She said she'd been trying to tell me something. She said she knew things about me that I didn't. She asked if I thought my overwhelming urge to stay was a mere coincidence.

I told her it was the usual bout of uncertainty I felt before a major change and blamed being raised with underdeveloped critical thinking skills.

She called me a liar, told me I needed to stay. She said it was like Jack had asked before leaving Austin, "Are you running toward something or running away?" She said I was running away and all I'd ever done was run away.

I got out from under the covers and slowly got up. I stepped over the General and Max, bent down, and turned a small fan on to drown out Charlotte's baleful grumbling.

I found the safety of my dogs under blankets and tried to fall asleep to the fan's hum.

Charlotte's Last Shenanigan

NEWS OF PRINCE'S death shocked the airwaves, making our exodus from Oregon much sadder. Cleaning the house from top to bottom, we listened to his hits as tribute.

I didn't listen to much Prince as a teen; he, his wardrobe, and his music were lurid and risqué. Listening to him as an adult was a treat. I loved *Starfish and Coffee*.

The General and I took a cleaning break and walked down Second Street toward Dutch Bros. for coffees-to-go. Coffee in hand, he looked at me and asked once again with his face, "Are you sure?"

I looked away. I knew he wanted to stay, and I knew part of me needed to stay.

I walked ahead, and he stepped up his pace behind me. Then he suggested strolling through a neighborhood near Mac's main drag.

On a dead-end side street, near a public tennis court, we stumbled upon a quaint, empty house for sale. The General walked around it, peeking in the windows.

"This is perfect. It's not unnecessarily huge like ours and it's closer to downtown," he said.

Everything was packed. Charlotte's Place was empty, clean. I'd heard the last of her whispers the night before while lying on the floor. I'd told myself I was ready to go, and there he was scoping out a house to buy.

I looked at him, tilted my head, and sighed. I was at war with myself and wondered which was the lesser of two evils—

leave behind the horrid creature Charlotte forced me to see, or stay and face my inner demons, come what may?

There was a certain intrigue that came with the thought of staying. Face my shit... But aside from the issues I knew I had, what *was* my shit? Charlotte was trying to tell me something, no doubt, but what? What did I need to fix?

Even though we lived near a local Kingdom Hall, I hadn't encountered any J-Dubs; that wasn't plaguing me. I was far removed from the Mallorys and the constant reminder that I'd been forced into perpetual orphanhood.

All reservations aside, I had a decent career that supported me across state lines; a great husband; two dogs I adored; and two kids who had love for me buried somewhere. What would a person with all those things need to fix?

I looked in the windows of this adorable house and toyed with the idea of owning it. I saw just where I'd put the couch, the key-holder, my seafoam, Formica kitchen table.

"What about Max? You know, he may *not* want to leave us if we're in Austin, he loves it there. And if we stayed here, where would we go? We're handing the keys over to the property managers today; we couldn't move into this place tomorrow," I said.

"I know, I was just thinkin'." He shrugged, sipped his coffee, and headed toward the main drag.

Back at the house, the kids had been waiting with electronic devices in hand, ready to go. The truck and cars were packed. The pups were leashed up.

As I stood at the front door, turning the lock, I shuddered. I walked toward my Toyota, and the screen door squealed in protest as it closed.

"I'll drive," Stormy said, hopping into the driver's seat.

We drove to Third Street toward the property management office. Since it was a Sunday, the office was closed. I stood at the drop box for what felt like an eternity while Charlotte, quoting Jack, whispered, "Are you running toward something or away from something?"

I looked at the keys and thought, *these might unlock a secret trapdoor that leads to inner growth.* Then, and not a second too soon, I opened the drop box, tossed the keys in, and stomped to the car.

"Let's go," I said to Stormy as I closed the car door.

With Stormy driving down I-5, I had time to look out the window and think about what I had done; what it meant. It meant I was flipping the bird to some part of me that needed something. It meant I was ignoring my superpower for the first time in a long time. It meant I was running away. Again.

Moving to Oregon, I thought the notorious rainfall and overcast skies would have nothing on my bull-headed will to conquer hardship. But just like Atreyu and Artax, while trudging through the Swamp of Sadness, I was overcome by the same melancholy that befell Artax.

Mac's comforting sorrow matched mine, and I wondered if I'd turned my back on an angel in disguise instead of the ominous demon I envisioned Charlotte to be.

Three hours into the drive, we passed signs for Enchanted Forest, one of Oregon's odd and unique amusement parks, and I started to cry.

"Bekah? You Gucci?" Stormy asked, looking at me. "Gucci" was a term she often used instead of "good."

I nodded, wiped the tears away from my face, and texted the General. "We need to go back."

"It's too late. You dropped off the keys. We need to be one hundred and ten percent Austin now," he replied.

I sighed and looked out the window; tears kept falling.

Things would be so much easier if I could get lost in some harmless caper with my very own Ethel.

Buying a failing dress shop only to come out broke, finding ourselves dressed as Martians on top of the Empire State

Building, selling Aunt Martha's Old-Fashioned Salad Dressing on *The Dickie Davis Show*, or ogling Bill Holden during lunch at the Brown Derby in Los Angeles.

As Stormy drove us from Oregon to Southern California, I wanted to stop along the way and play a game of hide-and-seek with an elusive sasquatch, hiding behind Douglas firs and whispering for my Ethel to "Be quiet! There he is!" But I had no Ethel, and Stormy drove us right along, taking us through crowded Los Angeles highways, without trepidation.

There was no time for a Lucy/Ethel shenanigan. There were places to go, things to do.

Tucson, Arizona was friendly, welcoming, and *very* warm. Southern California was warm, but not like Tucson warm. Tucson enveloped me in its cozy embrace, and I didn't want to leave. We decided to stay for two days.

Sitting in the hotel bar—Cosmo in hand, kids swimming in the courtyard pool—I unclenched and started writing again. Aside from the layover in Portland, I hadn't written at all in Oregon.

I let it all out. Things I was ashamed to think and afraid to say made themselves comfortable in a word document and I wrote uninhibited. I wrote about Charlotte. I thought if I could capture the horrid things she made me think and feel, I could say goodbye to her.

Only she wouldn't say goodbye.

She told me, while alive, she'd had a drinking problem; she was a bit unstable. She said she'd murdered her child. I turned away from my laptop after she explained in detail how she dragged a dead, bloody child down the hall, left it on the living room floor, and uncorked a bottle of wine. She'd hijacked my writing.

I slammed my laptop shut and gulped my Cosmo.

Stormy had always been an interesting girl with curious beliefs. To me she was merely a child of sixteen, yet she knew things about spirits, apparitions, and the inexplicable. It was one of the things that made Stormy, Stormy; she was like a mini medium.

Sitting at Caruso's Italian Restaurant, a Tucson landmark since 1938, I told Stormy all about Charlotte while drinking chianti. She listened intently and asked a series of clarifying questions.

"So, you felt random breezes...did you smell anything?" she asked, breaking her garlic bread in half.

"Sometimes," I said, pouring wine from my personal carafe into a glass. "It was a faint odor. Not foul."

"Did anyone else notice anything?"

"Liesel would run up and down the hall anytime there were odors or light breezes."

"I saw shadows and they felt..." Max searched for the right word, "dark?"

Stormy looked at her father.

"I saw and felt nothing. I have no idea what these two are talking about," he said, sipping his wine.

"You're a closed channel. You're not open to spirit-human interaction, so the spirit passed you by," Stormy said.

"Learn that from *Ghost Hunters*?" the General teased.

Stormy tilted her head and wrinkled her face in derision. "Ha-ha, Dad."

"Ooh, fettucine alfredo," the General said as his dinner was placed in front of him.

The three of us looked at him and shook our heads.

I told Stormy I had asked their auntie Diane for advice, and she'd instructed me to talk with Charlotte.

"And?" Stormy asked, making room for the waitress to set down her dinner.

"She, um, stuck around." I looked down at my four-cheese ravioli, sad that I'd suddenly lost my appetite.

"What was going on while she was around?"

"Tension, turmoil, discomfort," I said, poking at my dinner.

"Hmm," she said, cutting her chicken parmesan. "When was the last encounter?"

I sat, silently sipping my wine, and stared at the table. I looked over and noticed Max was also picking at his food with vacancy in his eyes.

I told Stormy I felt Charlotte in the house, full force, the night before we left Oregon.

"You didn't tell me that," the General said, twirling fettucine around his fork, using the dip of a big spoon the way I'd taught him, the way my family had taught me.

"You've been dismissing her since day one. Why would I tell you?" I said.

"Is that why you cried in the car?" Stormy asked.

Max looked up, eager for my response, and asked, "Do you miss her?"

I nodded in response to both questions.

Broaching the topic of Charlotte with Stormy set me on edge. All I wanted to do was forget the ghoul, forget all the tumult she'd unleashed inside of me.

The distraction of souvenir shopping was just what I needed. We strolled Fourth Avenue, and I purchased a sepia-colored Frida Kahlo portrait. The photo of Frida holding a gun, wearing a silk robe wide open down to her naval, was adhered to a piece of polished wood; it was perfect. *She* was perfect.

After dropping the kids off at the hotel to swim, the General suggested a walk. Blending in with Tucson locals, we walked up North Alvernon Way. Tucsonans were very friendly and genuinely happy; why shouldn't they be? They, too, owned the sun for a good portion of the year.

Seated at a hacienda-styled restaurant, attached to an upscale lodge, the General asked me what I thought of Tucson.

"It's nice. I like it. Why?"

"I've been looking around; the houses here are affordable," he said, scrolling through his phone to show me what he'd found.

I put my hand over his phone. "What're you doin' to me?"

"Just weighing all our options. Look at this house," he said, showing me a modest yellow house in a neighborhood he'd been eyeballing.

"You said you were 'one hundred and ten percent Austin.'" I humored him by swiping past photos of a house in the coveted Sam Hughes district.

"I just wanna drive by."

After lunch, I humored the General again when we walked back to the hotel, got my car, and drove around Tucson's most desirable neighborhoods. I could recall a time when humoring the General meant compromising sexual positions, involving leather chaps and small, vibrating butt-plugs. It was a much simpler time.

Keeping true to form, the General found the yellow house, parked, and began casing the joint. He lifted me off the ground from a stepstool using his laced fingers, and I peered into windows for him. It was cute and I wasn't humoring him when I gasped at the fenced-in backyard, encompassing matured lemon trees.

We strolled around the neighborhood, saying hello to folks getting their mail, watering their shrubs. I could see it, see us becoming Tucsonans. But the overwhelming guilt I felt while watching *Inside Out* with Max wouldn't allow me to settle him in another new city.

"It's picturesque," I said, amazed by the mighty saguaros and prickly pear cacti lining the street, "but we can't. Not now at least."

On one of our first dates, the General flat-out told me he was apprehensive about getting involved with someone who was such a "flight risk." He knew I was the type to pick up and beat feet. He wasn't wrong, but now he had the upper hand. Since he'd put a ring on it, binding me to his side, he started using my weaknesses against me—my love of travel, adventure, and excitement of the great unknown.

Saying no to this sudden detour pained me and surprised him. I was in love with the part of me that took off on a whim, settled into a new life, then changed my mind again because I could.

And now I had become this woman, this *grown-up*, with stepchildren. Their need for stability was unspoken, but it was there and loud as a fucking foghorn.

On the last leg of our drive back to Austin, I knew what was there waiting for me, and I wasn't the least bit excited.

This was around the time I started to fall apart; *we* started to fall apart.

Out of Sage

I WAS GRATEFUL for sunny, blue skies but disgruntled at the growth Austin had seen in the ten months we'd been gone. Being back didn't feel right.

Our mid-century apartment complex, The French Quarter, was smack-dab in the middle of a busy downtown street.

In the leasing office, getting keys and signing paperwork, I cried while looking at the General. He was suddenly a stranger to me. I was sick of him, his face, his voice, his accent; I was sick of everything about him by that point.

But it wasn't him, it was me.

I didn't know if my feelings were the remnants of Charlotte trailing behind me or if it was my inner compass, but I couldn't stand to be around anyone.

After loading the last of the furniture into our two-bedroom, second-floor apartment, overlooking a pool and dog park on the edge of the parking lot, my friend Opal texted.

"Wanna go to São Paulo with us?"

"Who's us?"

"Me and Blue."

Opal and Blue were two of my closest friends in Austin, excited we'd come back.

"Opal and Blue want me to go to São Paulo with them," I said to the General. I wanted to see them, but I also wanted to unpack and drink next to a fading Charlotte, alone.

"Get out of here, go see them. Max and I can unpack," the General said.

I texted Opal "Okay" knowing if I didn't, she'd come over anyway.

"I'll come get you."

I figured.

The sun beat into the car as Opal and I cruised downtown Austin. Even the warmth of Texas in April couldn't cure me of Charlotte's iciness.

When Blue saw me walk into São Paulo with Opal, she ran toward me, pulling me closer. I felt her shoulders shake and heard her sob. My face scrunched against my will and tears ran down my cheeks.

At a booth in one of Austin's many Brazilian joints, they both commented on my surliness.

"Hey, why aren't happy to be back?" Opal asked.

Staring at fried yucca neatly arranged around spicy queso, I sighed unsure about mentioning Charlotte; she'd clung to me, all the way from McMinnville.

Sipping my Mexican margarita, I said, "If I told you, you'd think I was crazy."

"Tell us," Blue said, leaning forward.

I told them about Charlotte, then nibbled on a fried yucca, avoiding eye contact. Their eyes felt heavy.

"I don't think you're crazy," Opal said.

"You don't?" I asked.

Opal shook her head. I looked to Blue for validation.

"I totally believe in spirits, hauntings, all of it," Blue said.

I nodded in gratitude as a tear slid down my cheek.

My voice shook and my face crinkled when I said, "Thank you." Charlotte was fucking real, and I knew it.

"What you need is to look forward to something, get back on track," Opal said.

Blue October at Stubbs BBQ would be enough to distract me from the gnawing ache I felt.

I hoped to find pieces of myself hidden somewhere between the notes and silence of my favorite songs. They'd helped me once; I was sure they could do it again. And goddamn did they ever do it again.

But after the lights, the energy, and the enigmatic voice of Justin Furstenfeld had worn off, I was back to shifting uncomfortably; disenchanted with myself.

I took to the drink once more—this time harder.

One of the things I liked about our apartment was its close proximity to alcohol. I frequented Little Woodrow's, a local pub, on my solo strolls. I'd sit at the bar with a book or my journal, sipping dirty martinis, rarely producing any written, coherent thoughts.

The General took to self-soothing aids of the greener, plantier persuasion while taking long walks with Liesel. Max was happy to be with his best friends once again, and Stormy, glad to be back in NH no doubt.

In Austin, it was easy enough to fall back into the quotidian drabness of previous routines and work schedules. What I struggled with was a new version of myself and finding a place to put her—she'd devolved in some inexplicable way.

When I wasn't working, I was drunk, alone. I knew I had a problem, and at the time I didn't care. Regardless of my new liquid diet, I was still working out like a maniac and had lost a considerable amount of weight; I was one hundred and fifteen pounds soaking wet.

Unable to shake the mournful tide from crashing on the shores of self-pity once again, I had a full-out meltdown in our bathroom. When I emerged, Max's jaw dropped.

"Um, wow. Did you just do that?" he asked, pointing to my head.

"Yeah. I guess I did." I chuckled nervously and ran my right hand over my shaved head in disbelief.

275

I didn't know then (and I'm still not sure now) what brought me to that deciding moment with the General's clippers, but one minute I had hair, and the next I didn't.

I only knew I was sick of everything—sick of the General, sick of the kids, sick of ailing dogs, sick of meal planning and working out, sick of moving, sick of *feeling*, sick of my hair, and sick of myself. I thought if I could get rid of one thing about myself, feel I had control over something, I'd feel better.

CODA International planned their annual conference in Austin for June and I'd decided to go. I'd never been. I was curious what hundreds of CODAs together would feel like. Not to mention, I always needed professional CEUs.

I went hoping to find "my people," hoping to connect with anyone who might have some insight as to why I was the way I was. I could always chalk my indecisiveness, inexperienced critical thinking skills, and emotional immaturity on being sling-shot from my J-Dub family, but beyond that, *why am I this way?*

Some CODAs said my issues were with having Deaf parents, to which I vehemently said, "No, I don't take issue with their Deafness, them, or what makes them who they are; it's the damn religion that left the scar."

I'd explain this repeatedly and they'd continue to shake their heads in disagreement. To find another CODA ex J-Dub would be like finding a unicorn—next to impossible.

But then I found one.

Stella was a beautiful, enigmatic young woman with long, dark hair, falling to the middle of her back, humungous brown eyes, and olive-toned skin. I don't remember how we met. I only know one minute I was alone, and the next minute there she was. Like magic. Unicorn magic.

The Deaf community is small. The J-Dub Deaf community is even smaller. It was no surprise to me that we'd grown up around the same people, though we didn't live on the same side of the country. She knew people from the snapshots of photos I'd kept in my phone, people that I didn't remember. She undoubtedly held a big piece of my life in her memories, and she was a mystery to me, a beautiful mystery.

She was scheduled for an activity while I had some free time. I sat at the hotel bar and stewed. Maybe having Deaf parents affected me more than I'd thought. It wasn't easy being such an indispensable part of my family dynamic. My parents leaned on me/us constantly. As a result, I rarely had privacy and sometimes knew more than I wanted to. Going from too much to absolutely nothing is hard. It'd be one thing if I didn't like my family, but I did even when I didn't.

After my drink was gone, I went outside and found Stella sunbathing on a lounge chair. She was looking at something small in the palm of her hand. I walked closer and could see something purple, shimmering, glistening in the sun. I sat next to her.

She looked up with a small tear in her eye and asked me if I'd met Pedro.

I shook my head.

She pointed just outside the pool area to the other side of the white iron fence and said, "Go see Pedro. You'll be glad you did."

I cocked my head in curiosity and headed to the other side of the fence. I stood where the grass met the pavement to the parking lot. Pedro was hugging a CODA as I approached.

Once the other CODA left, Pedro motioned for me to come closer.

I stood before him silently; I said nothing.

He began smudging with a Cuban cigar and said, "I ran out of sage."

That was fine because I had no idea what was happening.

Pedro looked into my eyes and said, "I know. I know."

Whatever skepticism I had quickly died, and I lost my ever-loving mind at the Radisson. Pedro placed his hands on my shoulders, drew me closer, and held me tight while monsters that had been living inside me for far too long began to howl and break away one by one.

"Those fuckers!" he shouted.

He knew, and I swear I didn't say one word. Not one word.

Pedro then taught me how to breath in order to control my emotions and bring my power back inside.

Once I calmed, he told me to choose a colored rock from a collection he had. I grabbed the first one that jumped out at me—a blood-red stone with white speckles.

I thanked Pedro, hugged him again, and asked, "Are you okay? Do *you* have everything you need?"

"Oh, yeah. Doing this is what I need," he said, smiling.

I felt lighter. Understood. Validated. Right. I didn't know what I was suddenly right about, but goddamn it I was right.

Back at the French Quarter, I was right about very little. The General and I were worlds apart.

Without a CODA family to fall back on for validation, I again found myself with strong drink in hand; only this time, I huddled in my walk-in closet with Squibbs, a laptop, the latest wacky, New Age personal growth book, and a list of people to send predatory "Hey, girl!" messages to.

Though the cult flag waved, I fell deeper into the online, fitness-coaching world. Top-earning celebrity coaches taught remote workshops on how the company structure worked. Having active coaches beneath you in the coach's pyramid—"to create a strong left-and-right-leg"—earned victory club points. Those points created volume, and that volume paid you in bonus checks signed by the CEO. The company was built on using your downline as props.

Attending those trainings drunk half the time, I didn't care what I'd heard. I scribbled notes in my journal as if my life depended on it. One day, I even called some how-to-climb-the-rungs gimmick and spoke with fast-talking strangers who tried selling me their own multi-level culting scheme.

Anything to distract me from the growing tension between the General and I because we, too, had run out of sage.

He had this way of erecting an impenetrable wall; cannons wouldn't make a dent. I hadn't seen this side of him before; it scared me. The same guy who melted on the phone with his daughter every night, the same guy who married me again on Oahu, the same guy who helped me shower each time I bled so much I could barely stand was also this callous, withdrawn, hardened man—unwilling to open himself up.

Something happened once we left Oregon.

And something else happened on a random day in July—we said goodbye to Squibbs. He'd stopped wobbling, pinballing down hallways, eating.

Lying with Squibbs, on the floor of Bluebonnet Animal Hospital (the same vet I'd once used for Bartok and Moron), his sweet soul went to sleep, sending us both into a downward spiral. It was the first time in seven years I'd ever seen the General sob.

Failing miserably to connect with anyone in the apartment or online, then coping with the loss of Squibbs, I reached out to Diane.

"Marriage sucks," I texted.

I explained that the General had shut down. I told her he was shunning and stonewalling me, which brought up too many feelings of abandonment; I couldn't take it.

Then she asked me something I wasn't prepared to answer.

"The things you expect him to do—are you doing them?"

I said I didn't know because I didn't.

The more I thought about it, the more I realized in some ways, yes. I'd expected him to open up, communicate, because goddamn it I was communicating. In fact, according to my first husband, I *over*communicated.

I'd bet dollars to donuts that my second husband would agree with my first, and someday they'd both raise a glass at my Celebration of Life and say in unison, "We couldn't shut the bitch up."

Diane asked if I'd be interested in going to a three-day personal development seminar she had once attended. I told her there was no way the General would concede; he wasn't even open to marriage counseling.

Then she said, "This isn't about him, it's about you. It only takes one person to change."

I, of course, was a bit leery. Not only was I to give a strange organization I'd never heard of five hundred dollars to help me fix something, but since joining Hard Bottoms, I'd become hypervigilant around anything that resembled a cult. Multi-level marketing; groups of well-intentioned CODAs; social media platforms; almost every group looked like a cult to me, complete with rigid structure and groupthink.

I asked Diane if the organization was a cult—knowing no one ever really believes they themselves are actually in one—and to my surprise, she said, "Some totally see it that way, but they won't shun you if you don't do anything with what you learn."

I was in. My curiosity had officially been piqued. A couple of weeks later I paid the five hundred dollars and registered for a seminar, slated for September.

The General supported my decision to attend. Truthfully, I think he and Max were relieved to be ridding the apartment of my presence for three days.

After Squibbs died, I got a tribute tattoo of his face on my back, and we decided to rescue another dog for Liesel's sake; she sulked for weeks, cuddling Squibbs' abandoned toys.

The Austin Animal Shelter was no place for me. Looking at those furry faces, begging for their forever family to find them, I wanted to take them all. The fact that I couldn't left a pit in my stomach.

We roamed that shelter for hours, making eye contact with every single pup. I wondered if my ability to feel what other people felt, to hear and sense apparitions around me, meant I could feel an animal's pain as well because being there was excruciating.

"We need to find a baby, quick," I said.

Then the General found him.

Sitting in cage was *the* dog, the General said. I was drawn to the grey, brindle pit bull next to the General's choice mutt; she was giving me her paw through the fence.

"What about her?" I asked the General, touching her paw as she whined.

He glanced over, then looked at our boy again. "No. This one. He sort of looks like Squibbs."

We brought the General's brat home the next day and it was love at first sight for Liesel.

Dexter Morgan was a two-year-old, medium-sized treeing feist; a hunting dog that's agile, fast, and can bring back a squirrel in seconds. Not that we needed any squirrels, but if we did, he would have been happy to supply them. He looked to have a bit of pit bull in him with the color patterns of a Rottweiler. One ear was crumpled, likely due to a fight or someone trying to crop it.

A week later, our vet treated Dexter for worms, pneumonia, ticks, fleas; you name it, he had it. The seven-hundred-dollar bill brought financial stress, but I didn't think twice about paying to treat him any more than I'd thought about paying five hundred dollars to register myself for some treatment.

The General wasn't so sure.

"I don't even know if I like him yet. Seven hundred bucks? And he gave his pneumonia to Liesel." The General shook his head while looking at Dexter, who was sitting quietly on the couch, crossing his white-socked, tan-freckled front paws, and smiling.

"I know, but she's on meds and he's definitely in his forever home now that we've *paid* the seven hundred. Who knows what his past home life was like to come with all that crap."

As it turns out, he was nowhere near two years old. Once Bubba Jones (one of Dexter's nicknames) recovered, he was zooming around the apartment, leaping over coffee tables and bent-over humans in a single-bound.

Definitely not two years old.

Sitting on a Time Bomb

ONCE SEPTEMBER CAME, I embarked on a three-day journey inward and it fucked my world up. To encapsulate all that took place in a hotel conference room with twenty-five strangers during that seventy-two-hour period would only cheapen it; there simply aren't enough words to adequately describe the experience.

But I'll try.

Using a visual technique we'd learned the first day, we each confronted a place only we knew about. Traversing my own past, I found and faced the armor I'd been wearing my whole life. Taking it off, I became weightless. It was surreal. At the end of that exercise, I opened my eyes and found myself, and others, balled up on the floor crying.

During the break, people didn't shy away from one another, embarrassed. They hugged each other, asking, "Doing okay?" Of course, even in my vulnerable state, surrounded by well-intentioned folks, I smiled and kept my distance because, cult.

I learned that the stories I'd told myself over the years were so rote my body had accepted them as truth. I'd become chemically dependent on my victimhood, had drilled each story into my head so many times the only thing that ever changed were the characters; the screenplays hadn't shifted one bit.

At home later that night, the General asked how it went. I grunted, headed into our bedroom, then completed our homework assignment: write a paragraph on resentment.

"I resent a small group of money-hungry, mind controlling men because they took away the best parts of me: my family, whom I model many of my redeeming, and not so redeeming, qualities after. This cult brainwashed my family so that they'll have nothing to do with me, and it's been damaging to my very soul."

I scribbled that, then went right to sleep.

On the last day, I was eager to find out what the hook-line was. So far, the weekend lessons had set me on the tracks to self-discovery while making meaningful human-to-human connections, the kind lost among the mob mentality of social media and needing to have a "strong online presence."

The classes hadn't felt gimmicky. I learned things about myself that were always there, waiting to surface. After a lesson underscoring that all humans are connected through energy—we're just wounded children, holding up mirrors for each other—there it was. A video advertising more classes, opportunities to "level up."

Let me say, this organization was very instrumental when it came to me recognizing my own bullshit, seeing my worth, changing the trajectory of my life—for myself. I can't thank them enough for some of the things I learned and was able to implement.

However, there are some cult-like practices weaved in, structurally. I'll agree with Diane: folks won't shun you if you don't do anything with what you've learned. Friendships don't end just because one person isn't buying in; people don't get disfellowshipped.

The foundation of their classes are born of love, connection, and the inner power we each have that we've unintentionally diluted living these mundane existences.

Therefore, I don't see them as a destructive cult. Yet some of their practices do fit a cultish mold. And of course, someone raised the way I was would most definitely notice.

Paying four thousand dollars more to "level up" felt...off. I understood that being on the ranch where they host intensive classes—providing transportation, room and board, food—would cost money, overhead. I understood footing that bill. But did it really have to cost so much?

Yes. It did. And if you bought the last two courses then and there, you got a discount. I was torn.

While there, I felt like I was finally catching up in life, I got the punchline, the train was going to stop and take me with it, at last. Everything I'd learned that weekend about the world and my place in it was truly invaluable.

But how the hell was I going to justify that much money to the General? We'd just moved back to Austin. "Moving trucks, security deposits, and driving across the country isn't cheap. Not to mention vet bills for rescue dogs," I heard him say.

I'd have an opportunity to convince the General, and maybe get him into some classes, the next night at our graduation ceremony.

Just before we left for the ceremony, I sat the General down and massaged his feet.

"What are you doing?" he asked.

"Just being nice. Are you complaining?" I kept rubbing.

"No. It's just, why?"

We'd been at odds since coming back to Austin, and there I was giving his hobbit-like feet a rub down, unsolicited.

I shrugged, put his socks and shoes on, and said, "We should get going."

A now thirteen-year-old Max—somewhat curious about my weekend whereabouts and sudden attitude change—tagged along.

The facilitator presented a truncated version of what we'd learned over the weekend. Once his presentation was over, everyone mingled while exchanging phone numbers and, of course, the back table was set up where people could sign up for the next classes.

The General faced me. "So, they're doing this introductory class again in a few months? I think I wanna take it."

My eyes bugged. "You do?"

"Yeah. If you wind up doing the next courses, I don't wanna get left behind. I don't want you to grow without me." He walked to the back table and signed himself up for the seminar I had just taken.

While standing at the registration table, in total shock of what the General was doing, I was reminded of the discount I could take advantage of by signing up for both next-level courses right then and there.

"I need to think about it," I said, feeling pressured.

I was not only taken aback by the General's willingness to enroll himself, but also stunned that he signed up for the seminar solely because he didn't want us to grow apart any more than we had. I needed time to process all that had just taken place.

While driving between campuses the next day, I got a call from a seminar organizer reminding me to "take advantage of the discount." The pressure was on, and sometimes split-second decisions need to be made. I gave her my credit card number while driving up South Lamar Boulevard.

The General's birthday was coming up and I was giving him something he desperately wanted—to be alone. Seminar or no seminar, things between us were still tense.

I'd been contacted by an interpreting agency in California wanting to book me for a weeklong conference in Boston. As in home? On somebody else's dime? Shit, yeah. I hadn't been in New England since 2013 when the General and I went home for Christmas, just after we'd flown Stormy up to live with Cassie.

I wanted to feel home again on my own terms. To breathe in that Dunkin'-Donuts-on-every-corner smell, to feel the rush of a Massachusetts driver cut me off in traffic while flipping the bird, and to squeeze in a trip across state lines and stand at my tracks in NH would be all right.

Just before I left Austin, the agency sent along itineraries, workshop schedules, and interpreting team names. They'd hired some familiar local New England 'terps. Not only would I be seeing my reinstated brotha-from-anotha-motha, Jesse, but I'd also be teaming with him.

Seems I wouldn't have to go across state lines to entertain ghosts of NH past—one of mine would be coming to me.

I sent Jesse a text asking if he'd seen the schedule and knew we'd been paired together. I wanted to coddle any discomfort he may have harbored while neglecting my own. He replied, saying he saw, and he was okay with the arrangement because we could "use that time to our advantage." I could feel Jesse's excitement as well as his sorrow, shaking me loose from the plastic bolts, screws, and flimsy contraptions lackadaisically holding me together.

I rattled again, looser, while recalling the three-day seminar. And that resentment paragraph I'd written? Still fresh in my mind. I wondered if anyone in my family had seen my apostate interpreting clip for Gregorio's *Truth Be Told* documentary trailer. I didn't dare ask, even if I had the chance.

Interpreting the conference wasn't what stuck with me; I couldn't even tell you what it was about. I'd been interpreting long enough to dismiss most of what I heard, processed, and released through my fingertips—my short-term memory was shot.

What I clung to, what I moved into my long-term memory and catalogued in my own personal Dewey Decimal System, was precious time spent with Jesse.

We walked the ground floor of the conference center and shopped at exhibit booths. I bought a fancy gadget to relieve back pain and muscle soreness—one that I never even used but had to have because one of my big brothers purchased one for himself. All these years and I still chased their shadows.

We took a drive and talked at length about what we'd been up to and how Mom and Dad were doing. Later that night, he texted how good it was to spend time with me, then he sent snapshots of framed photos of us over the years during many of our vacations and weekend getaways; the photos littered his nightstand.

It'd be easier if he hated me, hated what I "did to his God" like Luke or forgot I even existed like Mark. Instead, he gave in to his emotions—allowing them to lead the way while sitting with me in a place of love and compassion—even if it all ended once I boarded a plane back to Austin.

Christmas came around again, and Cassie had agreed to send Stormy to Austin. The General decided to fly Loretta down so we could all be together the way we'd been a few years prior.

Well, we were together, but it was nothing like it had been before. There was a tension so thick, the General and I took any opportunity to skulk off.

"I don't think my mom wanted to come," he said, strolling the snack aisle at HEB.

"She seems tired. Do you think she's okay health-wise?"

"I don't know."

"Maybe a drive to see the Christmas lights would lighten the mood," I suggested.

Reluctant to leave the kitchen, Loretta joined us for the Austin Christmas tour. I offered the front seat, she insisted on sitting in the back with Stormy and Max. When we stopped at various places to get out and sightsee, she stayed in the car.

She stepped out and walked to one place and one place only: the *I Love You So Much* mural on the side of Jo's Coffee where the General and I'd been married. We took turns posing for photos in front of the wall then convinced her to walk across the street to get Amy's Ice Cream.

There was something up with her physically; it was clear she didn't want to talk about it. Watching her felt like seeing an aged animal, sneaking off to "go peacefully" alone.

In the apartment, she typically sat at the table scoffing at her newsfeed anytime it featured the next "dumbass thing Trump was doing." At least her humor was still intact.

"She hasn't been the same since my stepdad passed," the General whispered as we lay in bed after a late-night game of *Clue* with the kids.

"I don't blame her. She's had a lot to deal with since then."

"She's giving up," he said, rolling over. "And we have front row seats."

The General released a few, quick snorts followed by heavy breathing. He always fell asleep as soon as his head hit the pillow. I never could and still can't.

With the streetlight coming through our bedroom window, I looked over at him, mouth agape, snoring peacefully.

I couldn't sleep. I lay there, wide awake, thinking about life, death, and what I was doing with my in-between.

J-Dub doctrines from my past haunted me that night. No matter what I'd learned during the seminar I had just taken three months prior, I still fought these unyielding, personal ghosts. No matter how long I'd been away, J-Dub credo made an appearance anytime a crisis was unfolding.

What happens when we die? Is there just a great, big void? Nothing? Do we go on? What happens just before? What do you feel as you're dying? What do you see? What's it like?

I closed my eyes and tried to lull myself to sleep, but the murky haze crawling behind my eyelids wouldn't allow it. I saw black with red speckles, dancing, poking, and prodding my cornea. Then I saw shades of blue and green, stone, azure, and turquoise.

Somewhere beyond a sea of mixing colors and my mother-in-law's face, it was 1996. I was working in a retirement home, caring for Alzheimer and dementia patients...

At change of shift, I drift from the nurse's station to one of the resident's rooms to get the daily report. On my way, I smell bleach and the lingering scent of sick diarrhea as I approach the room. The swishing of my white scrubs quiets and I hear voices as I get closer to the door.

"You can go now, Arthur, it's okay."

"You're not alone."

"We're here."

"We love you."

I step into the room, and as soon as my foot crosses the threshold, I look over at Arthur. His head moves slightly from the wall to the ceiling. His jaw drops, his eyes open wide, and he releases his last breath—right before my eyes.

The room is silent. A few of my coworkers sniffle. The shift RN gently takes his wrist to check his pulse. He's nothing but skin and bones. Arthur withered, day after day, growing weaker and weaker, yet, white-knuckled, he clung to life right 'til the very end.

Washing and preparing Arthur's body for the funeral home didn't bother me in the least. Washing him deceased didn't feel any different than washing him alive. Arthur wasn't Arthur; he was just a vessel, a shell. What made him who he was—grumpy sourpuss and all—was gone the moment the RN declared he had "expired," like cottage cheese.

In those moments—between life and death with Arthur—I wasn't afraid. Just morbidly curious about what he had seen when his eyes grew. What he felt as he exhaled one last time. Fright? Peace? Sweet relief?

Rolling around in the memory of Arthur holding on to dear life, I understood Loretta's plight. After becoming widowed *and* sick, what's left?

I didn't blame her for letting go decades before Arthur was willing to. But it was disturbing to watch her nonchalantly surrender her will to live, passing it off to an unknown entity eagerly waiting to devour what was left of her withering soul.

As much as I loved her and her company, there was nothing worse than watching her slip away.

Remember the Tin Man

IT WAS NOW the General's turn to look into the same mirror I had. Since someone close to me was attending the seminar, I was asked to be part of the volunteer staff. Being part of the staff meant I could observe the General's experience while keeping my distance.

Yes, challenge accepted. Plus, I wanted to shake off the remaining discomfort from Loretta's somber Christmas visit and replace it with intimidating self-growth.

While volunteering, I was privy to meetings before and after sessions. Hearing the facilitator's disappointment toward the group leaders for not enrolling more attendees into the next courses, forced that cult feeling to resurface.

On one hand, the facilitator stressing the need to enroll/sell the next classes sounded an awful lot like going door-to-door and peddling magazines, like some modern-day colporteur, or sending someone a "Hey, girl!" invite.

On the other hand, I liked what the institute was offering: freedom of choice, inner power discovery, responsibility, self-reliance, breaking down to break through, human connection, peace of mind, and personal growth unattached to the idea of God.

I couldn't dismiss my own recent experience; it helped me find that inner power and peace. What I'd learned during my weekend seminar was I could be responsible for the choices I made, or I could fall immobile and cling to my victimhood, blaming anyone who got in my way. That *was* powerful; unlike all I'd learned while growing up a Witness.

Fortunately, my upbringing, my personal experience with cults, made me rethink my almost-natural inclination toward rigid, prescriptive belief systems.

My inner struggle's timing was impeccable. Perhaps what I needed was to face all that systematic bullshit and see where I landed.

Just one month later, the General and my systematic bullshit landed in San Francisco.

The General was much more resistant than I was. Regardless of the experiences he'd had during his three-day class, and apart from what I experienced with him, he intentionally picked fights with me all the way to California.

"Carry your own luggage, and don't wake me if I fall asleep. I hate when you do that," said the guy who at one time turned down a free, first-class seat to snuggle with me in coach.

From the San Francisco airport, seventy-six strangers—life coaches included—rode on posh tour buses to a ranch hidden deep inside the mountains and valleys of California.

At the ranch, we collected our luggage then men and women were led to separate dorms. It didn't matter if you were married, there to work on your marriage—men in one house, women in another. Thank goodness because I was ready to sock the General right in his bulbous nose.

I went into the dorm I'd been assigned and realized (judging by all the camp-style bunkbeds) I wouldn't have a room to myself. I'd have roommates.

I walked deep into the belly of the dorm, further and further, until reaching the last room, hoping no one followed.

The room was connected to a locker-style bathroom. I'd chosen it because it only had two sets of bunkbeds and looked big enough to do my morning workout in. Three other women followed.

I threw my Darth Vader purse on the top bunk closest to the door, walked over to a dresser, and started unpacking my suitcase; we were scheduled to be there for seven days.

Somewhere in my mind, I envisioned the week being like my one and only experience at Environmental Camp in Maine when I was ten. We'd get three square meals a day, have time for arts and crafts, take nature walks through salt marshes, then someone would sing us to sleep while playing acoustic guitar.

But this was not that.

Once settled, everyone was summoned across the ranch to a conference room in the main house where we were given a schedule breakdown. Rules were set forth: men and women would remain in separate sleeping quarters; married couples were to act is if they weren't; cell phones were to remain off; no social media updates; and absolutely no alcohol.

"Be present. Be here, now."

While introducing ourselves, we were to tell seventy-six strangers what people would most likely hate us for if they were to find out.

I sat, hating many things about myself, unsure which shame-filled secret to share—my Dean years, the shit I did to Carter, my affair with Kelly, my humiliating engagement to Asshat, or the drunken mess I'd become.

One by one, each person shared a dark part of themselves. Stating what we thought we'd be loathed for felt more like us coming to terms with what *we* hated about ourselves.

After dinner, in the same conference room, we were given a lesson in choices. We were instructed, before any exercise or event, to state our full name and that we were choosing to do whatever we were about to do. That way, there was no one else to blame. Hence, personal responsibility.

During the next exercise, we had a choice: go all in or keep clinging to who we thought we were.

"What's the exercise?" someone asked.

"Doesn't matter. In or out?" a facilitator said.

Nonplussed, we each stated our full name and said we "choose to do this event." Everyone was spread out on the floor with a cushioned conference chair in front of them. The lights went dark, music clicked on, and Tracy Chapman sang, "Who stole your heart? Who took it away?"

"Now, go ahead. Scream!" one of the facilitators shouted.

As loud as I could, I bellowed into the chair while thinking about my absent family, my Dean years, what I did to Carter, Kelly leaving me in D.C., Asshat's gaslighting, the kids, photos of me face-down, Cassie's mirror of ugly truths, the distance between me and the General, and the fact that I felt no one would care if I died.

When the voices began to quiet, I heard the General roar from the other side of the room.

"Get it out; the hurt, the anger, the pain," another facilitator said, giving us license to go bonkers on the chairs placed in front of us.

Tracy sang, we screamed again, and I pummeled the chair until my knuckles went numb. I thought about switching fists, but my left hand is retarded; I would have missed the chair right in front of me.

"Get it out!"

Tracy's song started again, and we continued screaming and punching. I thought I was going to break my own hand. When I had nothing left, I collapsed under the chair. Tracy's song ended with, "Go find your heart and take it back."

We were exhausted, defeated. In puddles of our own tears. In the fetal position, I felt my right hand with my left; I'd broken skin, it was already swollen. When the lights came on, I saw I'd drawn blood. I looked around to see upturned chairs and people scattered everywhere in tears.

Released from that night's lesson, at 11 p.m., we shuffled across the ranch back to our dorms in silence as we'd been instructed. No one looked anyone else in the eye.

I crawled up to the top bunk, ignoring the "Do you need the bathroom?" whispers, and massaged my hand. I fell asleep missing my Tin Man, wondering how he was. I could still hear his cries echoing in my head. Did he hear mine?

Early the next morning, a facilitator walked through the women's dorm, stopped by each room, and said, "Morning, ladies! Breakfast is at eight, class is at nine!"

I was certainly awake early enough for a workout, but there was no way. My body was sore from the ass kicking I'd given to a chair the night before.

Breakfast was silent, aside from the clanking silverware and loud stares. I found the General; he avoided eye contact while wolfing down scrambled eggs.

Class started and the silence was broken when we were asked how we felt after the previous night's event. I hadn't had a chance to process it yet, I was barely awake. Rubbing my knuckles, I relived the late-night sparring session I'd had with an innocent chair. My hand had started changing colors, going through its own healing process; one my head hadn't caught up with yet.

The day was filled with lesson after lesson, exercise after exercise. I was hoping we'd have a break after dinner, but no.

Awkwardly, we stood in one big circle, on the hunt for a "buddy," a go-to person for the week. They couldn't be anyone we knew, they couldn't be anyone we might normally choose to talk to, and they couldn't be the opposite sex.

As I looked around the circle, some women eyeballed me, considered me. It felt like being picked last for dodgeball all over again.

Then I saw her. Across the way, our eyes locked and I knew she was my person. I don't know how I knew, but I knew. On the count of three we were instructed to approach someone in the room and ask if they'd be our buddy. They could say no, in which case the hunt would continue.

She won't say no.

Her eyes didn't look through me. There was something in her that was immediately tethered to something in me. My superpower had spoken. Decision made.

On the count of three, she and I walked doggedly toward each other and asked in unison to be buddies, then laughed.

Jennifer stood before me—long, brown hair, blueish grey eyes, lashes longer than I'd ever seen on a human, and a warm smile; she was gorgeous.

Was she really someone I wouldn't have talked to? Yes. Not because there was something wrong with her, but because I felt there was everything wrong with me. The mere sight of her was too good for me.

I wish I could say what we faced together that week was carefree and easy, but it wasn't. Jennifer was an unavoidable mirror all week long. She helped me realize how much I'd been trashing relationships for most of my life. Raised to be a door-slamming pro, I could cut people off on a whim, ignore their existence. Doing it whenever the ol' GB commanded it only meant I was bound to do it in my adulthood.

I didn't want to climb the pole. I did, but I didn't.

I had the protection—the hat, the gear, belayers down below literally tied to me with Jennifer cheering me on—I couldn't fail.

Maybe I wouldn't have failed if I hadn't seen the General, mere moments before it was my turn, climb that forty-foot telephone pole, stand at the top, turn around, jump, grab a trapeze with one arm, and start doing pull-ups on the friggin' thing. He left behind an impossible-to-follow act and fled the scene with his buddy, Stephen, just before my turn, barely interested in how my journey up the pole would go.

Heavily laden with rock-climbing gear, looking at the pole, I froze thinking that the General and I may not have been there for the same reasons. Whatever meaning he'd attached to making it up that pole, flying through the air with the greatest of ease, probably differed from mine.

With that stressing thought in mind, I reluctantly trudged toward the facilitator who'd been coaching folks before they headed up the pole.

He smiled at me with tears in his eyes. "I've been wanting to hug you all week."

"Me? Why?"

He shrugged. "I see pieces of me in you... I want you to try and remember little Rebekah. Use her memory to lift you up. Remember her on the playground, running around, having fun. When it comes time to lift yourself up, use your core, not your legs. As for the trapeze, think about what you want, in this moment, and jump for it."

In that moment, I didn't know what I wanted.

What am I jumping toward?

I walked to the pole and looked up at the foot-pegs lodged into the wood. Heart beating in my throat, I reached for a peg and started to climb, higher and higher, refusing to look down. Grabbing the platform at the top of the pole, I realized it was rickety. The friggin' thing spun.

I climbed up, put my feet on the small, circular platform one at a time, and steadied myself. As it wobbled, I sat in a yoga-chair pose for a split second. Inside that split second, directly across from where I was, I could see a photographer snapping photos of me from a hill. I attempted to push myself up and stand, but I lost my balance, the platform shook, and I fell backward.

I didn't stand. I didn't jump. I didn't grab the trapeze. I didn't do any pull-ups. I was lowered to the ground and met with sympathetic hugs. I felt like such a loser. Definitely not as cool as my husband.

I obsessed over why I hadn't channeled little Rebekah. Why had she and my superpower failed me when it came time to stand tall and own the moment? I'd thought hard, tried to see her on the playground but I couldn't.

At dinner, I listened in on a conversation between a couple of guys in my small group.

"I saw my five-year-old self. That was all I needed to stand and grab the pole," he said, buttering his bun.

"Yeah, I just couldn't get there, mentally," said another dude. "Maybe I didn't have good memories of that time in my life or something?"

Listening to them carry on while poking at my salad, I realized, I didn't go back far enough. I had been envisioning a timid version of me on the school playground. That girl had shut down, had already withdrawn, was unnerved around people. I'd gotten hung up on the word "playground," so all I could see was six-year-old Rebekah, wandering recess alone, looking for someone who wasn't *bad association* to play with.

Had I dug deeper I would've seen four-year-old Rebekah— my carefree train-track self—on the rails in her backyard. And she *did* have fun; it was mostly by herself at the tracks, but she was the one I should have summoned before climbing the pole. Not reserved Rebekah, roaming the playground alone.

Six-year-old Rebekah had already been exploited in the dark corners of her bedroom closet. Since that incident, along a twisted and thorny path, many unfortunate somethings had happened: my five humiliating Kingdom Hall tribunals, my scandalous Dean years, my string of sexual partners after Kelly, Asshat's bullshit.

I was mortified by all those things, and they each came in crystal clear the night we were instructed to share one shame-filled memory with our small group.

I wanted to vomit. I wanted to cry. I wanted to run out of the room to do both, in private. But what I did was tell one lewd Dean story, completely straight-faced. Emotionless. Like some news anchor.

I thought my memory would be the worst; everyone would see my disgusting, warped, slimy insides creeping up to the surface. But no. While others recalled their own dreadful stories, my body slackened. I wasn't the only one harboring awful secrets.

There was a certain peace in sharing our shame. To know that humans experience terrible things and can still move forward, proved there was some beauty in our breakdowns. The emotional collapse we each faced had purpose. For the first time, I could see Dean wasn't the catalyst for fucked up sex-capades. I had a choice, even if I didn't believe it at the time.

The next morning, one of the facilitators began class saying, "I want the three couples here to stand up, back-to-back, and at the same time, rate your relationship on a scale of one to ten. Ten obviously being the best."

The General and I looked at each other uncomfortably. Yes, I was there to repair my marriage, but I really didn't want one hundred and fifty-two ears and eyes on us while we did it.

"C'mon, we don't have all day. Let's go," the facilitator said, clapping her hands.

The General and I stood back-to-back, and when it was our turn, we shouted out a number. He said five. I said three. Out of the three couples, our relationship rated the lowest.

"Well, let's fix it. To the front of the room, let's go!"

The General and I walked to the front of the room and stood face-to-face, holding each other's hands, for an impromptu counseling session. In front of everyone, our marriage was pulled apart and turned inside out. It was Festivus—complete with the Airing of Grievances—we had a lot of problems with each other.

I laid into him.

"You didn't even care if I made it up the stupid pole," I said, tears running.

With knit brows he looked at me and said, "What?"

"You were all 'look at me catch the trapeze and do pull-ups.' Then you just left!"

I'd made up my mind that he didn't think our marriage was worth saving because of the pole.

"They were ushering me and Stephen to the next activity; we had to go!"

"Shit excuse—"

"Bekah—"

"You could've spared a fucking second!"

He squeezed my hands and said, "I was high—"

I rolled my eyes.

"On catching a younger version of *you*!"

"What?"

"Stan told me to visualize a little General then jump for what I wanted. A younger me saw a tiny you sitting on the trapeze bar, waiting for me to catch her."

I teared up.

"I jumped for what I wanted and what I want is *you*."

He squeezed my hands again. His eyes welled with tears.

The room fell silent.

No longer caring about ranch rules for married couples, the General kissed me, the same way he once had in the Funspot parking lot.

Everyone in the room cheered.

After couple's therapy, I realized it wasn't fair expecting the General to be and do everything. If I expected him to take care of himself and me, I needed to take care of myself and him. If I wanted him to pay attention to me, I needed to be attentive. If he stopped doing something, it was because I had stopped.

Again, with the mirrors. We were Lucy Ricardo and Harpo Marx doing their renowned mirror routine in the *Lucy and Harpo Marx* episode.

I was (and still am) indebted to the ranch for the things they'd helped me understand. At the same time, sharing such intimate parts of myself and my marriage felt invasive. I was broken down and emotionally vulnerable, repeatedly, all in the name of personal growth. They may as well have put me in the dungeon of shame and perched me in front of three elders.

The week quickly passed through my mind like a silent movie reel. There'd been publications given to us, specific ranch lingo taught, sleep deprivation, more classes offered, and the task of enrolling friends and family—mirroring Hard Bottoms and, of course, the *Society's* cult prescription.

I was grateful but leery. I didn't believe the coaches on the ranch had meant harm; I'd had a positive experience. But given all I'd seen and felt growing up, it was now a knee-jerk reaction for me to question anything that felt too dogmatic.

You expect me to draw in the people closest to me while submitting to a cultish, pyramid-like structure?

No. Sorry. I can't do it.

The Dark Side

BACK IN AUSTIN—sitting at my precious, Formica kitchen table, coffee in hand—I thought hard; then I saw the pattern.

Real cults and cult-like groups operate in the same fashion: find the downtrodden; give them bite-sized slivers of hope; break them down; allow them to make a mess of themselves whilst rewiring the connections in their brain (preferably to the organization's liking); continue feeding them bite-sized chunks of new information; keep them busy; keep them sleep deprived. Repeat, repeat, repeat.

Although some philosophies we'd learned seemed spot-on, I second-guessed myself over and over.

What if I'm just resisting? What if my "programs" have gotten the better of me? What if this is another way to cling to my victimhood?

I stopped and remembered all Joel and I had talked about, all the times he told me to trust myself. If my superpower was circumspect, there had to be a damn good reason.

I held fast to my cynicism, storing it in my mind's rolodex.

A month later, I readied myself for another flight to California. Alone. This seminar would be nine days; an opportunity to grow as a woman and leader with sixty-seven other women. No men.

I shelved any cult skepticism I harbored for the institute and started packing. I'd already paid thousands for the seminar, bought my flight, and obtained some of the random things on the institute's must-have list:

Handy wipes.

A headlamp.

Journal.

Formal gown.

Hiking boots.

Living will.

I was sitting on the couch, a document in hand, when Max came home from school.

"Whatcha lookin' at?" he asked.

"My living will," I said.

"Oh, is it for your Ladies Trip?"

"Uh-huh." Arranging my last wishes on paper, showing them to someone for approval, then getting them notarized made me anxious.

"After my homework's done can I skate to Hawk's?"

"Yeah, sure."

The General came home.

"Hey," he said, setting his welding backpack on the floor. He sat on the couch next to me, and asked, "You ready for this?"

"As ready as I'm gonna be." I sighed, looked at him, set the will down, and walked into our bedroom to sort through the clothes I had thrown around the room earlier.

Liesel lay on my pile of clothes in protest, little wiener arms stretched out over a pair of jeans, saying, "No, Mama, you stay home."

Part of me wanted to stay home. Stay who I was. Not grow. Trudge along the path well-traveled. Save myself from further humiliation and cultish vibes. But I'd already made all the arrangements and found subs for my interpreting gigs—I was going.

I got a cup of Peet's coffee after landing in San Francisco and collected my baggage.

Once I spotted the Royal Coach Limousine at the airport, I knew I was in for one hell of a week. I immediately noticed most of the other women were more put together than I was; hair done, make-up perfect, and outfit on point even if it was an '80s jogging suit with a visor.

I'd never been much into appearances unless you count old jeans, a '90s crop-top, a well-worn flannel, and combat boots stylish, which I do. That had always been more my speed—comfy, edgy, cute. Some women looked like walking Glamour Shots. And there I was—a grainy, campy, Old Western photo moving in real time, grating like sandpaper.

I knew I'd blossom in my own time, finding my way to a soft filter. But I'd always been a slow processor. Being on the ranch would undoubtedly speed things up, and I feared that I'd be pressured again in front of strangers.

The very core of who I was (am) rested solely on my own inner compass; Joel, and my train-track self, perched on a nerve in my brain, reminded me that I did know myself and could trust myself.

Observing other women on the way to the ranch, I realized that I had very little in common with them. Some were quiet, uncomfortable, and some were boisterous and domineering. I felt somewhere in between, wondering, *why am I here? I already know I don't fit in.*

Outside the dorm houses, still holding our luggage, we were asked to introduce ourselves as the "maternal granddaughter of so-and-so." It was the first time I'd ever introduced myself in that manner, the first time in years I'd said Grandma Nina's full name. I could smell lasagna and garlic bread, clearly see Lucille Ball frozen stiff inside a walk-in freezer, and hear Grandma's contained, raspy laughter. Tears welled instantly.

After introductions, we picked our bunkmates (this time I had five) and immediately received a lesson in masculine versus feminine energy.

I lean toward masculinity for very obvious reasons. Having revolted against being labeled a *weaker vessel,* was it any wonder why I flew into masculine without blinking? Needing to prove I was not weak or good for nothing? I thought not.

We looked at scans of men and women's brains, juxtaposed.

Neural pathways in men's brains look like a detailed grid map of a New York City borough. Women? Sweet Jesus, it's a wonder we get anything done. Our pathways look more like a map of Boston.

With each passing moment, I had to remind myself that I was better off listening to my superpower, which I learned was rooted in feminine energy.

Stubbornly, I'd ignore my gut just to put its accuracy to the test, and every time I did, I remembered why I shouldn't.

The endless cycle of trust-falls between me and my intuition was masculine in nature, and the trick laid in balancing both energies, which had always been my struggle.

By mid-week I was resentful, numb, tired, and stressed; disconnected from myself. I had no clue who I was, what I wanted, or why I was there. And that put me in no mood to accept unsolicited feedback from a conference room full of women.

But it happened.

We took turns drifting through the room, giving feedback to one another—based off our first impressions. What I heard about myself was a bit surprising, but not at all unbelievable.

I was chained, hard, angry, intense, rigid with a clenched jaw, piercing eyes, and an attitude. I reeked of low self-esteem, it was obvious I was looking outside myself for answers, and I was no one anyone wanted to meet in a dark alley.

Those mirrors were *not* shy; they were on motherfucking point. I was those things. I'd always known I wasn't an Olan Mills photo; I was an Old Western photo to the core. I just didn't know that anyone else knew it; I had no idea what I'd been projecting.

That night, laying on the top bunk, I wondered how gritty I really was. Why was I so stand-offish? Clenched? Pensive? Stifled and insecure? Why did I have such an incessant need for control? The more I thought, the more I realized that my control issues were nothing more than fear in disguise—self-denial.

The afternoon I confronted my mother was the day I almost threw up all over myself. We were instructed to say whatever we wanted to our mothers, eyes closed, sitting on chairs in a darkened room.

"In which language?" I asked before the exercise.

"Whichever language you used with your mother. This is for you," one facilitator said.

I started signing, asking Mom questions I knew she'd never be able to answer. I talked to her about the Closet Incident. My signing became sloppy sim-comming, then, I dropped the ASL altogether and screamed.

"I needed you and you didn't fucking hear me!"

I doubled over, held my stomach, and tried to control my breathing. When that didn't work, I gave in to the experience.

I remembered how his voice sounded, commanding my every move; his sinister grin; his fleshy little pecker on my exposed privates; warm liquid between my legs; the smell of urine; the disorientation that followed. Those few minutes in the closet felt like a lifetime.

I wished Mom could've heard me and stopped the start of a dreadful cycle in time. I ached knowing if that one specific thing hadn't happened, maybe none of the other fucked-up shit would've happened, and maybe I wouldn't have been so susceptible to the abuse that followed.

I sobbed, then felt someone come up next to me, placing something at my feet. I slightly opened my eyes and saw that it was a small, plastic waste can. Inside that moment, from the corner of my barely opened eye, I saw a woman fly out of the conference room in tears.

Festivus—we had a lot of problems with our mothers.

All of a sudden, a weight lifted, and I thought: how could I possibly be upset with my mother? She'd done the best she could with what she had. She didn't always hear me when I needed her (literally and figuratively), but she was as present as she could be; meningitis-stricken ears, doomsday cult, and all.

I forgave her just as quickly as I'd become upset with her; she was amazing, beautiful, and much stronger than I gave her credit for. Before she married my dad, she was a working Deaf woman—a Deaf runway model. In the '60s. With a toddler. She was totally badass.

The lights came on, the exercise ended, the room cleared. But I stayed behind.

"Why did you set a garbage can next to me?" I asked one of the facilitators.

"I've seen some women lose it, and emotion that intense sometimes comes out in the form of vomit. I saw that same outburst coming from you when you said she didn't hear you."

"Oh. Well, thank you."

I started to leave the room as she said, "Oh, Rebekah?"

I turned to face her.

"*I* heard you." She winked and bent down to pick up the waste can.

As the sun set, I walked the faded meditation maze. I paced that labyrinth for what felt like hours, wondering why it was so hard for me to just *be*.

I always felt like I needed to busy myself with some task, which usually left me irritated and exhausted. No wonder I seemed so intense and moody. I reflected on the feedback I'd received earlier in the week. They'd called me a "tough tita," aka: the girl you don't want to meet in a dark alley.

Am I really that hard?

At the time I wasn't sure. All I knew was I'd been pissed at myself all week for doubting my superpower. Whenever we were tasked with something—using an azimuth compass to navigate the outskirts of the ranch, climbing a rock with our bare hands, giving detailed instructions on how to cut an onion—I ignored what my gut was telling me, and I fucking knew better.

If walking that labyrinth taught me anything it was to continue trusting myself. I'd always known what was right for me, even if it wasn't right for anyone else. I didn't need to explain myself to anyone. My life didn't need to make sense to anyone except me.

Once the night sky fell, I promised myself that I'd be one hundred percent true to me—no matter what that looked like to anyone else. I'd made that same promise to myself at the tracks after my first judicial hearing with Trey, knowing that it wouldn't make sense to anyone on the outside looking in.

Once I landed in Austin, my intuition hit the ground running and went wild with things I'd been wanting to do. Things I'd told myself I either couldn't or shouldn't do reared their lovely, little heads and said, "Well, why not?"

Yes. Why not?

I called Paul at Bijou.

"I'm ready for my sleeve, Mr. DeMille."

He laughed into the phone. "Yeah? What're you thinking?"

"Vader. Stormtroopers. The dark side," I said.

"Badass. Send me some images, I'll start the design, and we can meet up sometime next week."

I texted images of Vader, stormtroopers, TIE fighters, and anything affiliated with the dark side. Once the design was ready and drawn up, I drove to the studio.

I saw the trace paper with all things dark side and fell over with glee.

"I love it!"

"I may use some fillers that aren't on the drawing, but we'll cross that bridge when we come to it," Paul said.

"I trust you; you're the artist."

"Now, are you totally sure about this? I mean, you've said your tats need to be covered for work and, well, this is a full sleeve. I'm going right to your wrist."

Looking at the design, I smiled and nodded my head. "I don't care anymore. This is something I've been thinking about for years. I want it. I'm so tired of worrying about what anyone thinks, and I don't mean that disrespectfully. But, like, if I can fall gracefully into who I really am, the me that I often don't let people see, maybe I won't feel, like, wound so tight. That make any sense?"

I thought if I allowed myself and my superpower to just *be*, maybe I'd accept myself more and feel softer, like that Olan Mills photo.

He nodded. "Makes sense. Let's set some dates, girlie."

Vader and I are kindred spirits. I'd always been drawn to the melancholy, the misunderstood, the macabre, the pain. I wanted to touch it, understand it, coddle it. This darkness has lived inside me since I was very young.

Vader wasn't born Vader, and villains aren't born villains. Villains are outliers, outsiders pushing against the norms of commonplace society, going against a well-established grain.

They're expected to toe the line with the mob, and when they don't, madness ensues.

Vader didn't fit in, and he was resisted. As much as he tried to fall in line, he wasn't meant to; there was no place for him there. Forced into a mold he couldn't shove his foot into comfortably, he became distraught, misplaced, scared, and alone with powers he himself didn't understand.

Until he figured his shit out.

That felt so much like me. A born outsider. An outlier. An unintentional misfit.

It was time to glide like Vader with poise and purpose.

After several three-hour sessions with Paul the Magnificent, Vader and all things dark side decorated my entire right arm from my shoulder to my wrist.

I stood in front of his full-length mirror, ogling his work.

"Oh, my god." Tears welled. I wished I could remove my arm to hug it.

"The mandala on your elbow's not necessarily dark, but I think it fits."

"I love it. Especially the little midi-chlorians. That's exactly how I pictured them. And just *look* at Salacious B. Crumb!"

Paul grinned, swiveled in his chair, and began cleaning his station. The General stood next to him, talking about the next piece he wanted.

I stood at the mirror, in love with who stared back.

You can come out now, Beks.

311

Acknowledgements

I'd be remiss if I didn't thank some deserving folks. I know, this part blows, still, but I could not have done this alone.

First and foremost, I thank you, Dear Reader. You have no idea how much it means to me that you're holding this book.

Mom and Dad, I'll never stop loving you, thanking you. To all my brothers, especially Jesse, 53.

Kayli Baker, what can I say? Not only do you copy edit and proofread (so many times) but you've become a very close friend. I love that we text about non-book stuff, like, all the time. A million times thank you. Big INFJ love.

Jo Harrison, I'd go insane if I had to format this shit myself and you know that. Your patience and mad skills are still unparalleled. You're a queen. Ryan Ashcroft, the cover designs are friggin' stellar. I love and appreciate your work, sir. Lauren Sapala, you're the queen of everything. Like always.

J.A., Melissa, and the little Plosker, I love all of you, like, so much. Thank you for your continued friendship, love, and support. Patricia Kirsch, Katherine Turner, Jas Hothi, and all my writing buds—I don't know if I could do this without you. Seriously.

Sarie Hill, thanks for doodling warped images of me that I've been able to use and friending me in Oregon. I love you and your art.

Asshat, thanks for showing me how to trust my inner compass. With you, there were so many opportunities.

Travis, thanks for still being a friend. Without knowing it, you taught me how to stop myself from door-slamming. Jodi

313

Rhodes, twenty-three years of friendship and you may never know how much I love you. Here's to twenty-three more.

Kara, my woman, I love you. Mama Yvette, Kym, Aunt Kathy, Gianna, Gregorio Smith, Kyria Abrahams, the city of Austin, the city of Tucson, the state of Oregon, Charlotte (yes, I'm thanking a ghoul), Remy and her wine crew, Diane, Blue, Han, Opal, Jay and Shari, Pedro, Stella, Jack, Paul the Magnificent tattoo artist, Jen Derickson...thanks for the support, I love you all. I've learned a lot.

Joel, I've tried other therapists; you're still my favorite. Steve Hassan, thank you for being a cult expert.

Hard Bottoms, thanks for showing me cults exist pretty much anywhere you look; mine feels less special now and there's a certain power in that. Thanks also to Mr. Khaki, Mr. Navy Blue, and my one-time interpreting team for reminding me why I'm no longer a J-Dub.

PSI, thank you for taking me in and letting me find my own way, judgment free. I will be forever grateful to that ranch. To my buddy, Jennifer, what can I say? You continuously hold up important mirrors for me, you hold my busted bits of glass with such care. I love you. And Stephen, thanks for bringing out a softer side of you-know-who. I love you, too, buddy.

Thanks to my step kids, Max and Stormy, for being pretty cool, little mirrors. I still learn tons though you're both all grown up now. Rest assured, any pain I felt or mistakes I made as an inexperienced stepparent were the result of my own baggage. I needed to write it to understand it, and in so doing, I grew up, too. Any injuries, real or imagined, have since vanished, and I couldn't be prouder of who you've each become. I hope you know I'm crazy about you both. I luve you more than I could ever tell you. I'll also thank your mom, she held up an important mirror...thanks, Cassie.

Bartok, Moron, Squibbs, Liesel, and Dexter, thank you for being what makes my heart beat. Words can't express how this fur-mom feels.

Thanks to my train-track self; I got you, girl.

Last, but certainly not least, my General. I don't even know what to say. You know I luve you even though, some days, I wonder why. You get me, you let me be me. Marriage is hard. Even knowing how hard it can be, even knowing that sometimes I'd love to strangle that thick neck of yours if I could just get my fingers around it, I'd marry you again; *I choose to do this event.* Hell, I said enough in the book, right? Let's not get mushy.

A Note from the Author

Thank you so much for reading *Mirrors Strike Back,* the sequel to *Train Gone.*

I believe we're all just shifting; looking for a place to rest our darkness, confronting the mirrors and busted glass within ourselves, and the ones other people reflect.

I used to think that I'd never bust out of my mirror-walled cocoon. Forever doomed to peel my inside layers apart, baring a hole just big enough to peek outside and watch all the other butterflies, who seemed to get it, flit around. I was sure my fate was sealed, destined to twist and contort in my own constricting shell.

Alas, the mirrors I confronted inside myself, and the ones other people held up made it easier to accept who I am at my core. After years of navel-gazing and pondering the enigma that *is* me, my cocoon is finally opening. My wings will be shimmering black with tiny spikes. (Touché, Lauren; you're probably not wrong about that).

To have this thing, this being, this darkness inside me is not intentional. I didn't create it; it created me, and I'm okay with that. But for the longest time, it was a part of me that I didn't understand. I wondered if there was something wrong with me.

I'm no Joel, and maybe I've got this all wrong, but what if I'd never confronted the mirrors in that closet? What if the people placed in my path never showed up? Would I have seen all I needed to see? Would I have grown? And since writing is another mirror, what if I'd never written about any of it?

For fellow ex J-Dubs, life does go on outside Kingdom Hall walls and it can be beautiful. I won't lie, it's also hard. Being stonewalled sucks. Losing family sucks. And unfortunately, sometimes shit just keeps circling back. But things can get better once we acknowledge our shit, allow the experience, let it pass, and create something new. It can be done. First step is to stop denying ourselves, ugliness and all.

As for my previous career reservations, they've dissipated. Like I said, things get better when we acknowledge our shit, allow the experience, let it pass, and create something new. Me sitting in my resentment was necessary. Once I examined what ailed me, I realized the issue wasn't my career choice or the community I served, it was my own bullshit.

The Deaf community raised me. Those are my people, my home. I feel nothing but gratitude for folks who trust me the way that they do. My job is *literally* connecting humans to other humans. It doesn't get any better than that.

If you, Dear Reader, know anyone that could benefit from this book—the first installment, this sequel, or both—I hope you'll pass it along, and tell them it's never too late to know and be who they truly are.

I hope that you'll post a review on the interwebs. To keep up with future book releases, please add yourself to the free mailing list on my website: www.rebekahmallory.com